Catholic Social Teaching:
An Historical Perspective

Marquette Studies in Theology
Andrew Tallon, editor

Frederick M. Bliss. *Understanding Reception*

Martin Albl, Paul Eddy, and Rene Mirkes, OSF, editors. *Directions in New Testament Methods*

Robert M. Doran. *Subject and Psyche*

Kenneth Hagen, editor. *The Bible in the Churches. How Various Christians Interpret the Scriptures*

Jamie T. Phelps, O.P., editor. *Black and Catholic: The Challenge and Gift of Black Folk. Contributions of African American Experience and Thought to Catholic Theology*

Karl Rahner. *Spirit in the World.* CD

Karl Rahner. *Hearer of the Word.* CD

Robert M. Doran. *Theological Foundations. Vol. 1 Intentionality and Psyche*

Robert M. Doran. *Theological Foundations. Vol. 2 Theology and Culture.*

Patrick W. Carey. *Orestes A. Brownson: A Bibliography, 1826-1876*

Patrick W. Carey, editor. *The Early Works of Orestes A. Brownson.* Volume I: *The Universalist Years, 1826-29*

Patrick W. Carey, editor. *The Early Works of Orestes A. Brownson.* Volume II: *The Free and Unitarian Years, 1830-35*

Patrick W. Carey, editor. *The Early Works of Orestes A. Brownson.* Volume III: *The Transendentalist Years, 1836-38*

John Martinetti, S.J. *Reason to Believe Today*

George H. Tavard. *Trina Deitas: The Controversy between Hincmar and Gottschalk*

Jeanne Cover, IBVM. *Love: The Driving Force. Mary Ward's Spirituality. Its Significance for Moral Theology*

David A. Boileau, editor. *Principles of Catholic Social Teaching*

Michael Purcell. *Mystery and Method: The Other in Rahner and Levinas*

W.W. Meissner, S.J., M.D. *To the Greater Glory: A Psychological Study of Ignatian Spirituality*

Virginia M. Shaddy, editor. *Catholic Theology in the University: Source of Wholeness*

Thomas M. Bredohl. *Class and Religious Identity: The Rhenish Center Party in Wilhelmine Germany*

William M. Thompson and David L. Morse, editors. *Voegelin's **Israel and Revelation**: An Interdisciplinary Debate and Anthology*

Donald L. Gelpi, S.J. *The Firstborn of Many: A Christology for Converting Christians.* Volume 1: *To Hope in Jesus Christ*

Donald L. Gelpi, S.J. *The Firstborn of Many: A Christology for Converting Christians.* Volume 2: *Synoptic Narrative Christology*

Donald L. Gelpi, S.J. *The Firstborn of Many: A Christology for Converting Christians.* Volume 3: *Doctrinal and Practical Christology*

Stephen A. Werner. *Prophet of the Christian Social Manifesto. Joseph Husslein, S.J.: His Life, Work, & Social Thought*

Gregory Sobolewski. *Martin Luther: Roman Catholic Prophet*

Matthew C. Ogilvie. *Faith Seeking Understanding: The Functional Specialty, "Systematics" in Bernard Lonergan's* **Method in Theology**

Timothy Maschke, Franz Posset, and Joan Skocir, editors. *Ad fontes Lutheri: Toward the Recovery of the Real Luther: Essays in Honor of Kenneth Hagen's Sixty-Fifth Birthday*

William Thorn, Phillip Runkel, and Susan Mountin, editors. *Dorothy Day and The Catholic Worker Movement: Centenary Esssays*

Michele Saracino. *On Being Human: A Conversation with Lonergan and Levinas*

Ian Christopher Levy. *John Wyclif: Scriptural Logic, Real Presence, and the Parameters of Orthodoxy*

Michael Horace Barnes & William P. Roberts, editors. *A Sacramental Life: A Festschrift Honoring Bernard Cooke*

Catholic Social Teaching:
An Historical Perspective

by

Roger Aubert

David A. Boileau
Editor

Charles E. Curran
Preface

Marquette University Press

MARQUETTE
UNIVERSITY

PRESS

Marquette Studies in Theology No. 40
Series Editor, Andrew Tallon

Library of Congress Cataloguing-in-Publication Data

Aubert, Roger.
  [Selections. 2003. French]
  Catholic social teaching : an historical perspective / by Roger Aubert
; David A. Boileau, editor ; Charles E. Curran, preface.— 1st ed.
    p. cm. — (Marquette studies in theology ; no. 40)
Includes bibliographical references and index.
  ISBN 0-87462-692-7 (pbk. : alk. paper)
 1. Sociology, Christian (Catholic) 2. Catholic Church—Doctrines.
I. Boileau, David A., 1930- II. Title. III. Marquette studies in theology ; #40.
  BX1753.A8914 2003
  261.8'088'282—dc22

                                    2003020047

Association of American
University Presses

MARQUETTE UNIVERSITY PRESS
MILWAUKEE

The Association of Jesuit University Presses

Dedicated to

Wilhelm Emmanuel Baron von Ketteler
Bishop of Mainz
1811 - 1877
Great Predecessor
of
POPE LEO XIII
and
All Who Hold in High Respect
The Social Teaching of the Church

Contents

Dedication 7

Editor's Preface
David A. Boileau 13

Preface
Charles E. Curran 15

Monsignor Ketteler, Bishop of Mainz, and the Origins of Social
Catholicism
Monseigneur Ketteler, évêque de Mayence, et les origines du catholicisme social, dans *Collectanea Mechliniensia,* t. 32 (1947),
pp. 534-539. 23

Franco-Canadian Catholics Faced with the Social Question: An Island of Catholic and French Civilization in North America
Les catholiques franco-canadiens face à la question sociale, dans
La Revue Nouvelle, t. 12 (1950), pp. 430-438 29

Recent Contributions to the History of Social Catholicism
Contributions récentes à l'histoire du catholicisme social, dans *Collectanea Mechliniensia,* t. 37 (1952), pp. 493-505 41

A History of Christian Democracy
Une histoire de la démocratie chrétienne, dans *La Revue Nouvelle,*
t. 25 (1957), pp. 558-571. 55

On the Origins of Catholic Social Doctrine
Aux origines de la doctrine sociale catholique, dans *Dossiers de l'action sociale catholique,* t. 43 (1966), pp. 249-278. 75

Social Christianity
Le christianisme social, dans *XIIIe Congrès international des sciences historiques, Moscou, 16-23 août 1970, Moscou, Éditions "Nauka,"* 1970, 23 pp. 113

The Beginnings of Social Catholicism
in *The Church in a Secularized Society (The Christian Centuries, Vol. 5), Paulist Press,* 1978, pp. 144-164.
(Translator: Janet Sondheimer) 135

Development of the Social Teaching of the Church in Europe from Leo XIII to Pius XI
Développement de l'enseignement social de l'Église en Europe de Léon XIII à Pie XI, dans *L'Église et la question sociale aujourd'hui, Fribourg [Suisse], Éditions universitaires,* 1984, pp. 23-37.
.... 161

The Encyclical *Rerum novarum:*
Culmination of a Slow Maturation
dans *De "Rerum novarum" à "Centesmus annus." Textes intégraux des deux encycliques avec deux études de Roger Aubert et Michel Schooyans (Conseil Pontifical "Justice et Paix"). Cité du Vatican,* 1991, 189 pp.
.... 181

The Great Themes of the Social Teachings of the Popes from Leo XIII to Paul VI
Les grands thèmes de l'enseignement social des papes, de Léon XIII à Paul VI, dans *La Foi et le temps [Tournai],* t. 22 (1992), pp. 242-279.
.... 205

Some Reflections on the Historical Perspectives of Catholic Social
Teaching
David A. Boileau 241

Index 283

Contributors 290

Editor's Preface

During the last ten years, many meetings, seminars, conferences, and books have been conducted and written to celebrate the hundredth anniversary of Pope Leo XIII's encyclical *Rerum novarum* (May 15, 1891). We hope in this book to give the reader an historical background to this celebration. No other historian in Catholic circles enjoys the reputation of Canon Roger Aubert. Thus, we are presenting ten of his articles that have to do with Catholic social teaching.

These articles give very measured descriptions of the struggles, defeats, and successes that mark the birth of Catholic social teaching. Their reading should produce great wonder and awe at the stance taken by the Church over the last one hundred years. That they have not been adhered to and that they are called "our best kept secret" underlines the fact and the struggle that we all have to become truly Christian.

Charles E. Curran, one of America's foremost Catholic ethicists, enlightens and frames Canon Aubert's essays with background, clarity, and awe. His respect for the good Canon should enhance our own.

In my own way, I have tried in the concluding essay to point out a number of things. First, the social teaching of the Church has a rich pre-Leonine period beginning with Benedict XIV (1740-1758). Second, the encyclicals are eclectic in origin and, thus, several substantive contradictions occur. Nor is natural law or Thomistic neo-scholastic thinking sufficient to explain the corpus of papal thought.

Throughout the history of the encyclicals, the popes, basing themselves on the life and words of the Lord Jesus, spoke a loud "No" to an excessive individualism; a decided "No" to attempts to privatize religion; a "No" to an espousal of rights with no corresponding duties; a "No" to a positivism in law, in politics, and in economics, which render it unaccountable to moral scrutiny or humanity. And finally, a "No" to civil rights without moral obligations.

We point out, too, in our essay the range of Catholic social teaching, of texts from an ecumenical Council, of seven types of texts from the magisterium, to texts of bishops and Bishops' Conferences. We have added to these numbers the work of social, philosophical, and theological authors who address themselves to this very theme. Many conferences celebrating the centennial of *Rerum novarum* were held by those who made up the nonofficial teachers of the Church and its social doctrine. How to celebrate this anniversary, how to reevaluate it, and how to make it relevant to our day remains the task before us.

With the good Canon and Professor Curran, we, too, are convinced the Church has something of importance to say to our world. How to get it heard is the task. It is my hope that these essays will assist in that task.

I wish to acknowledge that permission has been obtained from *Collectanea Mechliniensia*; from *La Revue Nouvelle*; from *Dossiers de l'action social Catholique*; from *Paulist Press and Darton, Longman and Todd, Ltd.*; from *Editions Universitaires* in Fribourg, Switzerland; from the *Pontifical Commission of Justice and Peace* in Rome; and from *La Foi et le Temps* in Tournai, Belgium.

Of course, a grateful thanks to Canon Aubert, who gave his blessing and encouragement to this enterprise. I cannot thank Curran enough for his insightful preface. Many thanks to my secretaries at Loyola University and especially to Dr. Sharon Harbin, who really put it all together. My French professor, Dr. Howard Margot, gets a loud round of applause for all his help.

An historical perspective is always a good way to begin any enterprise. It is a pleasure for me to present Canon Aubert's historical perspective to you, dear reader. What is of value here is attributed to the Canon, the mistakes and final responsibility for the texts are my own.

Rev. David A. Boileau
New Orleans, Louisiana
Easter, 2003

Preface

Catholic social teaching refers to the documents of the hierarchical magisterium of the Roman Catholic Church dealing with social issues. The tradition began with the original encyclical of Leo XIII in 1891, *Rerum novarum*, and many subsequent papal documents were written on the occasions of the anniversaries of *Rerum novarum*. There is no canonical or official list of the documents belonging to Catholic social teaching, but commentators generally include, in addition to the encyclicals and documents from the popes on the social question, the Pastoral Constitution on the Church in the Modern World, of Vatican II, and the 1971 document from the International Synod of Bishops.

These documents have developed considerably over the years. In 1891, *Rerum novarum* dealt with the grave problems arising from the Industrial Revolution and the plight of the worker. In this context, Leo XIII called for limited state intervention to protect the rights of workers and supported the need for unions. *Quadragesimo anno*, Pope Pius XI's encyclical in 1931, continued to address the problems of an industrial society but now in the context of a worldwide depression. Pope John XXIII and his successors broadened the topic of Catholic social teaching to include the whole world and the question of social justice for all. The later documents of Pope Paul VI and Pope John Paul II have also incorporated some of the significant methodological shifts initiated by the Second Vatican Council (1962-1965) such as greater use of Scripture and growing recognition of a more historically conscious methodology. In the course of the development of these documents, the Catholic Church also changed its appreciation of democracy and the importance of freedom, equality, and participation. Leo XIII proposed an authoritative, or at best a paternalistic state in which the ruler instructed the ignorant multitude how they should act. In the late 1940s, Pope Pius XII cracked open the door to a greater appreciation of democracy, while John Paul II has strongly supported democracy throughout the world but with certain critical comments. Thus, the documents of Catholic social teaching contain a continuity of general approaches and perspectives together with a measure of discontinuity involving even the teaching on particular issues.

In the United States, and on the level of the Church in general, official Catholic social teaching has been called the Church's best kept secret. Catholics are very familiar with official Church teaching on sexual issues and personal morality, but Catholic social teaching is not that well known in the pews. One seldom hears homilies or sermons on the subject. In the presidential election in 1928, a reporter asked Al Smith, the Roman Catholic, Democratic candidate for president: What the hell is an encyclical? Today, thanks especially to the pastoral letters of the United States bishops on peace and the economy in the 1980s, Catholics in the pews and the general public in the United States are more familiar with Catholic social teaching; still, awareness of this teaching lags behind the Catholic awareness of hierarchical Church teachings in other moral areas.

Catholic scholars in the United States have paid attention to these documents over the years, but with some significant developments and changes. As time passes, Catholic social ethicists are giving more importance to these documents. Note here the distinction between the broader discipline of Catholic social ethics and the more narrow 'Catholic social teaching,' which refers to the teaching found in these hierarchical documents.

John A. Ryan was the most significant figure in Catholic social ethics in the United States in the first half of the twentieth century. Ryan, a priest of the Archdiocese of St. Paul, Minnesota, served as professor of social ethics at The Catholic University of America and as the director of the Social Action Department of the National Catholic Welfare Conference (NCWC), the national arm of the U.S. Catholic Bishops. In these two different roles, Ryan was both the leading theoretical scholar in Catholic social ethics and, on the practical level, he explained and applied Catholic social ethics to life in the United States. Although people in the pews seldom heard about Catholic social ethics, church professionals, lay activists, and Catholic scholars were familiar with this teaching especially through the work of the Social Action Department.

Ryan's most scholarly books, *The Living Wage* (1906) and *Distributive Justice* (1916), pay little or no attention to Leo XIII's encyclical *Rerum novarum*. *Distributive Justice*, in its almost 450 pages, mentions *Rerum novarum* only three times (p. 7, n. 15). However, by the middle 1930s, Ryan made official Catholic social teaching a primary source in his writings.

A number of factors help to explain the growing importance of Catholic social teaching in the writings of John A. Ryan. First, as the 20th century developed, papal teaching in general played an ever-increasing role in Catholic theology and life. Second, there now existed two papal encyclicals (Pope Pius XI wrote *Quadragesimo anno* in 1931 on the 40th anniversary of *Rerum novarum*) dealing with social ethics, so there now came into existence something of a critical mass of social teaching. Third, some people in the church, including cardinals and bishops, attacked Ryan as being too progressive, so he then used the papal mantle to justify his own positions. Thus, in the United States by the middle of the twentieth century, Catholic scholars and activists were aware of the papal encyclicals and tended to give them a primary role in their approach to social issues.

John F. Cronin (1908-1994), a Sulpician priest who served as associate director of the Social Action Department of NCWC, published his *Social Principles and Economic Life* in 1959. All seventeen chapters of this book begin with extended citations from the papal encyclicals and other documents. Thus, in the middle of the twentieth century, papal teaching occupied the central place in the discussion and application of Catholic social ethics in the United States. In 1971, Cronin perceptively pointed out a significant problem in his (and others') approach to the documents of Catholic social teaching in the earlier years. Cronin recognized that his earlier work was based on a "limited and fundamentalist" ecclesiology and an unsophisticated hermeneutic. "It never occurred to us that these documents were both historically and culturally conditioned." Cronin recognized the need for Catholic theologians to become more sophisticated and critical in their analysis of Catholic social teaching.

Today, students and scholars of Catholic social teaching bring an historical and critical hermeneutic to their study of Catholic social teaching. This explains why such interested persons can learn so much from the historical work of Canon Roger Aubert, Emeritus Professor of History at the Louvain University in Belgium. The Catholic world today recognizes Canon Aubert as the premier church historian dealing with nineteenth and twentieth century church history. In this book, David Boileau, Professor and Chair of Philosophy at Loyola University New Orleans, has translated and made accessible to the English-speaking world ten articles of Canon Aubert dealing with Catholic social teaching. Scholars in the English-speaking world can and will learn much from this broad, deep, and perceptive historical knowledge of Roger Aubert.

These articles were all written for a particular purpose and on a particular occasion and do not intend to propose a fully systematic historical study of Catholic social teaching. Likewise, they bear their own historical and cultural limitations. Also, as one would expect, overlap and repetition frequently exist. A neophyte should not come to these articles to begin the study of Catholic social teaching. However, those interested in Catholic social teaching will find here a veritable gold mine of historical knowledge.

Most English-speaking students of Catholic social teaching are not familiar with the French language writings of Aubert, which focus on the European scene, and therefore will now have their first opportunity to learn from them. These essays primarily look at the origins of Catholic social involvement in the 19th century before, during, and after *Rerum novarum* with much less attention to the more recent documents. As one would expect, Aubert's historical judgments are well founded and nuanced. He avoids any triumphalism and recognizes both the strengths and weaknesses of this tradition of Catholic social teaching. His evaluation of *Rerum novarum* well illustrates this approach. *Rerum novarum* reveals a relatively timid attitude that today appears at various points as manifestly obsolete. However, it opened doors and was a decisive step pointing the Catholic Church in the right direction.

In general, Aubert traces a trajectory in this tradition evolving toward what he calls social democracy. One might have expected that Catholic social involvement would come to the fore in the ranks of those liberal Catholics who in the nineteenth century attempted to reconcile the Church with democracy. In reality, the call for Catholic involvement in the social sphere in middle and late 19th-century Europe came primarily from more conservative Catholics who were strongly interested in preserving the old order and suspicious of any rapprochement with the new democracies. Aubert describes their approach in accord with the old adage, "everything for the people, nothing by the people." Such an approach appealed to the corporative society and the guild structures of the Middle Ages. But even this approach was too much for some Catholics, as exemplified in the School of Angers that insisted on private institutions and the growth of a true Christian spirit among employers as the way to solve the social problem.

In *Rerum novarum*, Leo XIII definitely came down on the side for the need of some state intervention. He recognized aspects of the corporative or guild approach but did not totally support his organic corporative approach as illustrated by his support for the worker organizations or unions. The term "Christian democracy" at this time was a very controversial term among Catholics. History recognizes that Leo XIII was not a democrat; rather, he held an authoritarian or at best paternalistic view of political society that was structured from the top down. The authorities constituted by God had to instruct the "ignorant multitude." In his 1901 encyclical, *Graves de communi re*, which bears the English title *On Christian Democracy*, Leo XIII accepted the term Christian democracy but gave it a very restrictive understanding. The term means nothing more than charitable, Christian action among people, and should not be involved with any political meaning.

However, after Leo, Aubert traces the evolution toward Christian democracy ("everything for the people and by the people") that was not without serious ruptures and problems. Pope Pius X, in keeping with his doctrinal integralism, strongly opposed Christian democracy. The movement toward Christian democracy was quite successful in Belgium, and also made progress in Germany, but experienced real problems in France and Italy. However, after World War I, the trajectory toward Christian democracy became more inevitable and resulted in the Christian democratic movement that was so prevalent in Europe after World War II. In these articles, Aubert touches only very briefly on the post-World War II scene. However, Professor Samuel Huntington of Harvard has pointed out that, to the surprise of many, the Roman Catholic Church has been the strongest institutional force in the latter part of the twentieth century in favor of democracy throughout the world. Aubert sees in this evolution toward Christian democracy in the social teaching of the Church a good example of the "living tradition" that characterizes the best of Catholic self-understanding.

Aubert's articles show both explicitly and implicitly how, especially in the beginning, the papal documents learned much from what Catholic theologians and social activists were saying and doing. Sometimes the impression is given that papal and hierarchical documents simply come from the top down in some type of vacuum. The very way in which the papal documents are drawn up adds to this impression. A few theologians are asked secretly to propose drafts, but it is only later that word leaks out as to who was involved in the drafting process. Aubert here concentrates especially on the drafting of *Rerum novarum* and also *Quadragesimo anno*. Especially in the case of *Rerum novarum*, Aubert shows how the drafters learned from other Catholic theorists and activists so that the final encyclical, in reality, relied heavily on the broader dialogue and discussion within the Church.

In my judgment, contemporary ecclesiology calls for a more explicit recognition of this dialogue and a structure that carries out such dialogue. The drafting of such documents should come, in the first place, from a public and larger group representing all areas of the Church and contributing from their knowledge and experience on the local level. The draft then approved by the pope would be made public and sent to all the churches in the world in order to receive comments and suggestions. On the basis of these comments, the final document would be published.

The above approach would have three distinct advantages over the present process. First, the method itself shows how the hierarchical magisterium is in necessary dialogue and contact with others, thus underscoring the fact that the Church is the whole people of God. Second, such an approach indicates that the whole process of teaching involves more than just presenting a final document to the world. The very process of raising consciousness about social issues adds a great deal to the way in which teaching is understood. Third, the final document would be more truly received and owned by the whole Church and thus have a greater impact on the life of the Church.

Perhaps the biggest contribution of the translation of Aubert's articles comes from making English speakers aware of the historical developments that occurred throughout Europe in the early development of Catholic social teaching. This historical knowledge aids English speakers interested in Catholic social teaching in having a more critical and historically conscious hermeneutic. Let me illustrate the many important contributions with two significant examples I found in Aubert's essays.

The first example considers the composition of *Rerum novarum*. Today we recognize that Leo XIII's support of labor unions in this document is one of its most significant contributions to Catholic thought and life. However, the first drafts of *Rerum novarum* called for a guild system in which workers and employers would be part of the same association. A few days before the publication of the encyclical, Leo called for a change that had enormous ramifications. He specified that the professional associations that he hoped would grow and develop could be "either composed of workers only, or mixed bringing workers and employers together at one time" (p. 111-112). Thus, only at the last minute did the encyclical clearly support independent labor unions.

A second illustration concerns the drafting of the encyclical *Quadragesimo anno* in 1931. Scholars in the United States generally attribute the drafting of this encyclical to Oswald von Nell-Breuning, a German Jesuit. However, the reality is a bit more complex. In 1986, the late Richard McCormick and I published an English translation of an article originally written by Nell-Breuning in *Stimmen der Zeit* in 1971, describing his work in drafting the document. A few years later, a friend sent me a reference to P. Drouler's *Le Père Desbuquois et l'Action Populaire, 1919-1946*, which describes the much more complex process that preceded the final version of *Quadragesimo anno*. Aubert cites this same source in describing the composition of the encyclical.

Father Ledochowski, the Jesuit General, was in charge of the drafting process and under secrecy commissioned Nell-Breuning to do the first draft. However, this draft was judged too theoretical and too obtuse, being based on the somewhat particular social philosophy of the author. Ledochowski then asked Father Desbuquois, the head of the famous

French center in Paris, *l'Action populaire*, for a more concrete draft. He also had the Belgium Jesuit, Albert Muller, work with Nell-Breuning on reworking his first draft. Aubert accepts Drouler's description of Muller as "the veritable orchestrator of the whole, combining the elements furnished here and there and bringing them the nuances required by the Vatican" (p. 245). Apparently, there were eight successive versions of the encyclical. These two examples thus illustrate the many significant historical realities and nuances that one will find in these essays.

Any English speaker interested in Catholic social teaching will learn much from these essays about the historical development of Catholic social teaching. David A. Boileau and Marquette University Press deserve our thanks for making these essays of Canon Aubert available to the English-speaking world.

Charles E. Curran
Elizabeth Scurlock University Professor of Human Values
Southern Methodist University
Dallas, Texas

Monsignor Ketteler, Bishop of Mainz, and the Origins of Social Catholicism
1947

Whatever interest the Liberal Catholics of France and Belgium may have taken, toward the middle of the 19th century, in the poverty of the working class, it is not in this direction that one should look for the true origins of the social movement which would gain momentum in the heart of the Catholic Church during the second half of the century, culminating in the solemn publication, in 1891, of the encyclical *Rerum novarum*. It is a German prelate, Wilhem-Emmanuel von Ketteler,[1] bishop of Mainz, who had the honor of being the first to present the social question very clearly as a problem of justice and not of charity, and even to face head on the necessity of basic reform.

Three phases can be distinguished in Ketteler's social accomplishments. The first is during the period when he was still only a modest parish priest exercising his ministry among the factory workers. His sympathy for the working class had manifested itself at the time of the Revolution of 1848, when following the Frankfurt riots, he had, at the victims' funeral oration, absolved the working classes of all responsibility for this crime: "The thoughts which provoked these acts did not sprout in the hearts of our people. I know the German people. I do not know them, it is true, through the popular assemblies, but I know them through their lives. I have consecrated my life to the service of the poor, and the more I have learned to know them, the more I have learned to love them."[2] A few days later, at a Catholic assembly meeting in Mainz, after toasts to the Pope and the episcopate, Father Ketteler had risen and made a toast to "the poor people." So it is no surprise that, called to preach the Advent sermons at the Cathedral of Mainz, he decided to use the opportunity to broach the social question, by explaining to his audience, steeped for the most part in the purest sort of liberalism, the theory that private enterprise is free from any control, the Catholic doctrine of property. He doubtless condemned the thesis of budding socialism, "Property is theft", but he also attempted to show how this communist theory, which began to spread around 1848, was born of a partly legitimate reaction to a false interpretation of the rights of ownership. Inspired by Thomist doctrine, at the time almost forgotten, he condemned as a "perpetual crime against nature," the modern conception that makes an owner the absolute master of his property, cut off from all social function, excused from all social responsibility. He showed that "the true and complete right of property belongs only to God, that man's right is limited to usufruct (humans have only use, not possession), and that man is obliged, for this usufruct, to recognize the order established by God." In other words, to take into account first and foremost "the common Good of all."

There is thus something that needs changing in the current social order. But "whatever talent as a precursor he revealed already, the Ketteler of 1848 went no further than the presentation of the doctrine; he was not yet on the path of social action."[3] Having little or no confidence in the effectiveness of political reforms, he awaited the salvation of a resurgence of Christian spirit, of an "inner reform of the heart," which would spontaneously lead people of good will to change the way they acted.

Assigned as a priest in Berlin in 1849, then, in 1850, bishop of Mainz, while still giving himself primarily to his pastoral ministry, he continued to follow closely the progress of ideas in the social arena, and especially the socialist concepts of Lassale. It is on his advice that, in 1863, the dean Heinrich lead the General Assembly of German Catholics meeting that year in Frankfort, to suggest that Catholics give more attention to the social problem. Shortly thereafter, Doellinger made a motion at the Munich Congress of Catholic Intellectuals that the clergy become more deeply involved in this matter.

Happy to see German Catholicism going in this direction, and wanting to channel his good will into constructive projects, Ketteler decided to publish a book in which he summarized the results of fifteen years of reflection on the social problem. His book, *Die Arbeiterfrage und das Christenthum*, appeared in the Spring of 1864. This

time, Ketteler was not content to hope for a change in men's hearts:
he considered profound institutional reform. He declared that Lassale and the other socialist theorists "have the indisputable merit of
having depicted, in terms as energetic as they are true, the situation
of the working classes reduced to the bare necessities." This situation
is an inevitable consequence of the salary system as it was conceived
in liberal economics, which applies to workers' remuneration the
same fundamental principles that rule the fluctuations in the price of
goods, "that is to say supply and demand ruled by competition, this
last reducing salaries to the extreme limits of possibility." It would be
necessary, believed Ketteler, for workers to organize manufacturing
guilds, in order to become themselves entrepreneurs and share directly
in the profits of labor. The problem was finding the necessary capital
for these associations of manufacturers. Ketteler refuses to ask them
from the State, as Lassale was proposing. First because of theological
scruples, because he wonders if the money necessary for transforming the poor into proprietors can ever be gotten from the rich, but
above all for a reason of appropriateness: "Ketteler's very instincts,
so quick to oppose any absolutism, dissuaded him still, at that time,
from entrusting the centralized State with finding the solution to the
social question. Because he was hostile to absolutism, he opposed,
on the part of the proprietor, the *jus abutendi* and, on the part of the
employer, the exploitation of human labor — from this comes his
robustness as a social theorist. But because he was against absolutism,
also, he did not want a State subjugating the rich by its fiscal demands
and the poor by its free benefits."[4] He believed that the real solution
would consist of the well-to-do classes, having become aware of their
social duty, spontaneously furnishing the working classes with the
necessary initial funds for the founding of the guilds, of which the
workers would thereby become the owners.

Socialists and Catholics discussed Ketteler's work with sympathy;
they approved its fundamental tendencies, while having various reservations as to the possibilities of their realization. Ketteler himself, in the
months that followed, applied himself to specifying more concretely the
actual workings of the associations he hoped to see founded all over.

But soon, the bishop of Mainz realized that, whatever the future
held for his plans, he should not have any illusions about the time that

would be required for such profound economic and social reform. Now it was necessary, in the meantime, to prepare with all speed, and try to improve as much as possible the workers' situation in the context of the present industrial system. As early as 1865, Ketteler begins to be concerned with this new aspect of the problem, and very soon realizes that the only means of obtaining tangible results is to lead workers into forming powerful organizations, capable of discussing working conditions and of demanding the appropriate improvements. He even admitted later that the intervention of the State could be useful, in order to counterbalance the power of the employers. "In 1869, Ketteler, ever more practical, preaching before an audience of workers in a pilgrimage chapel, details, as would a professional agitator, those demands that the workers must present to the public authorities beginning immediately, and which their rudimentary organization is perhaps already capable of making come about. Higher salaries; shorter work hours; Sunday rest; outlawing of child factory labor; outlawing of the labor of women and young girls; such are the workers' demands that Ketteler judges the most immediately achievable, and of which he seeks to show, from the height of the pulpit, in the name of religion itself, the undeniable fairness."[5] A vicar of Aix-la-Chapelle wrote to him a bit later on this subject: "Coming from lips other than yours, our Catholic bourgeoisie would not have been able to stand hearing such truths."

That same year, 1869, Ketteler prepared a detailed report for the Conference of German Bishops meeting in Fulda, in which he asked the episcopate to back a program of reforms that demanded, among other things, benefits sharing, salary increases tied to seniority, measures favoring the mothers of families, the enactment of State legislation with a view to limiting the hours of work, or closing unhealthy locations. He further asked that "in each diocese there be several clerks invited to the study of economic questions, and that a priest or Catholic layman be especially assigned to study the state of the working class; that from time to time, conferences gather these specialists from various dioceses among them, and that thus, the German Church would have before its eyes, endlessly completed, endlessly renewed, the map of the workers' world."[6]

Ketteler's last years brought him to a further specification of the State's role in the solution to the workers question. In his book, published in 1873, *Die Katholiken im Deutschen Reiche. Entwurf zu einem politischen Programma*, which was to serve as platform for the Center Party, he challenged the latter to clearly set itself on the path of progressive social legislation, while awaiting the cooperative reorganization of the working class, which he had wished for ten years earlier. With great intellectual precision, he himself elaborated a series of legislative bills favorable to the working class:

> The very progress of his thought and the urgent need for imme-
> diate remedies led Ketteler to let go of his systematic suspicions
> concerning the State. It is in the middle of the *Kulturkampf*, it is at
> the moment when Catholics were singularly authorized to distrust
> the State, that this bishop hoped for the creation of a corps of labor
> inspectors charged with overseeing the passage of social legislation.
> After having for many long years worked for tomorrow, the social
> ideas of Ketteler were working for today.[7]

Death surprised Ketteler on July 13, 1877. He was busy writing a brochure on the relations between Catholic workers and the Socialist Party, in which he sought to distinguish among the socialist demands those which seemed to him legitimate, half-legitimate, and illegitimate. He left German Catholics a social doctrine, based on the principles of St. Thomas, and a very concrete social program, which the Center Party would defend courageously in the years to come.

In 1890, the head of this party, Windthorst, re-editing the 1863 book on the workers question, could write in the preface:

> It is for us a lasting glory that a prince of the Catholic Church
> first had the courage, at a time when the doctrine of Manchester
> completely dominated public opinion, to plant the flag of Christian
> social reform, by judging fairly what was true in the criticism that
> Lassale leveled against the current state of affairs and the current
> ideas and in pointing out as well, in the theories of Lassale, their
> errors and their weaknesses. I know of no more efficacious invita-
> tion to working on the vital questions of the Christian social order,
> the interests of the poor and the weak; I do not know of a more

luminous explication of that which is insufficient, exclusive, and defective in the Liberal and Socialist solutions.[8]

Notes

[1] The basic biography concerning Msgr. Ketteler (1811-1877) is P. Pfuelf's work, *Bischof von Ketteler*, 3 vol., 1899, to be complemented by F. Vigener, *Ketteler*, 1924. In French, worth noting are E. de Girard, *Ketteler et la question ouvriere*, 1896; J. Lionnet, *Un évêque social, Ketteler*, 1905; G. Goyau, *L 'Allemagne religieuse*, t. III, chap. II: La formation sociale des catholiques allemandes; as well as a collection of translations of selected pieces concerning political and social problems: G. Goyaux, *Ketteler* (La pensée chrétienne), Paris, 1908.

[2] Cited in G. Goyau, *Ketteler*, p. xxi.

[3] G. Goyau, *L 'Allemagne religieuse*, t. III, p. 124.

[4] Id., *ibid.*, p. 136.

[5] G. Goyau, *Ketteler*, pp. xli-xlii.

[6] Id., *ibid.*, p. xliii.

Franco-Canadian Catholics Faced with the Social Question: An Island of Catholic and French Civilization in North America 1950

The Catholic Church in Canada, with its 6,000,000 faithful, comprises a bit more than four tenths of the population, and it is, as in the United States, an expanding Church. However, and following the historical antecedents, it presents itself in very particular conditions. In effect, despite the fact that modern Canada is a state where the British element is predominant, such element has not played the role of "catalyst" in the presence of all ethnic elements as it has in the United States. The French, descendents of the 55,000 colonists who occupied the country when Louis XV ceded these "few acres of snow" to England, have always opposed with their last breath any absorption. They continue to form a "nation" of intense local patriotism. The French owe this patriotism to an exceptional birthrate (families of 12-15 children are not rare), which neutralizes the fact that immigration favored the British element almost exclusively. They also owe this patriotism to a constitution that accords equal rights entirely to the two groups, especially two basic groups — the family and the school.

Now, this often-prominent duality finds itself also in the ecclesiastical plan. The 4,500,000 Franco-Canadians, practically all Catholic (97% in 1940), are indeed intent on marking their distance, not only from the Protestant majority, but also from the 1,600,000 English speaking Catholics, who are for the most part from Irish origin. In the past, this situation has created difficulties in the bilingual dioceses where certain anglophone bishops supported by the United States episcopate have tried to encourage assimilation. The Holy See first envisioned this solution as wise outside the province of Québec, purely French, but later it was revised. At present, the Holy See is systematically naming Franco-Canadian bishops wherever the majority of the faithful speak French; in other words, where compact francophone minorities exist. Rome does not hesitate to detach the existing dioceses and place them under the jurisdiction of a bishop who speaks the French language.

Thus, two catholic communities are created, living in good understanding, but extremely different in character. The English speaking community is more characteristic of American catholicism, while the French speaking community presents with an individuality that is completely unique. The Church has succeeded in surrounding the Franco-Canadians with a "sanitary rope" that carefully isolates them from the double danger represented by Anglo-Saxon Protestantism and the free thinking French. The Church has especially succeeded in making them accept a tight network of ecclesiastical influences. A network that is practically impossible to escape, extending not only to primary through post-secondary education, entirely in its hands, but also to family, social, political, and economic life. In the province of Québec in particular, entirely French and enjoying political autonomy, there is the formation of a society that in the middle of the 20th century continues to be motivated almost entirely by Catholic principles. The influence of Catholic principles has everywhere else progressively weakened over the course of the past century. Franco-Canadian catholicism has been compared to Spanish catholicism "by the manner in which it units the people, culture, and the Church into an organic whole."[1]

However, it has to be recognized that this situation, enviable in more than one respect, is not without inconvenience:

> Due to circumstances, moreover, to salvage the race that was entrusted to it, the Church has been amenable in assuming these excessive functions, which are in truth abnormal, and in which it no longer desires to partake.... The clergy tolerates no activity independent of itself. If independent activity arises, it slips in, imposes itself, preventing the good arrangement from operating efficiently.[2]

The observations of André Siegfried, one of the best connoisseurs of things Canadian, perhaps are somewhat influenced by his Protestantism. However, taken together, they are incontestable; as was recently demonstrated again by the "crossroads" of catholic intellectuals in attendance in Montreal February 16 through 19.[3] An elite laity is beginning to assert itself against an excessive clerical rule, which was tolerable only as long as isolation was maintained. Now, this becomes more chimerical from year to year, due to the prodigious economic development of the country, which employs all modern influences.

From Patriarchal Regime to Industrial Civilization

Over the course of the last decades, the economic development of Canada has been prodigious.[4] This country, which 40 years ago seemed confined to the exploitation and sale of its thus said "primary" resources, grains, lumber, cattle, fur, has been abruptly transformed into a great industrial nation. Progress slowed over the course of the war of 1914, but during World War II, it sped up. Despite all contrary prognostics, progress has expanded further these last few years. "Secondary" industrial production (finished and semi-finished products) grew from 3.3 billion dollars in 1938, to 9.2 billion dollars in 1946, and reached more than 15 billion in 1949. The very recent discoveries of enormous petroleum reserves, iron, titanium and pitchblend, have excited still more imaginations, which are dominated, more or less, by an impracticality of production, which influences opinion.

The old province of Québec has not escaped this progress, which in a few years has moved Canada from an agriculture state to an industrial state. From 1901 to 1948, the proportion of the population devoted to agriculture has diminished to almost half. The urban population currently exceeds 63%. Contrary to what many people think though based on data not all that old, "it is a fact," the episcopate recently affirmed in a collective letter, which we will return to later, that "the majority of our people live neither in the country nor from agriculture."

These economic data have their repercussions at the moral and religious level. "In the past, the city retained something of the rural spirit. Little influenced by grand commerce, grand industry, it called more to the village type than the properly urban type. Today, everyone can observe, it is the country that takes up, more or less, the spirit of the city."[5] Consequently, the rural family type is disappearing to make room for the individualistic family of the working classes. Individualistic families where each child, earning his living, can boast of independence with regard to parents and where the house is more a hotel than a home. Furthermore, the rapid increase in urban population has created a severe housing shortage with all its disastrous consequences: crowding together of families, who favor the limitation of births, neglecting the home, which accentuates juvenile delinquency, alcoholism, and the loosening of morals. Franco-Canadians, long term isolates, find themselves at present threatened in their turn to growing materialism and are strongly tempted to turn their backs on the conception of life that was theirs until recently. André Siegfried characterized this as follows:

> It is a catholic conception, united in one tradition that came straight from old France… It holds from this fact the respect of values outdated perhaps a little, but especially in the new world: the acceptance of hard work; the praise of thrift and budgeting, best said a sort of asceticism; the doctrine of a large family considered a Christian duty; a sense of proportioned ambition.[6]

In face of the structural transformation of the country, the Canadian episcopate had the wisdom to understand that it would do no good to confine themselves with their sterile regrets in a past gone by. It was a movement toward the best possible adaptation to inevitable progress. Progress analogous to this past century in Western Europe, the only difference being it was accomplished in Canada in one generation, while the same progress for us took more than a hundred years. The experience of what happened in Europe permitted the Canadian episcopate to recognize easily what it was necessary to do and necessary to avoid. If the Church in the 19th century lost the working classes, it is in large part because European Catholics only opened up to dealing with social problems after a half century of delay, leaving the field open to materialist socialism. The Franco-Canadian hierarchy understood right away that the only means to avoid an analogous catastrophe, the gain of communism, was to this time become resolutely engaged in, without wasting any time, the path of social catholicism.

Under the intelligent and dynamic leadership of Msgr. Charbonneau, archbishop of Montreal since 1939, the initiatives themselves multiplied. One such initiative was the episcopal commission for social action, which did not hesitate on more than one occasion to talk about the replacement of the capitalist regime rather than its reform. Another initiative was the sacerdotal commission of social studies, charged with thoroughly examining the doctrine of the encyclicals and applying its principles to Canadian situations. Then, the development of Christian unions; systematic organization of catholic Action specialists; special encouragement to the L.O.C. (League of Christian Workers, probably women) and to the J.O.C. (Young Christian Workers), which demonstrated promising progress during the Week of International Studies in Montreal, 1947. I have on occasion these past years, encountered in Paris or Rome dozens of Canadian priests. I was amazed to observe how many of them planned to take advantage of their trip to Europe to make contact with, sometimes prolonged, the *Centrale Jociste du Boulevard Poincaré*. This was considered by all of them as one of the high places of the apostolate in the modern world. The Canadian clergy, who in certain relationships, for example, from a cultural point of view, to us seem sometimes as latecomers in relationship with European clergy. This was apparently so in the social domain as was contrary to the avant-garde. They were ready to take part with lucidity of the times in our most profound experiences and lessons suggested by our errors and faulty moves so frequent in this domain in the past 100 years. It must be recognized that this deliberate orientation, common and social in the Canadian Church, especially in Québec, has been facilitated by two facts. First, the clergy finds itself, through its origin, a lot less cut off from the working masses than was the case in France and Belgium. Following this, a large part of industry finds itself in the hands of English or American capital. We understand that in the face of strange patrons, Protestants, and, in general, anonymous patrons, the priest coming from the people spontaneously takes the side of the common folk, his fellow Catholics and compatriots. "The alliance of the presbytery and the palace," which was so deadly for us, never had the occasion of reproducing itself in Québec.

The asbestos strike, which caused such an uproar last year, marvelously illustrates the very clear attitude from a social point of view that the Franco-Canadian clergy deliberately adopted despite opposing resistance from several conservative groups. These groups complained that the Church betrayed their hopes by not limiting itself to engaging the workers in patience and resignation.

The Asbestos Strike

On the 13th of February, 1949, in the asbestos factories of Johns-Manville Corporation located in the province of Québec, there erupted a strike that would last longer than four months. The Jesuit Canadian review, *Relations*, characterized it as "one of the more important events in the social history of Franco-Canada." Other than diverse claims concerning salary, paid leave, and social security, above all, the workers complained about the indifference of the mining company to taking safety measures likely to diminish the terrible ravages produced by the dust: tuberculosis and asbestosis (an illness similar to silicosis). They were also exasperated by the more or less reactionary attitude of the provincial government, led by Mr. Duplessis. He had among other things and in the context of a ridiculous anticommunist struggle, tried to impose a labor code that was clearly from capitalist inspiration, hostile to the right of trade-unions. This explains why the workers undertook the strike without seeking recourse in governmental arbitration, in which they had no confidence.

Despite the violent accusations of the directors of Johns-Manville, who tried to distort the meaning of the workers' demands by presenting them as a communist-inspired assault on the rights of private property, and in spite of the hostile attitude of the government, which declared the strike illegal and did not hesitate to send in the police to support the strikebreakers, the ecclesiastical authorities supported the strikers, aware that their possible failure would have gravely compromised the labor organizations of Catholic workers, in their eyes the principal safeguard against the communist threat. On the 29th of April, the Sacerdotal Commission on social issues issued an appeal to the faithful that they might warmly support the collections organized for the families of the strikers and several bishops prescribed that a supper be held every Sunday to this end. On the 1ˢᵗ of May, Msgr. Charbonneau stated in the Cathedral of Montreal: "When there is a conspiracy to crush the workers, the Church has the obligation to intervene," and he demanded labor laws "giving priority to man rather than to capital." As for the diocesan journal of Sherbrooke (diocese where the asbestos mines were located), it did not hesitate to print: "The unions will have the victory: because truth, justice, and right are for them, even though the powerful, the very rich, armed with narrow legal formulas, are against them." And it was in all sincerity that an almoner of the C.T.C.C. (a Catholic labor organization) could declare to the strikers, during a distribution of aid: "The Church, which we represent, is with you."

This clear intervention by the hierarchy evidently upset the government of Québec, which had already been displeased by the earlier declaration of the Sacerdotal Commission on social issues stating that the famous Labor code was unacceptable in its nonconformity to principles of Catholic sociology. It tried by various means to put pressure on the bishops to stop encouraging the strikers by making collections for their benefit, and it went as far as canceling the subsidy of 50,000 dollars granted to the Faculty of Social Studies of the University of Québec. However, the bishops held their ground and it was in fact the archbishop of Québec, Msgr. Roy, who, after several fruitless attempts, managed to make Johns-Manville accept a compromise that recognized the strikers' principal demands. The agreement, signed July 1ˢᵗ, after 138 days of the strike, at one o'clock in the morning, was received by the working populace with displays of enthusiasm that lasted all night and ended at eight o'clock in the morning with a solemn mass of thanksgiving, while the press of the day saluted the archbishop of Québec as the indefatigable mediator who had well deserved the workers' gratitude.

The Resignation of Msgr. Charbonneau and
the Collective Letter of the Episcopate

A few months later, an unexpected event shocked the province of Québec: this past February, we learned in fact that Msgr. Charbonneau, the most remarkable figure of the Canadian episcopate, had just announced his resignation, at barely 58 years of age, being obliged, the archbishop was told, "to take a long rest necessitated by overwork and a state of extreme fatigue." Everyone knows that, contrary to what happens in the Anglican Church, it is very rare that a Catholic bishop retire strictly because of his advanced age or his bad health (although the case is not unheard of: we remember the resignation, in 1945, of Msgr. Delmotte, bishop of Tournai, felled by illness). It was immediately assumed that other reasons must have been involved in making such an unusual decision, all the more because it was known that two ministers of the Duplessis government had taken advantage of their stay in Rome, at the beginning of the Holy Year, to submit a report more than a hundred pages long containing numerous and severe criticisms of the stance taken by the hierarchy, and by Msgr. Charbonneau in particular, in the recent social conflicts. The leftist press did not fail to quickly talk about the influence of Wall Street on the Vatican, and, without going to the same extremes, many wondered with a certain uneasiness if the archbishop's decision had not been made under pressure from the Holy See, which would disavow the progressive position of the Franco-Canadian episcopate and demand a reexamination of the general lines that had been taken to that point.

Various clues seem nevertheless to indicate that such an interpretation of Msgr. Charbonneau's resignation are far too simplistic. Certainly, those informed know that the true motives are not reasons of health, about which in any case no one had heard a word before the resignation. Several bishops reproached the metropolitan for seeking to impose his personal views concerning the apostolate in a manner that some found a bit authoritarian. Others feared that the tension between the government and the archbishop postponed indefinitely the decision on the University of Montreal's new status, expected to mean a great deal for the Church. Perhaps it is also necessary to take into account the support given the last few months by Msgr. Charbonneau to the demands of the catholic educators — in fact rather poorly paid — at the risk of hurting the interests of certain religious communities. In short, in Rome it was judged opportune to see removed, in a spirit of appeasement, a personality whose intransigent positions had earned more than a few enemies. However, one can hardly say that his social orientation has been disavowed by Rome. When the American magazine *Time* insinuated that the apostolic delegate, who seems to have played an important role in the archbishop's decision, had vainly tried to effect a modification of the latter's position concerning labor issues, Msgr. Antoniutti did not limit himself to "categorically denying" it, but added, which is more important, that he had "always approved and encouraged Msgr. Charbonneau's very charitable attitude toward all the victims of war, strikes, and social injustice."[7] Moreover, the Roman Jesuits' *Civiltà cattolica* had published in December a detailed study of the asbestos strike, approving the hierarchy's position without reservation, and everyone knows the close ties that exist between this quasi-official revue and the Curia. It has also been observed that other prelates became even more directly involved than the archbishop of Montreal in this sad affair, and that they are still at their posts: Msgr. Roy, Archbishop of Québec, and especially Msgr. Desranleau, Bishop of Sherbrooke, who, returning to Rome at the end of the strike, had totally backed the workers: "Capitalism," he had told them, "is the cause of all our misery. We must work to replace it.... You have begun the struggle against this menace. You must not give up. You know that beating a retreat is neither Catholic nor Canadian, even when it lead to death."[8] Msgr. Roy did not hesitate either to make the government face its social responsibilities. Speaking at the Congress of the Professional Association of Industrialists, after having declared himself in favor of basic reform guaranteeing workers not only benefits, but a voice in a company's operations, he added that if, in countries where there is not a Catholic majority, it is hardly possible to implement the Church's social doctrine, except in a partial fashion, the province of Québec, having a Catholic population, Catholic institutions, and a Catholic government, owed it to itself to thoroughly apply this doctrine and to testify before other nations that this is the only path to salvation for modern society.[9]

However, another fact still more arguable has come to confirm that, regardless of questions of personnel, nothing had changed in the Franco-Canadian Church's social politics the publication of a collective letter by the Episcopate of the Province of Québec on "the workers problem in regard to the Church's social doctrine."[10] This very long document — the summary alone is 7,000 words — after painting a picture of the present state of proletarian life, sets forth what a Christian revival of the worker should be, by indicating to each his duty: to the workers, to the employers, but also to the State; for the bishops do not hesitate to make each face up to their responsibilities, and if blame is still assigned with moderation, it is assigned in each case where it should be. The letter reacts against the "naïve sentimentality" that would have us believe *a priori* every workers' complaint, but also disapproves those who "give themselves over to the impression that the worker is asking for favors when he demands *that which is due to him,*" and it asks of everyone, including the public powers, "a comprehensive understanding, which prevents shouting about communism as soon as it is a questions of worker's demands." One of the characteristic traits of this document is the psychological understanding of the labor problems it is examining. The bishops of Québec have understood that, even when salaries are fair, the worker in the modern world continues to be treated like a pariah, a condition that dehumanizes him; thus, they call sincerely for the establishment of a:

> ...'Christian worker's lifestyle' that corresponds on another level to what used to be our agricultural society. As it still is for that part of our faithful who live in rural areas, the worker will feel that he has his place in society. He will not be a man without attachments, uprooted, ignored.... In better economic circumstances, his family will no longer appear to him as a constant problem and even sometimes as an obstacle to a normal life; a better organized profession, a stronger involvement in his city and his country will make him love his profession, his city, and his country, because he will understand his belonging to these institutions that will have given him the place he deserves. In short, he will be proud to be a worker, because his identity as a worker will give a meaning and value to his life.

The press has especially emphasized the insistence put on basic reforms:

> Basic reforms will be aimed at involving workers more and more in the life of the business, in such a way that all those who participate, employers and workers, build their community of activity and interest, through a form of association that will unite them more effectively than the current salary-based system.
>
> It must be observed that the simple salary system, in an economy impregnated with economic liberalism, tends to foster class warfare, to dig a chasm separating capital from labor.... By gradually leading organized workers to share in the management, the profits, the property of a business, we will contribute greatly to the much desired reestablishment of trust among collaborators in a common endeavor.

This clear invitation to finding a solution to the problem, in accordance with the views of Rome, in the spirit of the cooperative guilds, did not go without raising objections on the part of the Anglo-Canadians, always ready to suspect fascism behind professional guilds. Even socially progressive Catholics have expressed their reservations, pointing out that Québec was neither an island nor an oasis and that it was perhaps presumptuous to suggest the establishment of such a system in the heart of North America, on the border of the United States. Equally worth remembering, is the observation formulated by the excellent American Catholic revue, *Commonweal.*

> If Franco-Canadian labor is to participate to any degree in management, it must be educated to assume its new responsibilities. In Québec this problem poses particular difficulties, for in that Province, education beyond the elementary level has traditionally been for the élite and not for the masses. Québec's network of classical colleges, culminating in her two French-speaking universities, guards a priceless heritage of true education as opposed to mere instruction. It has produced an élite of deeper culture and more mature taste than can be found on the English-speaking side. But it is ill-suited to the vast mass of the people without marked intellectual aptitudes who must earn their living by ordinary trades and skills. Education in Québec today is being adapted to meet new

industrial and democratic needs. The equivalents to high-school classical courses are being provided; technical and trade schools are being developed; and the universities are doing good work in economics, sociology, industrial relations and similar subjects. It is clear, however, that this trend must be speeded up, and that some form of higher education must be made general if the papal program of professional organization is to be put into practice.[11]

The problems are thus very real, but have never stopped energetic and farsighted men. And as the Catholic leadership in Canada possesses these qualities, it seems high likely that Christopher Dawson is right when he states that the Franco-Canadian Church "represents and retains something that the modern world, and especially the American world, greatly needs, and it is possible that it has an important contribution yet to make to the civilization of North America."[12]

Notes

[1] C. Dawson, *Roman Catholics in the Modern World*, in *The Geographical Magazine*, London, April 1950.

[2] A. Siegfried, *Le Canada, puissance internationale*, Paris, 1937, p. 56.

[3] See the account given in the review of Jesuit Canadians, *Relations*, Montreal, in the April 1950 issue.

[4] You will find some details on this subject in the works published during his embassy term, Francisque Gay, *Canada XXᵉ siècle. Aujourd'hui. Demain*, Paris, 1949.

[5] Chanoine Lionel Groulx, *Aux tournants de l'histoire*, in *Relations*, March 1950, p. 62.

[6] A. Siegfried, *op. cit.*, p. 55.

[7] Cited in *La Documentation catholique*, May 7, 1950, col. 616.

[8] Cited in *The Tablet*, March 18, 1950.

[9] *Relations*, December 1949, p. 322.

[10] One can find the text in *La Documentation catholique*, May 7 and 21, and June 1950. The *Bellarmine* Edition of Montreal has published also this text in a pamphlet of 80 pages.

[11] *Commonweal*, April 21, 1950, p. 41, Vol. LII, No. 2.

[12] Article cited from *Geographical Magazine*.

Recent Contributions to the History of Social Catholicism 1952

The days of "the history of battles" are definitely over. The great interest it evokes today concerns the history of civilization, the history of customs and ideas, and this is a good thing. Social history in particular is garnering more and more attention, and this is normal for an era in which civilization is taking an increasingly "pro-workers" direction and in which the confrontation between traditional points of view and the Marxist solution is constantly played out.

Numerous works have appeared concerning the onset of new problems posed by the industrial revolution of the 19th century, the life of laborers in this period, the origins and development of Marxism, the evolution of the labor-union movement, etc. In this vast movement of ideas and action, the part played by Catholics long remained, unfortunately, rather modest; it was nevertheless far from being zero, even before the solemn warning for Christian conscience that was the encyclical *Rerum novarum* of 1891. But too few serious histories have until now appeared on this particularly current aspect of the history of the contemporary Church. We are therefore that much happier to be able to point out the recent publication of two important works on certain aspects of the movement which would culminate in the publication of Leo XIII's famous encyclical.[1] We will use the occasion to add a few remarks about the present state of the history of Catholic social action in our country.

* * *

The general outline of the history of Social Catholicism in France during the last thirty years of the 19th century had long been known, when it was fully articulated by the publication of Mr. Henri Rollet's thoroughly researched book, which rests on a quasi-exhaustive documentation, in part unpublished.[2] But for the previous period, that of the first dawning of awareness among French Catholics of the workers problem, not a single comprehensive and critical study existed, and the rare works which incidentally touched on the question had extremely limited perspectives. The question was moreover not an easy one to treat, first because every study on the origins of a movement demands painstaking research of widely dispersed sources, next because the boundary between nascent Social Catholicism and traditional charity is not always clear.

A young French historian, whose merits have just been confirmed by two successive nominations, one to a chair at the French University of Sarrebruck, the other to the co-editorship of *Histoire de l'Église* founded by Fliche and Martin, J.B. Duroselle has for a number of years dedicated himself to the systematic scouring of not only books, brochures, and newspapers, but as well to a large number of unpublished manuscripts and private papers, and he has succeeded in presenting the results of his research in a huge book crammed with details and facts, but with a clarity of conception and an ease of presentation which mark the greatest achievement of French science.[3] Even while putting back into their true context, with every desirable nuance, the few names that were already known, such as Lamennais, the viscount Armand de Melun or the group from *L'Ère nouvelle*, he reveals to us "an unexpected swarm of characters and explosion of works whose usual lack of success did not generally discourage further initiatives."[4]

Even before 1830, some lay Catholics had begun to become aware of the sad social consequences of the industrial revolution and of the inadequacy of traditional assistance in the face of the new forms of misery. From this moment on one can speak of a "Catholic social movement," which thus appears to be about as old as Socialism *per se*. This movement, which develops little by little under the reign of Louis-Philippe, results from the juxtaposition of two quite distinct currents which, for reasons having to do primarily with differences of social milieu, have hardly any contact with each other: one of a more conservative orientation, the other constituting the first manifestation of Christian Democracy.

Certain legitimists, who are happy to point out the malfeasance of the Orleanist regime by stigmatizing its contempt for the misery of the working classes, try to promote remedies: Villeneuve-Bargemont insists, one of the first, on the necessity for State intervention in the industrial sector; this is also the opinion of Armand de Melun, the devoted auxiliary of the famous Sister Rosalie, the founder of the *Société d'Économie charitable* [Charitable Economy Society], whose practical mind had soon grasped the full magnitude of the new problems and the necessity of moving from the charitable domain to that of social justice. A very active group forms around de Melun, especially from 1845 on, one which takes the initiative in diverse concrete projects and will soon promote various legislative reforms. But this legitimist group remains too paternalistic all the same, only conceiving of improvements for the working classes in terms of the "patronage" of the ruling classes. On the other hand, some quite bold views are to be found: first, among some of the collaborators or sympathizers of *L'Avenir*, of whom the most remarkable is Charles de Coux, who by 1830 is proposing the rights of unions and universal suffrage as remedies; second, and especially, among the various cells of "Christian Socialists," convinced of the necessity for profound social reforms, which will not only attenuate the severity of the workers' regimen, but will also radically modify the relationship between capital and labor. Among this last group, the majority are former Saint-Simonians or Catholic Fourierists; one of the most typical figures is Buchez, medical doctor and philosopher converted to Catholicism, who has many contacts with the workers belonging to Republican societies and who, convinced of the Christian origins of the principles of 1789, dreams of reconciling Catholicism and the Revolution.

It is not possible to mention, even briefly, all the initiatives minutely examined by Mr. Duroselle: let us confine ourselves to pointing out again the social role of the Conferences of Saint Vincent de Paul, where militants were prepared for Catholic Workers societies, and the efforts of several Liberal Catholics, gathered around Ozanam, to establish bridges between conservative Social Catholics and Christian Democrats.

Finally, it is important to notice the extent to which the clergy is absent from these first attempts at Social Catholicism. Besides, it is more a matter of ignorance than of ill will: the lower clergy is recruited almost exclusively from the countryside, and even when it exercises its ministry in an industrial center, it easily categorizes as a peasant the worker who fights, drinks, and is thriftless; as for the upper clergy, it in most cases conserves the attitudes of the class to which it is linked by origin or education.

Then came the revolution of 1848, whose causes, unlike those of 1830, were as much social as political. The Christian-Democratic milieus took advantage of the euphoria, based on romantic idealism, of the first weeks of the Second Republic, which translated into an aspiration of seeing all the classes, fraternally united, working together for the good of everyone. The "Christian Socialists" were very active: some collaborate on the workers' newspaper *L'Atelier* [The Workshop]; others, like the journalist Chevé from Nantes, are clearly inspired by Proudhon's ideas and even collaborate sometimes on his newspaper; Fr. Chantôme founds the *Revue des réformes et du progrès* [Review of Reforms and Progress], Victor Calland the *Revue du Socialisme chrétien* [Review of Christian Socialism]. For their part, Ozanam and a young professor at the Sorbonne, Fr. Maret, supported (timidly, it is true) by Lacordaire and approved by Msgr. Affre, found a new daily, *L'Ère nouvelle* [The New Era], favorably received by the young clergy, whose aim is to defend not only the particle of truth in the principles of 1789 and the advantages of the Republican regime, but also various social reforms considered revolutionary at the time: workers' sharing in the benefits and management of enterprises, the organization of arbitration, assistance to the unemployed.

Every sort of hope seemed permissible, but the riots of June and the panic which ensued brought this élan to a dead halt: the Democratic-Christian movement found itself caught up in the general backlash against everything that was closely or distantly related to Socialism, and that which subsisted after the fall of *L'Ère nouvelle* was put to death by the coup d'État of 2nd December, which completed the ouster of the Republican Party. Christian Democracy, whose roots in the country were not very deep, was not able to reorganize like the anticlerical Republicans; its life languished thereafter, punctuated only by the publication of a few unremarkable works, and Mr. Duroselle even believes that it is difficult to establish a connection between it and the second Christian Democracy of the end of the century.

During the Second Empire, there will be nothing to represent Social Catholicism except the conservative, paternalist-leaning current, which to be sure involved a great deal of generosity, but whose influence remained extremely limited. There is besides nothing surprising about this considering the group's lack of doctrine: its leaders have only a summary knowledge of economic science, even though it flourished in this period, and their numerous writings testify as much to the imprecision and inefficiency of their thinking as to their good intentions. They had neither their Marx nor their Proudhon; the theory which most inspires them is that of Le Play, whose scientific character leaves something to be desired and which, combined with a strict interpretation of the *Syllabus*, contributes to directing them toward "counter-revolutionary" doctrine, hostile to the rights of man and to democratic egalitarianism.

Their action appears as hesitant as their ideas. Although Melun partially succeeds in directing the *Société d'Économie charitable* toward truly social activities, the Society will remain until the end torn between different solutions: the old method of "patronage" of workers' organizations by the ruling classes, support of workers who aspire to free labor unions, and the development of mutual funds. In this last area, certain results are obtained, at least in the provinces, but Catholic mutual aid societies do not manage to penetrate seriously the world of the working masses.

As for the priests, too rare, who are given to the popular apostolate, they seek above all to "bring the working class back to Catholicism by forming the more malleable minds of the young workers,"[5] and their attention is much more given to religious education or "honest recreation" than to popular education or the material improvement of the young workers' lives. Moreover, if Maurice Meignen appears as a precursor when he decides to give the young workers greater autonomy in running the circles he had founded, his methods remain an exception. On the whole, nowhere, except among a few little-known writers whose work goes unobserved, is put forward the idea that it is by conferring the responsibility for Catholic Social organizations on the Catholic workers that de-Christianization and class struggle will be avoided and that a real improvement of society will be realized. Now, it is at precisely this moment that the workers movement in France and in all of Europe is evolving in a direction which is increasingly opposed to paternalism: it is not surprising that the workers adopt a reticent attitude toward Catholic social initiatives and that the latter do not succeed in reaching the true working elite.

It must be added, to conclude, that these very limited efforts are the work of a small minority who, before 1870, are not able to interest the majority of Catholics in their efforts:

> Doubtless the latter, on the occasion of a sermon on charity, or out of politeness toward a friend, will sometimes loosen their purse strings. However, in general they are indifferent to the efforts aimed at improving the workers' lot. They believe that the workers' misery is analogous to secular poverty and do not understand its new character, its links to the Industrial Revolution. They believe that charity is sufficient for all. The evangelical saying easily appeases their conscience: *The poor will always be among you.* After 1848, the fear of the Socialist menace also constitutes an excellent alibi. Is it a selfish attitude, the defense of a class? There is maybe some of this, but also and especially, we think, a total incomprehension of the problem. At a time when the industrial proletariat, the craftspeople of certain great centers, and the milieus of the heads of industry are almost all strangers to the Church, this incomprehension is not surprising. [6]

This last remark gives the tone of Mr. Duroselle's work: there is nothing accusatory about it, as was the case for example for that unfortunate *Histoire des catholiques français au XIXe siècle* [History of French Catholics in the 19th Century] by Guillemin. No, it is as objective and impartial as is possible, a meticulously established account, in which the author seeks to comprehend rather than condemn. But one has to admit, after having reviewed that long series of experiments, as generous as they were ineffective, that there is nothing shocking in the fact that the after-1870 generation, the generation of Albert de Mun, de La Tour du Pin, and Léon Harmel, could easily believe that before it, nothing had been accomplished.

* * *

Circumstances lead French Catholicism in the 19th century to concentrate more and more on the bourgeoisie. The attitude of the clergy toward Social Catholicism, that of the episcopate in particular, was in part influenced by this fact. We can find the counter-proof by studying the situation in America. There, as in France, the hierarchy was by 1870, with very few exceptions, prone to cast a wary eye on attempts at organizing labor and the demands of workers, because social ideas were most often propagated by anticlerical revolutionaries whose radical tendencies appeared threatening to the Church. However, unlike that of France, American Catholicism, made up especially by the mass of poor Irish emigrants and concentrated in the ports and industrial cities of the Northeast, had a decidedly proletarian look. The bishops therefore found themselves obliged to take a much keener interest in the problems of labor, and thus became aware of the legitimacy of many of the workers' demands and of the danger there was for the Church in remaining indifferent to them or, worse still, seeming to oppose them. This is what clearly comes to light in a recent dissertation from the Catholic University of Washington dedicated to the *affaire* of the Knights of Labor,[7] one whose abundant documentation gathered from the archives of the different dioceses permit an insider's appreciation of the American hierarchy's attitude in the face of developments in the workers movement.

Around 1875, the discontent among the common people, brought about by the industrialists' practice of salary "dumping," had led to the creation of workers' associations dedicated to defending more effectively the workers' interests, and a great number of Catholic workers had joined the most important of them, the association of the Knights of Labor. The danger of indifference, which for Catholics could result from their participation in a society not under the direct control of the clergy, of apparent compromises with socialist and anarchist doctrines, and especially the secret-society-like practices adopted by the organization to protect itself from the capitalists' retaliation, all had worried a certain number of ecclesiastics. As the organization had branches in Canada, Msgr. Taschereau, Archbishop of Québec, queried the Holy See in 1883 to find out what position he should take;[8] as he had insisted on the secret-society-like characteristics of the Knights of Labor, he was answered that they immediately fell under the authority of canonical condemnation that forbade Catholic participation in associations of this type, suspect of having ties to Freemasonry. Likewise, in the United States, certain bishops, those of St. Louis and New York among others, were hardly in favor of the Knights of Labor, too revolutionary for their likes. But the majority of the bishops, who appreciated the Catholic sensibilities and moderating influence of the head of the association, Terrence Powderly, believed it dangerous for the Church to appear to be siding with the excesses of liberal capitalism by taking a position against the principal organization for workers' rights. Also, under the pretext that the Papal decree of 1884 only applied to the situation in Canada, they refrained from taking measures against the Catholic members of the association (around 1885, they were 500, 000 out of 700, 000) or against the Catholic papers which supported its actions. In 1886, however, the Prefect of Propaganda asked them to send to Rome an informed opinion, which definitively would be examined and decided by the Holy See. For a moment, they feared the worst, but the intervention, at once firm and skillful, by the Archbishop of Baltimore, James Gibbons, succeeded in counterbalancing the unfavorable opinions of Msgr. Taschereau and those who shared his views.

Gibbons took advantage of his stay in Rome at the beginning of 1887, on the occasion of his elevation to cardinal, to appeal personally to the Pope and among the Congregations, and above all he submitted to the Holy See a report on the question, which made a profound impression and which had to be considered all the more seriously in that it was shortly thereafter, due to an indiscretion, published by the press. Found in this document is, according to Gibbons' biographer, "not only his qualities as a statesman, a confident logic and intelligent perspicacity, but also a rare honesty in exposing the dangers of a condemnation, an honesty which is almost audacious."[9] This report concluded in these terms (A.S. Will, *The Life of Cardinal Gibbons, Archbishop of Baltimore*, trans. A. Lugan, Paris, 1925, p. 146):

> Finally, to sum up all, it seems to me that the Holy See could not decide to condemn an association under the following circumstances:

1. When the condemnation does not seem *justified* by either the letter or the spirit of its constitution, its laws, and the declaration of its chiefs.

2. When the condemnation does not seem *necessary*, in view of the transient form of the organization and the social condition of the United States.

3. When it does not seem to be *prudent*, because of the reality of the grievances complained of by the working classes, and their acknowledgment by the American people.

4. When it would be *dangerous* for the reputation of the Church in our democratic country, and might even lead to persecution.

5. When it would probably be *inefficacious*, owing to the general conviction that it would be unjust.

6. When it would be *destructive* instead of beneficial in its effects, impelling the children of the Church to disobey their Mother, and even to enter condemned societies, which they have thus far shunned.

7. When it would turn into suspicion and hostility the singular devotedness of our Catholic people towards the Holy See.

8. When it would be regarded as a cruel blow to the authority of the Bishops in the United States, who, it is well known, protest against such a condemnation.[10]

In 1888, the Holy See officially decided the question by authorizing Catholics to be members of the Knights of Labor. The authorization was indeed presented in a conditional manner, since it was made known to Gibbons that there was a desire to introduce several modifications into the statutes of the association, in order to dispel "any hint of Socialism or Communism"; but in fact they did not urge this clause, which was interpreted by Gibbons as a purely formal precaution.[11]

Gibbons' intervention had been decisive in achieving this happy outcome, even according to the testimony of the Roman personalities who were closely involved in the negotiations. It will be noted however—this is one of the most original results of Browne's book—that the groundwork had been efficiently laid by the autumn of 1888 by two other American prelates present in Rome, Msgr. Keane and the famous Msgr. Ireland, and that moreover the difficulties faced by the Archbishop of Baltimore were less formidable than has been thought until now. A large part of the episcopate in the United States believed as he did that it were better if the Church did not intervene, and when in Rome, Gibbons was able to draw support from this community of views, which had notably appeared during the meeting of American archbishops in Baltimore in October 1886. It was besides easy to show how much distinguished the Knights of labor from the secret societies prohibited by the Church (the book is crawling with unpublished details about the close contact between Powderly, the head of the Knights of labor, and the ecclesiastical authorities). Besides, it would be wrong to see Gibbons as a decided champion of the workers' cause, as was for example Manning in England during this same period. The argument clearly showed that, although the Archbishop of Baltimore judged a condemnation of the Knights of labor to be inopportune, as it ran the risk of discrediting the Church among workers, he did not *positively* support their actions and long preferred to wall himself in with an attitude of prudent reserve—"a masterly inactivity," he called it; and once the question was settled, his interest was moreover increasingly drawn to problems other than the social problem.

Whatever the interest may be in these findings, the difference in attitude between the majority of the American hierarchy and the majority of European bishops regarding the workers movement remains nonetheless significant and invites reflection. One should also take note of the personal role that Leo XIII played in the final decision, a role that Soderini had already explicitly exposed.[12] Historians of Social Catholicism are right to consider the Knights of Labor incident as a noteworthy element in the pre-history of the encyclical *Rerun novarum*: it contributed to increasing the Pope's awareness of the acuteness of the workers problem and of the urgency there was for the Church to take a position. The manner in which the incident was decided permits us to glimpse that, although the supreme authority remained very prudent concerning its principles and feared any compromise with the revolutionary doctrines of socialism, it intended, on the other hand, to distance itself from the abuses of the capitalist system. Msgr. de T'Serclaes, in his biography of Leo XIII, which was written under the Pope's supervision and which can be to a certain extent considered the "memoirs" of the Sovereign Pontiff, concluded his account of the Knights of Labor affair in these terms: "It should be deduced from this attitude of Rome that she did not, in principle, condemn the efforts of workers' organizations made outside of her bosom, and that she was far from putting her power at the service of capital against the claims of labor. Labor and capital are two forces that the Church considers with an impartial eye, and with the urgent desire to see them both serve the prosperity of nations and the needs of souls." [13]

* * *

After having read the two works analyzed, extremely different as to the scope of the subject and the spirit of synthesis, but both conceived according to the rigorous demands of the scientific method, we regret all the more intensely that, until now, no comparable work has been attempted concerning the situation in our country. "In the domain of the historiography of the workers movement, practically everything remains to be done concerning Belgium," wrote Fr. Scholl recently, [14] adding that the little that exists was the work of Socialists rather than Catholics. There is however no lack of printed and unpublished documents which would enable the writing of a certain number of objective and detailed monographs on the different currents of Catholic social thought in Belgium in the era of Charles Perrin, on the social interventions during the Catholic congresses in Liège, and on the influences, French and especially German, which were felt there, on the initial reactions of the clergy and of Belgian Catholics to the encyclical *Rerum novarum*, on the works of Bishop Doutreloux, of Msgr. Pottier, or of Fr. Daens, on the beginnings of Christian labor unions, etc. These sorts of monographs, written not as propaganda or in the form of panegyrics, but with the soul desire of knowing and understanding "what really happened," will permit us to present with nuances and exactitude the evolution of the Catholic social movement in Belgium in the course of the last century.

We are happy, from this perspective, to salute the publication of Fr. Scholl's study on the workers' movement in the Turnhout district during the last quarter of the 19th century. [15] The work is however a little disappointing, first because it deals with a minimally industrialized region, next because the author was not able to rely on sources other than the local press, having found no archival documentation, private correspondences, minutes of meetings, or other papers of the *Volks-bond* [Popular League] founded in 1893 under the impulsion of the doyen Adams and of H. Proost, "the only great lay figure in the social movement of the district before 1900." As it is, with its restrained perspectives and limited documentation, the work is nevertheless not without interest. Written by a man who received a solid education in history and who lives in close contact with the workers movement, it contains numerous circumstantial and lively details on the economic and social situation of the region, on the attitude of the local bourgeoi-sie, on the first strikes and their consequences, on the appearance of Socialism in Turnhout and in Arendonk, and especially on the fruitful work accomplished, before 1900, by the *Volksbond* and the various associated movements. Studies on other, more industrialized regions, able to rely on a more extensive unpublished documentation, will be well advised to follow the plan and method of Fr. Scholl. Besides, he promises us himself other works, which we hope to see soon and which, if they are done with the same care, will be extremely useful for arriving at a precise and nuanced[16] understanding of the beginnings of the Catholic social movement in Belgium.

Notes

[1] A summary sketch on *Les antécédents de l'encyclique Rerum novarum* will be found in *Collectanea Mechliniensia*, July-August, 1948, pp. 565-573.

[2] H. Rollet, *L'action sociale des catholiques en France (1871-1901)*, Paris, 1948.

[3] Jean-Baptiste Duroselle, Professor at the Université de la Sarre, *Les Débuts du Catholicisme Social en France (1822-1870)*. Preface by B. Mirkine-Guetzévich and Marcel Prélot (Bibliothèque de la Science Politique. Quatrième série. Les grandes forces politiques). XII-788, pp. 22. Paris, *Presses Universitaires de France*, 108, Boulevard Saint-Germain, 1951. It is necessary to search really meticulously in order to find, here and there, a few small errors: for example, p. 693, Msgr. de Ségur is ranked among the "social bishops," although he was never more than a prelate; or p. 337, the social tendencies of the Catholic newspaper of Toulouse, *Le Réveil du Midi*, in 1848, appear exaggeratedly minimized, if reference is made to P. Droulers' attentive study on the question published in the *Bulletin de Littérature Ecclésiastique* of 1950 (see especially pp. 96, 99, and 103, n. 7).

[4] B. Mirkine-Guetzévich and M. Prélot, in J.B. Duroselle's preface, *op. cit.*, p. xi.

[5] On this subject, note the pertinent remark made elsewhere by Duroselle: "Did not the semi-failure that marks this immense effort originate in the artificial character which it presented? Exercising the intellect without dreaming of reforming social conditions by fighting for justice, for the improvement of material conditions, resulted either in uprooting from their milieu those who persevered, or in the

young people abandoning their missions as soon as they felt in solidarity with this milieu" (in *Revue d'Histoire de l'Église de France*, 1948, t. XXXIV, p. 61).

[6] J.B. Duroselle, *op. cit.*, p. 701.

[7] H.J. Browne, *The Catholic Church and the Knights of Labor* (Studies in American Church History, t. XXXVIII). xvi-416 pp. Washington, The Catholic University of America Press, 1949. The work, extremely valuable for its exhaustive documentation, has unfortunately a character that is too analytical, limiting itself to recounting minutely factual details, without attempting to situate them in the social and economic context of the era or to illuminate them with some few psychological portraits of the principal protagonists, without ever, moreover, stopping to take stock.

[8] One can no longer speak, as has been done in the past, of a Roman condemnation provoked by the Canadian hierarchy: Taschereau was in reality the only one to intervene, and furthermore, he at first limited himself to simply posing the question to Rome, without presenting a list of charges.

[9] A. S. Will, *Vie du cardinal Gibbons, archevêque de Baltimore*, trans. A. Lugan, Paris, 1925, p. 146.

[10] Cited in A. S. Will, *op. cit.*, pp. 145-146, from the text published in the press. The original English version given by Browne (*op. cit.*, pp. 365-378) included a few slight differences, the newspaper version having attenuated certain expressions: these differences are however minimal. Concerning the conclusions that we cite here, the original contained a ninth one: "It would be almost *ruinous* for the financial maintenance of the Church in our country and for Peter's Pence."

[11] Gibbons wrote to the rector of the American College in Rome: "The decree is in substance that *tolerandi sunt*, provided some verbal changes are made in the constitutions of expressions that might be distorted into a bad sense. The particular expressions are not even indicated. Hence I infer that the emendations are suggested to save the Holy Office from a charge of inconsistency, and to get out of the difficulty as quickly as they can" (cited in H. Browne, *op. cit.*, p. 327).

[12] E. Soderini, *Il Pontificato di Leone XIII*, t. I, Milan, 1932, pp. 370 and 372.

[13] Msgr. de T'Serclaes, *Le Pape Léon XIII*, t. I, Paris-Lille, 1894, p. 43.

[14] S. Scholl, *Rond de historiographie der arbeidersbeweging*, in *De Gids op maatschappelijk gebied* (a historiographical summary of the workers' movement), in *The Guide on Social Matters*, February-March 1952, p. 179.

[15] Dr. S. H. Scholl, O. Praem. *De Geschiedenis van de Arbeidersbeweging in het Arrondisement Turnhout vóór 1900* (the history of the workers movement in the district court of Turnhout before 1900). 188 blz. 23 x 15 1/2. Turnhout (*Verbond der K. A. J.*, Korte Begijnenstraat), 1950.

[16] I mention among others, in another article by Fr. Scholl, this reflection which it would be so interesting to see fleshed out scientifically (in part already done by Adams, the dean of Turnhout): "And now the priests.... We no longer believe that the large opposition against everything that was of the workers came from the priests. This is pure fabrication and deceit and was frequently used against the Catholic Religion by other parties in a very unloyal manner. It is true that the higher church hierarchy did not take any initiative and certainly was very cautious; that Msgr. A. Lauwers, Msgr. Van Lerberghe, Dean De Grÿse, Dean Adams (to name merely some deceased) certainly fought as honestly and stubbornly for the interests of the workers as Vandervelde, De Paepe, Anseele, de Brouckère: that there were

several priests, who have done more for it than the future history books will tell. True as well that there were several priests that did nothing for it and that only a few truly offered opposition (*The Flemish workers movement before 1914-1918*, in *De Gids op maatschappelijk gebied*, November 1951, p. 1052).

A History of Christian Democracy
1957

It has already been more than a year since publication of the work in which Mr. Maurice Vaussard retraces, with broad strokes, the difficult birth and slow progress, the hopes and the vicissitudes of Christian Democracy in France, Belgium, and Italy.[1] However, it is not too late to call attention to this book. In fact, although it will teach but few things to experts, all those — and they are many — who have not had the opportunity to follow closely the monographs on this subject (whose number has been increasing the last few years) will take great interest in this first attempt at a synthesis, by an author having been closely involved in the events about which he writes but who, although he makes no attempt to hide the fact that he was "actively committed," gives proof throughout this book of a fine objectivity, avoiding the twin dangers of idealization and too acerbic criticism, which certain disappointments might have justified. The public at large will particularly appreciate this introduction, generally well documented, clearly conceived and acceptably wriitten, to the history of a movement whose influence on Church and State has been steadily increasing for a good half-century.

It is typical to link Mr. Vaussard's work, now complemented by a parallel volume on political Catholicism in Germany with the same general title[2] — with that which was written a few years ago by two specialists in political science, justifying the publication of the fine work by Mr. Duroselle on *Les débuts du catholicisme social en France* in the section of the *Bibliothèque de la Science politique* dedicated to the *Grandes forces politiques*:

> As far as Catholicism is concerned, the political and social movement to which it gave birth counts among the most important in the Western World. It is currently [1950] active, under various names and with a few subtle differences, in all of Western Europe. However, this capital phenomenon, even should it be limited in

its duration, appears to some as being episodic. They see in it only an avatar of traditional clericalism, or again as a sort of interim between the declining reign of 19ᵗʰ century forces and the rise of those which will dominate the second half of the 20ᵗʰ century. Its success would be principally due to the weakness of its rivals: to the great schism which divides socialism and communism, to the retreat of liberal radicalism. The error thus committed, concerning the existence and the essence of a movement and of an authentic and autonomous political doctrine, stems primarily from a general ignorance of its origin and its development.[3]

Even if one believes it necessary to voice one or the other reservation concerning Mr. Vaussards' book — we will see moreover that all which have been voiced are not equally pertinent — it remains that thanks to him it is henceforward possible for anyone to acquire easily an exact overview of this origin and development, and that here is a title worth knowing by all cultivated people who are interested in the world that is being made and the Church's role in that world.

* * *

It is in Germany and in Belgium that Christian Social Works were the most pronounced, but it is in France that the movement was born and that there appeared the greatest number of tentative efforts, diverse and often ephemeral but often suggestive in one way or another — for translating the Christian-Democratic idea into action in an original manner. Four well-informed chapters trace this tormented history, doubly disappointing because of the lack of intelligence generally displayed by the conservative Catholic milieus but also because of the utopian and doctrinaire stances taken by too many Christian democrats who, as so often in France, have a tendency to build little chapels of intolerance against all those who think differently.

The minutely wrought and quasi-definitive works of Mr. Duroselle and of Mr. Rollet permit us from now on to follow in detail *the contrastive elaboration of a Christian Democratic philosophy in the course of the 19ᵗʰ century.* Two parallel currents, almost completely unaware of each other for reasons having primarily to do with differences of social milieus, develop during the second third of the 19th century. One, rather close to pre-Marxist Socialism, progressive and generous, had its moment of glory in 1848 with the newspaper *L'Ere nouvelle*, which truly deserves the label "Christian-Democratic," but which disappeared in the reaction that followed the great fear of the right-thinking under the Second Republic. The other, more timid and pa-ternalistically leaning, but which in the short term does not want for effectiveness in the domain of charity or of educating the masses, and which will continue with new nuances, in Albert de Mun's *Œuvre des Cercles*, and in the corporatist (and monarchist) group assembled by La Tour du Pin, handicapped by the memories of a so-called Christian past that keeps them from facing the future head on. Then, toward the end of Leo XIII's pontificate, encouraged by the encyclical *Rerum novarum* and by pontifical directives in favor of "rallying" to the Re-publican regime, outdoing the already more audacious initiatives of Léon Harmel, promoter of workers-only unions, a group appears, few in number but very active, too noisy for the taste of some, convinced that the realization of a social order of Christian inspiration in no way required taking a reactionary stance against the Democratic current issued from the revolution of 1789 (as so many Catholics of the time still thought), and judging that, on the contrary, it was important to frankly accept all that was of value in that ideology. This was the era of the *abbés démocrates* [Democratic Priests], shouldered moreover, or at least spurred on, by a handful of lay people coming from diverse social milieus: intellectuals like Georges Goyau or Henri Lorin; employees like Marius Gonin, workers, and even industrialists; this was the era of Workers' Congresses and Democratic union, with the founding in Paris, in 1895, of a Christian-Democratic Party (still-born, moreover). It was the golden age of Marc Sangnier's *Sillon*, and of the enthusiastic awakening of a part of Catholic youth to these ideals.

Sangnier's supreme ambition, Mr. Vaussard who knew him well tells us, was "to penetrate the milieus of non-believers and to make it experimentally evident to them that one can be both fearless Chris-tian and unequivocal Democratic Republican." A generous ambi-tion, which inevitably makes one think, *mutatis mutandis*, of that of certain Progressive Christians, fifty years later, of the tragedy of a movement like *Jeunesse de l'Église*. Then as now, there was an often dishonest campaign of denigration on the part of *good Catholics, bad Christians,* more sensitive to their reactionary prejudices than to evangelical imperatives; but then as now, it must be added, stances that were too independent combined with clumsiness of expression, which betrayed a certain laxness in doctrine, "would fatally disturb all representatives of religious authority who were anxious to keep Catholic youth guarded in a nursery under their exclusive control, or having a secret nostalgia for the monarchy, intending in the strict sense to maintain the indirect power of the Church in temporal affairs." Pius X's condemnation of the *Sillon* in 1910, was a hard blow for the Christian Democrats. However, it would be unjust to reduce the history of Christian Democracy in France *from the death of Leo XIII to the Treaty of Versailles* to this one negative aspect. One cannot forget the rapid success, under the impetus of a team of worthy directors, of the *Semaines sociales,* whose pioneering role during these years is easily underestimated today. Neither can one neglect the slow progress of the Christian labor unions, which would permit the founding, in 1919, of the *Confédération française des travailleurs chrétiens* [C.F.C.T., French Confederation of Christian Workers]. Finally, one cannot neglect, despite the few results they obtained, the persevering action in Parliament of a small group of Catholic deputies who continue Albert de Mun's effort at initiating social legislation effectively protecting the workers' interests.

Chapter 3, full of interesting judgments and observations, retraces the highs and lows of the Christian Democratic idea between the two World Wars. The progress made by members of the Christian labor unions, supported by that of the *Jeunesse ouvrière chrétienne* [J.O.C., Young Christian Workers], is a favorable factor. However, it remains rather modest,[4] but it points the way for the future. Still, the center of interest during this period moves toward the political scene, where young Christian Democrats hope to realize their ideals thanks to the tiny *Parti démocratique populaire.* Much influenced, thanks to Marcel Prélot, by the ideas of Don Sturzo, the inspiration of Italian Christian Democratics, "going beyond the bounds of Social Catholicism, which was suspicious of the political arena, and organizing into a coherent whole the tendencies that were not exempt from confusion of the first Christian Democrats," the P.D.P. presented an attractive program, seriously thought of even while it remained perhaps a little too preoccupied with generalities. However, despite the promising start, this minuscule parliamentary group accomplished almost nothing. It certainly was lacking the support of a considerable portion of Catholic opinion, asleep in its social immobility and continuing, for the most part, to pursue the old theocratic dream, under the renewed and so-illusory guise of the *Action française*. But there were also other reasons for the P.D.P.'s lack of effectiveness, belonging only to it, and which are easy to identify with the passage of time: the lack of a long parliamentary tradition, which German and Belgian Catholics benefited from; the lack also of an undisputed leader, as Don Sturzo was for the Italian *Populari*; the low profile of most members of the group, a group poorly balanced moreover by the preponderance of Alsace-Lorrainians; the negative effects from the suppression of proportional representation; the psychological difficulty of associating with the Socialists given their persistent anticlericalism, aggravated by the unabated chauvinism of the popular Democratic leaders, who remain insensitive to pontifical warnings, and which leads them on more than one occasion to retreat to the right. The relative failure of the Christian democrats at the parliamentary level between the Wars nevertheless had an advantageous counterpart in the creation of a dynamic press that permits the gradual penetration of their ideals into milieus that until then had remained indifferent: weeklies, *La Vie catholique* [Catholic Life] and especially *Sept* [Seven] and *Temps présent* [The Present Time], in which collaborated a team of intellectuals, argued about in traditionalist Catholic milieus but incontestably brilliant; and a daily, *L'Aube* [Dawn], founded in 1932 by Francisque Gay, and whose foreign politics editorials by Georges Bidault quickly grabbed the attention of both political chroniclers and of Parliament.

The name Georges Bidault leads us naturally to Chapter 4, the Exercise of Power by the *Mouvement Républicain Populaire* [M.R.P., Popular Republican Movement]. The long-awaited breakthrough finally arrived, but under conditions which foreshadowed the "semi-abortion," to say the least, of the great hopes that had animated the combatants of the secret army. Born of the Resistance, of the refusal of most of the Christian Democrats to accept the defeat as irremediable, and the Vichy regime as definitive, the M.R.P. originally wanted to be a movement more than a party. It dreamed of gathering French Catholics around a progressive and Christian social ideal, freeing them from the outdated formulas that had for too long kept them looking inward in an uneasy circumspection as they confronted the modern world. However, it was quite naturally led toward politics, "understood not as a career, still less as a battleground for settling old scores, but as the privileged, irreplaceable means of realizing" their program. But we know the fundamental ambiguity that, even more than for our *Parti socialiste chrétiens* [P.S.C., Christian Socialist Party], weighed on the M.R.P. from the start: a party with a progressive program but elected for the most part by conservatives who, if they had indeed managed to forget this or that, had nevertheless not learned a great deal. It is also fair to remember that unlike its Belgian, Italian, or German counterparts, the M.R.P. at no moment had the entire responsibility of power, and that compromises, the poison of coalition governments, were therefore fatal. However, it must be added that if "the curve of events," as Étienne Borne said, can in part excuse the weakness of accomplishments, it is not possible to minimize the responsibility of men. Run principally "by jurists and publicists," the M.R.P. was not able to make the effort of thought required by the situation: it sidestepped some real problems of the post-War period and exhibited a disconcerting ignorance with respect to economic questions, which today condition internal and international politics. Its actions were thus handicapped, but also its power to influence. One reads with interest the comparison, suggestive and distressing, between *Le Monde* and *L'Aube* of the post-War period sketched by Mr. Vaussard, who further observes that "during these ten years, not one work of any worth was published by a leader of the M.R.P." Following a series of missed opportunities, which are recalled without passion but with just severity, it had to be admitted that, despite several non-negligible accomplishments, the Christians' presence in government had not effectively changed many of the defects of the pre-War political and economic regime. And the M.R.P.'s attitude concerning colonial problems and, soon, the war in Indochina, was still more disappointing and still less in conformity with what should have been a politics of Demo-Christian inspiration. We know how, following so many successive disappointments, the party's disintegration came about, some of its members moving to the R.P.F.

while others joined the *Jeune République* of Mendès-France, hoping to find there the realization of the ideal of social and international justice which the M.R.P. had espoused at its birth.

Disappointing story, we said at first. And yet, Mr. Vaussard, at the end of this first section, refuses to conclude on a pessimistic note:

> Some will conclude from this the failure of Christian Democracy, with or without the confessional label. We do not think it so. The idea remains not only viable, but fertile. It was incarnated, in France and abroad, in too many worthy men that a setback here or there should spark a condemnation without appeal of the ideal that motivated them. If democracy without epithets is already, as has been said, the most difficult regime to realize usefully, in the dignity of human institutions and gestures, how much more so is authentically Christian democracy! The effort of translating it into actions must always be made anew, as for the Christian confronting himself the effort of living his Evangel.

* * *

We will pass more quickly over the second part, dedicated to Belgium. In effect, the history of Catholic efforts *from Catholico-Liberal union-ism to organized Christian Democracy* and that of the vicissitudes of the *P.S.C. after World War II* are better known to the readers of the *Revue Nouvelle*. It is besides also the weakest part of the book and the one that would call for the most explication. Outside too-numerous errors of detail,[5] I for my part especially regret to find so little on the Catholic efforts aimed at obtaining universal suffrage. To be sure, alongside the Liberal opposition, there was a vigorous Catholic opposition to these demands, but it cannot make us forget the struggles led by the *Jeune Droite* during the twenty years preceding the War, nor the ear-lier attempts of Adolphe Dechamps and the group *Universel*, around 1863-1864, to give a more democratic base to the actions of Catholics. I also regret that there is no mention of the creation, in 1895, by the Catholic government, of a Ministry of Labor. This action, at that time, was not so lacking in originality, since Mr. Vaussard considers as one of the claims to fame of Fr. Lemire, one of the best-known French democratic priests, the fact that "by 1899, he was demanding that parliament create a Ministry of Labor" (p. 53). Clearly, the author was handicapped by the almost complete absence until recently of serious works on the history of Christian Democracy in Belgium,[6] but he also seems to have ignored certain works that could have provided a precious connecting thread. I am thinking for example of the *Histoire de la Belgique contemporaine*, published in three volumes from 1928 to 1930 under the direction of Canon Deharveng and especially of the little book, so perspicacious and so serene, by Mr. Franz Van Kalken, *Entre deux guerres. Esquisses de la vie politique en Belgique de 1918 à 1940* [*Between Two Wars. Sketches of Political Life in Belgium from 1918 to 1940*] (Brussels, 1944).

The reservations concerning the part dedicated to Belgium do not however prevent our pointing our numerous very pertinent remarks found throughout these pages. On the imminently bourgeois character of political, economic, and social life, more pronounced in Belgium than anywhere else in the 19th century, having for consequence a lasting narrow-mindedness in the face of the Social Problem. On the much more realist character, on the other hand, of Verhaegen's *Ligue démocratique belge*, compared to the French *Œuvre des Cercles*, "perhaps because instead of having been created like the latter under the impulsion of officers and aristocrats in a great capital, (it had) as its chief an engineer in an essentially industrial city," where Socialism was already in full bloom. On the stagnation of the Catholic Party between the Wars, in which:

> The predominance that the Flemish Question attained over all others for almost twenty years combined with what has always remained of clericalism in the Belgian Catholic world — where the advantages of political power are only with great difficulty dissociated from the purely religious demands of Christian faith — to lower the modest level of exterior vital signs of this Catholic world closed on itself.[7]

On the novel and progressive character, too much forgotten today, of the Van Zeeland experiment of 1936, whose program was rightfully considered by many young Catholics to be a practical application of the principles of the encyclical *Quadragesimo Anno*; one can dislike Mr. Van Zeeland, but one can only subscribe to Mr. Vaussard's affirmation when he writes that, for the period between the Wars, "his ministry represents the only truly constructive period seen by the country since 1921." On the quasi-impossibility, in the short term, of seeing constituted in Belgium a labor movement of the English type, gathering into one deconfessionalized party all of the progressive elements in the country, due to the persistence "as much of the old Socialist anticlericalism as of its contrary, the clericalism of the peasant masses and of the middle class bound by the influence of the clergy." Or the tendency of the Christian Democrats, stronger in Belgium than in France, "to consider the social encyclicals of Leo XIII and Pius XI to be compendiums though they were only outlines," such that "instead of using them as a point of departure for personal edification, they often stereotyped the teaching of them."

* * *

Italy forms the third panel of the tableau. This third part is assuredly that which will seem the most original to readers, it is to be hoped numerous, of Mr. Vaussard's work. Italy, in the French-speaking world, is a land of art and tourism, but how little its history and especially its recent history are known! Mr. Vaussard is on the contrary a specialist on Italian questions, who, besides studies on Italian Jansenism in the 18th century, has already published a noted volume on *L'intelligence catholique dans l'Italie du XXᵉ siècle* [*Catholic Intelligence in 20th Century Italy*]. Thanks to his reading and his personal contacts, he is in a position to evoke, in a detailed tableau replete with concrete data, the social and economic conditions in Italy before 1880, region by region,[8] and to reveal in a hundred or so pages the essential history, over the course of the last century, of Catholics' reaction to the *Risorgimento* and its Liberal aspirations, then to the nationalist ambitions of the early 20th century and to the Fascist Revolution, finally to the rise of Communism and to the drama of unemployment and the peasants' misery, especially in the *Mezzogiorno* [i.e., southern Italy], systematically disadvantaged during the entire last century by the allied egotism of the bourgeoisie and the working class in the north of the Peninsula.

Three chapters retrace the principal steps in that history: The Comportment of Catholics confronting the Liberal State from 1870 to 1918, that is to say during the period dominated by the Roman Question, which risked drawing away attention from other important problems comportment characterized especially by the abstention on the political level of a large number of Catholics following pontifical directives, then by the timid awakening to social issues with the *Œuvre des congrès*, and finally by the crisis of the first Christian Democracy under Fr. Murri around 1900;[9] *Ascension and Decline of the Italian Popular party (1918-1925)*, or the brief revenge of Christian Democracy, purified thanks to the strong personality of Don Sturzo,[10] the only truly profound thinker of Latin Christian Democracy, the worth of whose theoretical body of work and the realism of whose practical action the author never ceases to praise throughout his book; finally, after the slow death of the Popular Party during Mussolini's rise and the return of those Christian Democrats who were not exiled to clandestine activity or to the discrete protection of *Action catholique*, is *The Rebirth and Evolution of Christian Democracy after the Fascist Interruption*, slice of contemporary history, in which are found chronologically and logically reclassified, explicated and critiqued impartially, numerous facts that we had read in the press over the last ten years but often without possessing the connecting thread that gives them their meaning: succession of the different De Gasperi cabinets, gradual unraveling of the *Democrazia cristiana* in relation to the Communists and winning of the absolute majority; establishment of an agrarian reform analyzed at length by Mr. Vaussard, who explains the advantages[11] of it very well but also the disadvantages; temptation of bourgeois-ification and *arriviste* mentality among the new Christian Democratic leaders and dangerous tendency among a good many of them to place the anticommunist struggle on the level of propaganda and parliamentary tactics rather than on that of ideas and doctrinal confrontation; uneasiness within the party between the wing favoring a move to the right (Pella), encouraged by a portion of the conformist religious press, and the one wishing to remain faithful to the original inspiration, truly democratic and truly Christian (Dossetti); triumph of the "youths" and the elements of the popular base during the Congress of Naples in June 1954, which gave the secretariat general of the party to Mr. Fanfani, one of the former leaders of the progressive tendency that was expressed in the *Cronache sociali* [*Social Chronicles*].

Whatever the limitations, the delays, and the imperfections in the contemporary realizations of Italian Democracy — Mr. Vaussard tries in no way to dissimulate them — one remains struck, in reading this synthesis, by the positive results of those ten years of preponderantly Democratic-Christian government. And one takes with some melancholy to comparing this "efficiency," to use a term in vogue, with the quasi-immobility of our P.S.C. governments. Truth to tell, to be fair, it must also be considered that everything needed to be done in Italy and that it was therefore easier to make progress than in a country already largely democratized, as is Belgium. And the fact of having a knife at the throat due to the immediate character that the Communist danger presents in Italy certainly facilitated things by silencing certain recriminations when faced with the necessity of choosing between two evils the one which seemed the lesser. But it must not be forgotten moreover the particular difficulties which the proximity of the Vatican might have constituted for the leaders of *Democrazia cristiana*, and the pretexts for timidity some could have found in the authoritative advice of personalities who were more or less close to the Sovereign Pontiff, who sometimes excel at passing off their personal opinions, or even their prejudices, as the expression of orthodoxy or at least of official doctrine.

It is besides one of the particularly interesting aspects of this history of Italian Christian Democracy that it was more tightly dependent on the interventions of the Holy See than in the other countries where the movement existed. Professor Latreille put it well:

> If in Belgium, one can see Catholics, who are conscious of their autonomy as citizens, practically ignore an encyclical that impedes their political action, as happened with *Mirari vos*, on the peninsula the least word falling off the lips of a Pontiff, a sign coming from the high spheres of the Vatican, are orders which cannot be contradicted, which one cannot neglect to register, but with which one can sometimes find an accommodation. A simple *non expedit* kept

Catholics away from the parliamentary battle for more than thirty years, but not from municipal struggles nor from civic action. Of course, an attempted action like Don Sturzo's is only conceivable from the moment when a Pope, Benedict XV, authorizes the establishment of the Italian Popular party (which intends not to be a confessional party) and up until the day another Pope, Pius XI, withdraws his powerful protection and leaves the last few *popolari* alone to face the fascist tide.[12]

Let us note on this subject that the confessional percentages of the Christian Democratic parties could perhaps have more strongly held the attention of Mr. Vaussard, and not only in the case of Italy. One of his critics[13] reproached him for not having put enough emphasis on the fundamental handicap that every Christian Democratic party suffered from and that condemned them to immobility: "It is not making a pejorative judgment to say that insofar as the electoral mass of the Christian Democratic parties will vote for them for religious reasons, their leaders must be absolutely docile, in all domains, to the injunctions of the hierarchy and the Holy See, under the pain of losing the support that carried them to power." There is certainly truth in this remark and one could illustrate it from history. However, one could also retort that the confessional influences can equally act in a constructive way to the extent that the hierarchy hopes to see the social doctrine of the Church realized institutionally — and the hypothesis anyway has nothing chimerical about it — the support that it brings to a Christian-Democratic party can win for it many conservative voters, who would have denied their votes to the progressive program of the party but who accorded them to it for religious reasons, and can thus give it a parliamentary power it would otherwise never have obtained. The social realizations, relatively modest but incontestable, of Belgian and Italian Catholics in power were in part made possible by this. There is also a history lesson therein before which one cannot close one's eyes, especially when considering head on the paucity of effective French realizations in spite of so many programs each more advanced than the other.

* * *

We cannot finish these already long pages without mentioning an aspect that Mr. Vaussard takes especially to heart and which few reviewers of his book seem to have noticed. Vice-president of the French chapter of *Pax Christi* after having been the founder of the *Bulletin catholique international*, he has for a long time closely followed the development of nationalism throughout the world, stigmatized the responsibility of the European ruling classes, including Catholics, for the rise of militarism since Napoleon the First's establishment of obligatory conscription, and deplored the minimal response to the warnings of Leo XIII and Benedict XV aimed at trying to save the glory of Christian civilization through peace among the great powers. While studying Christian Democracy, he especially concentrated on discovering what attitude its leaders adopted in this regard in the various countries. As he explains from the first lines of his introduction, "as it is hardly arguable that the major problems" faced by Catholic bourgeoisie in the 19th century, as for all of bourgeois society, "have been of an economic nature and a military nature, it is on these two problems that we will first focus our attention." He observes, and the thing has often been mentioned, the egotism of the bourgeois classes, ill-advised besides for it resulted in the rapid loss of the considerable privileges acquired after the Revolution of 1789: "the renunciation of immediate gain in favor of greater social or international balance is not put into practice by almost any representative of the so-called elite leadership — be they Catholic, Protestant, or atheist — does not enter into the plans of any great States." However, he also observes, and the thing will be more surprising, that on the international level the Christian Democrats did not often display any more perspicacity than the conservatives and that, despite a certain number of exceptions — especially in Belgium and in Italy[14] — many of these generous Catholics did not lend as attentive an ear to papal calls for peace *and for the establishment of conditions conducive to peace* as to their calls for greater social justice. The importance that Mr. Vaussard attaches to this aspect of the problem appears when we see him considering the year 1917, year of the failure of Benedict XV's attempt at mediation, as a year "as crucial as 1848," the year of failed social revolutions that pushed frightened Catholics toward the right and after which the working class began to detach itself from the Church.

* * *

Writing in a Belgian revue, there is a last point to which I would call attention for an instant. In the Belgian section of *Témoignage chrétien* [Christian Witnessing], Mr. Gérard-Libois reproached Mr. Vaussard for presenting to his readers something other than that which his title announces: "It is no longer about the history of Christian Democracy, but about the political action of Catholics. The two topics are interesting but it is regrettable that the second is given to us bearing the label of the first."[15] What should we make of this criticism?

When one speaks of Christian Democracy in Belgium, one thinks either of efforts made aimed at realizing the betterment of workers in a Christian context, or of political tendencies elsewhere baptized "Catholicism of the Left." When Mr. Vaussard's work is broached from this perspective, one cannot help being shocked and disappointed: the P.S.C. is presented as typical manifestation of Christian Democracy, which is doubtless not completely false, but cannot in spite of everything fail to astonish all those who are used to hearing about the permanent tension within this party between the "Christian Democratic" wing and the conservative wing, and who observe — to their delight or chagrin — that up to the present the latter is far from letting itself be dominated by the former; and Mr. Van Zeeland appears as a Christian Democratic personality, which will further stupefy those who are accustomed to the Belgian vocabulary in this matter. But precisely, in order to understand Mr. Vaussard's point of view, it is necessary to forget our Belgian purview and this is moreover quite educational.

In 1831, Belgium adopted a constitution of the liberal type to which it has since remained faithful and, in spite of a few periods of rather superficial agitation,[16] Catholics never rejected the political ideal of a constitutional monarchy in which public opinion as represented in parliament has the predominant role in running the country, and in which it is through parliamentary action that efforts are made to obtain institutions acceptable to a Christian conscience. The only problems that divided Catholics were, in the context of this regime, those pertaining to the scope of reforms to be introduced for the benefit of the working classes, and the name "Christian Democracy" was used to designate the tendency favoring the extension of social legislation, universal suffrage, and more recently, the establishment in Belgium of an authentic social democracy of individualist inspiration (as opposed to a social democracy of the statist type, represented in it radical form by the popular democrats of communist inspiration, but toward which the Socialist Party seems to likewise be leaning more and more if not in theory then at least in fact).

The problems that Catholics found themselves confronted with in France and Italy were rather different. The regime itself was in question. From the monarchists of the *Action française*, deaf to the warnings of Pius XI — not to mention supporters of the Vichy regime — many French Catholics only saw salvation for the Church and society in a chimerical return to the monarchist regime of the *Ancien régime*, still much better in their eyes than the Republic under the Empire. In Italy, no sooner had they stopped criticizing the constitutional monarchy in the name of a sort of pontifical theocracy, rather poorly defined besides, than many Catholics began throwing themselves enthusiastically into fascist authoritarianism, which they expected to protect moral values effectively. A farsighted nucleus resisted these mirages of monarchy protecting the Church or of the providential man and, believing that in the long run the Church had everything to lose and nothing to gain by allying itself with regimes that too evidently contradicted the aspirations of their times, affirmed against wind and tide that the important thing was to reconstruct, on the foundation of all that was worthwhile in those modern aspirations, a society that was both democratic and Christian. The problems of workers' rights had their place in these preoccupations but the question they had to envision was more vast: it was Catholics' options faced with Democracy in its totality. A Frenchman having closely followed the internal struggles of his country for a half-century and having been interested for many years in Italian questions, it is normal that it is from this more general and more strictly political angle that Mr. Vaussard approaches the problem and the history of Christian Democracy — it must be added besides that such is the sense that the term most often has in France today — and it is likewise normal that the P.S.C. and the Van Zeeland experiment of 1936 appear, from this perspective, as "Christian-Democratic" realizations.

* * *

These few remarks, like the rest of our summary moreover, permit us to glimpse that Mr. Vaussard's work has interest as more than a retrospective. Despite the lacunas that we have mentioned in passing, it is stimulating to the intellect and full of lessons for the present and the future. One of the principal lessons is doubtless the observation that he returns to on several occasions, of the great danger that Christian Democracy is exposed to for lack of doctrinal understanding. Whether we are talking about Belgian Catholics, ripened by the almost continuous exercise of political power since 1830, or French and Italian Catholics, who due to local circumstances, very different moreover in each country, only came to it very late but how precisely would have had the leisure to reflect on it, he believes that he must diagnose, despite the wonderful exception of Don Sturzo, a common weakness at the doctrinal level, from which their action greatly suffered. Because they were unable to elaborate a coherent political and social doctrine the equal of Liberalism and Marxism, they have as yet produced hardly anything but militants and politicians, and almost no statesmen. The future of Christian Democracy is at risk and the profound reasons for the disappointments and the retreats of the last years are doubtless largely to be found in this fact. This is not a new idea for the readers of the *Revue Nouvelle*, who know how much this problem occupies our staff. May the lessons of the past, distant and recent, so opportunely recalled by Mr. Vaussard, stimulate the zeal of the responsible parties in this direction.

Notes
[1] Maurice Vaussard, *Histoire de la démocratie chrétienne. I: France, Belgique, Italie* (Collection *Esprit*). Paris, Éditions du Seuil, 1956, 336 pp.
[2] Joseph Rovan, *Histoire de la démocratie chrétienne. II: Le catholicisme politique en Allemagne*. Paris, 1956. We have unfortunately not received this work.
[3] B. Merkine-Guetzévitch and Marcel Prélot, preface to J.B Duroselle, *Les débuts du catholicisme social en France, 1822-1870*. Paris, 1951, pp. vii-viii.
[4] The proof of this is in the fact that the Matignon accords in 1936 were concluded between management and the C.G.T. "as if the latter had a monopoly on representing labor."
[5] Here are a few of them: p. 135: The Bishop of Liège, Van Bommel, is called vicar general of Malines; p. 147: Cardinal Mercier is said to be, in 1905, recently

promoted to the Archbishopric of Malines; p. 154: the *Patriote* was not the only major French-language Catholic daily before 1914, it suffices to mention the *Bien public*; p. 171: the author only sees the military or international aspect of the royal question; to grasp the latter exactly in its psychological reality, one cannot minimize the tension at the level of internal politics between King Léopold and the parliamentary milieus; p. 172: it is already known that the quadripartite Van Acker ministry, with U.D.B. participation, was not the first postwar cabinet, but only the third; p. 175: the U.D.B. had in reality one elected member in the 1956 elections; p. 180: it was a bipartite Liberal-P.S.C. cabinet and not a tripartite cabinet that passed the popular consultation; p. 185: it was the low-clergy rather than the "religious authorities" who "openly" supported the Léopoldists by intervening in the political struggle; p. 186: it was after April 15, 1950, that the P.S.C. won an absolute majority in both houses; p. 187: it is Mr. Auguste Cool and not Mr. P.W. Segers who is president of the C.S.C. Minor details, one admits, but which are irritating to the reader and that disagreeably recall the so-often deficient information of the best French newspapers when it comes to events in Belgium.

[6] We think it worth mentioning at this moment that a doctoral dissertation in history on the beginnings of Christian Democracy in Belgium (until 1909), by Mr. Rezohazy, is forthcoming.

[7] A very accurate statement. Let us add nevertheless that Mr. Vaussard, like the French in general, does not seem to have sufficiently realized the democratic and even Christian-Democratic aspect of the Flemish Movement, which was much more than a simple reaction against French culture. Whatever may have been the political exploitation that followed, the movement had at its base both a concern for folk education and a preoccupation with bridging the divide in Flemish country between the French-speaking social elite and the masses of workers or peasants: concern and preoccupation which on the whole left indifferent both the liberal conservatives and the Socialists, who were hardly given to preach the coming together of classes.

[8] Because, in this only recently united country, the problems are posed very differently in the rich Piedmont and in the still half-feudal Neopolitan provinces, in Venice impoverished by Austrian domination and in Tuscany, which benefited from the enlightened despotism of its sovereigns and from the intelligent paternalism of its great landowners, not to mention the Papal States. As far as these last are concerned, Mr. Vaussard is perhaps a little severe. In effect, the political regime that deprived the lay element of all effective participation in government was an intolerable anachronism; but recent works have shown the undeniable administrative effort accomplished during the half-century before 1870 and it does not appear that the common people have gained much in the new system, but on the contrary.

[9] For this period, the author could have perhaps taken advantage of the numerous monographs published in the last few years by a constellation of young historians on the Italian "Catholic Movement" in the second half of the 19th century. It is in any case a shame that the only bibliographic reference found in his notes is to the dated work by E. Vercesi, *Il movimento cattolico in Italia* (Florence, 1923). One would like to have at least seen mention made of Fausto Fonzi's excellent sketch, *I cattolici et la società italiana dopo l'unità* [*Catholics and Italian Society Since Unification*] (Rome, 1953). Mr. Fonzi's work is all the more interesting in that he arrives at the same conclusions as Fr. Van Isacker in his book *Werkelijk en*

wettelijk land. De Katholieke opinie tegenover de rechterzijde, 1863-1884 (Anvers, 1955): the adversaries of the *transigenti*, that is the partisans of a reconciliation between Catholicism and Liberalism, were not merely backward reactionaries who lacked understanding of their era; many among them sought, in reaction against the "legal country" constituted by a narrow bourgeois oligarchy, to build on the "real country," on the working masses who were still deeply Christian, and were led, by tactics or by conviction as the case may have been, to undertake the improvement of the workers' lot: they were reactionary relative to the ideology of 1789, but the ultramontane conservatives generally showed themselves to be more open to social problems than Liberal Catholics and it is from their ranks that came the future pioneers of Christian Democracy, against which these same conservatives, twenty years later, would indignantly revolt before seeking, under the pontificate of Pius X, to organize through an alliance with the Liberals (known as the "pact Gentiloni") the defense of the established order.

[10] Don Sturzo, Don Murri, one notices the preponderance of ecclesiastics as leaders of Christian Democracy from the beginning in Italy. In France, on the contrary, from Ozanam to A. de Mun, from L. Harmel to M. Sangnier, the names of laymen mark the route.

[11] In particular this one, too little noticed by those who only see the "socialist" aspect of this agrarian reform: "The agrarian reform initiated by the Christian-Democratic government proceeds from all the other directives and aims at much more than the breaking up of a few *latifundia*. It addresses itself more to people than to things. One would hardly be exaggerating to say that its ultimate goal, alone capable of ruining the revolutionary hopes of the Communists, is the formation of an Italian middle class that this country has long lacked (...). The development, already begun, of an agrarian middle class, following that of industry and the technical professions attached to it, would forge the best instrument of resistance both to the excesses of capitalist power and to the downward leveling resulting from the economic consequences of the two World Wars in the countries ruined by them — continued inflation and proletarianization of the bourgeoisie. A new ruling class would be born from a better distribution of national wealth and, at first, from a more rational exploitation of the ground" (p. 292).

[12] In *Le Monde*, February 7, 1956.

[13] Michel François in *France-Observateur*, April 5, 1956.

[14] Mr. Vaussard is especially hard on French Christian Democrats. He makes an exception for Marc Sangnier after the War of 1914. He has been reproached for not giving full credit to the pacifist and internationalist inspiration of the *Sillon* from before 1914, in which the chauvinist tendency represented by Henri du Roure may have been less widespread than he seems to say.

[15] From February 17, 1956. Developing his criticism for the particular case of Belgium, the author continues: "It is not surprising, under these conditions, that the veritable problems of structure faced by the Belgian Christian-Democratic movement are eluded or poorly framed. What place and what theoretical and practical influence does this movement occupy in the Catholic population? What relations have been established between the socioeconomic branches of Christian Democracy (not to mention the educational and apostolic movements which are institutionally linked to them) and the elements which are their spokesmen and

their representatives both in Parliament and in the P.S.C.? How has this problem been treated since the school war?"

[16] Campaign against the constitution led by the ultramontane Catholics of the Périn-de Hemptinne faction around 1870-1880; more recently, the Rexist endeavour.

On the Origins
of Catholic Social Doctrine
1966

From 1848, the year in which Marx published the *Communist Manifesto*, to 1891, the year of *Rerum novarum*, more than half a century went by. These two dates have often been contrasted to point out how late the Church, by comparison with the Socialist movement, came to recognize the workers problem. In reality, however, the situation is more complex than this, although it is undeniable that the Church allowed itself to fall behind Socialism in this domain.

Although by 1830, theoreticians and militants like Robert Owen and the Chartists in England, Saint-Simon, Fourier, or Proudhon in France are denouncing the injustices of Liberal Capitalism, although, in spite of the reactionary wave that followed the crisis of 1848, Marx succeeds with true revolutionary genius in setting up, by 1864, the First International, and in gradually raising up in a common hope the industrial proletariat, revolted by their "undeserved poverty," the majority of Catholics and most of the ecclesiastic authorities, until the end of the century, refuse to recognize the necessity for "fundamental reforms," and consider as dangerously revolutionary the efforts seeking to modify institutionally the workers' condition. This is moreover less due to selfishness or to ignorance of the actual situation than it is to a lack of understanding of the new problems posed by the Industrial Revolution. Many are indeed aware of the lamentable condition of the workers, but the only solution they can think of proposing is private charity. Even after 1891, when the supreme authority will have finally taken an official position, they will still hesitate to admit that morality and religion have a role to play in the organization of economic and social structures, and that there are remedies for the workers' poverty other than charitable work.

But it would be a distorting simplification to forget that a more farsighted minority of lay people, priests, and bishops—who were also part of the complex reality we call the Church—awakened rather quickly to veritable social concerns by perceiving that the workers' question was a problem not only of charity but of justice. It is in these limited but active milieus, some open to a certain socialist influence, the majority in energetic resistance against it but thus always in a position of dependence, that little by little were elaborated a Catholic social doctrine and Catholic social action that received their first official expression in Leo XIII's famous encyclical. It is in briefly recalling these efforts, initially dispersed, then gradually convergent, that the few pages which follow are dedicated.

*   *   *

J.B. Duroselle's work on *The Beginnings of Social Catholicism in France (1822-1870)*[1] [*Les débuts du catholicisme social en France* (1822-1870)] has revealed in that country, as early as the second quarter of the 19th century, thus in a period contemporary with the beginnings of Socialism as such, "a stirring of personages and an explosion of works whose lack of success did not generally discourage further initiatives."[2] This movement is born of two entirely independent sources. On the one hand, the legitimist milieus, naturally hostile to the French Revolution, which denounce the suppression of corporations and the traditional legislation of labor as the source of Liberal exploitation of the workers. On the other hand, the milieus which can already be referred to as Christian Democrats, gathered around the *Avenir* of Lamennais, around the converted Saint-Simonian Buchez, who wants to reconcile Catholicism with the ideals of 1789, around the Catholic disciples of Fourier, like Arnaud de l'Ariège, who seek the synthesis of pre-Marxist Socialism and evangelical inspiration.

As for as the hierarchy, the studies of Fr. Paul Droulers[3] permit us to sketch a tentative outline, rather disappointing it must be admitted. Many bishops do not react any differently from the Cardinal d'Astros, Archbishop of Toulouse, who while often deploring the rapid de-Christianization of the working class and its increasing poverty in his mandates, does not dream of establishing a link between the two, and, for the remedy of that poverty, sees no other solution than a moral and spiritual one: resignation on the part of the poor, charity from the rich. While he favors workers' organizations which have purely religious goals, the Cardinal takes no interest in mutual aid societies, which were flourishing however under the July Monarchy. He is opposed *a fortiori* to any idea of institutional reform that would be undertaken in the name of social justice. Doubtless, the moral aberrations of certain Socialists of the time partially explain his mistrust; doubtless as well, as is the case for the representatives of the Holy See in France during the same period,[4] the social aspect of the proletariat problem appears to him in fact to be linked and confused with the political aspect, generally revolutionary in its ideals and its methods and which evokes therefore the horrors and the persecutions of 1793. But there is still something else which can explain his reticence, and that of many of his colleagues, when faced with any attempt at modifying the established order: an almost unreal hyper-spiritualism, which makes him ignore everything at the level of the profane. He does not notice that the new situation created by the generalization of the capitalist economy poses a moral problem and that this is one of those "mixed" questions toward which the Church cannot remain indifferent.

There are however one or two exceptions worth noting. Here and there, in the regions where large industries are developing, a few prelates intervene with a certain amount of vigor: the Cardinal de Croij in Rouen; Msgr. Affre in Paris, who can distinguish between good industrialization in and of itself as a progressive factor, and an economic system based entirely on profit and ignoring the dignity of man; Msgr. Belmas and then Msgr. Giraud, in Cambrai, the latter by 1845 invoking the entire labor question; the Cardinal de Bonald in Lyons, who openly regrets the direction of the new industrial economy and who is not afraid of giving a certain moral support to strikers. But most of the time, the episcopate thinks it sees the profound root of the evil in the employers' lack of a moral sense, the problem of future social reforms is seen principally in the "clerical" aspect of the violation of the Sunday repose, and extremely rare are those who, like the Archbishop of Paris, question the very system of Liberal economics. At least one must observe that in this period in which large industries were still in their infancy, a few bishops had "realized that it was one of their functions to speak out in the name of Christian doctrine, at least at the level of principles, in this temporal domain of economic and social industrialism, precisely because the human being is at once body and soul and cannot be completely divided" (Droulers).

The Revolution of 1848, which gave a free rein to the aspirations of Romantic Socialism, at first favored the Christian-Democratic current, which could count on the support of Msgr. Affre, among others. It found for several months an organ of expression in the newspaper *L'Ère nouvelle* [*The New Age*], founded by a former Menaisian, Fr. Maret with the collaboration of Ozanam, and edited by Lacordaire. *L'Ère nouvelle*, whose title was a program in itself, meant not only to defend the truth of the principles of 1789 and the advantages of the Republican regime, but equally to promote various social reforms considered revolutionary at the time: the participation of the workers in the rewards and management of businesses, the organization of arbitration, and assistance to the unemployed.

This program, approved by the Archbishop of Paris, met with an enthusiastic reception, especially among the young clergy. But the interest raised by *L'Ère nouvelle* and by this or that provincial Catholic newspaper defending comparable ideas cannot erase the fact that most Catholics, like the great majority of the nation moreover, while they were comfortably resigned to the momentary disappearance of the monarchy, feared more than anything seeing the bourgeois republic transform into a social-democratic republic. Without sharing the simplistic and incomplete views of Henri Guillemin,[5] it must be recognized that, very careful of maintaining the order and intangible character of the "sacred dogma of property," not dreaming of making a distinction between the extremist demands of the partisans of Communism and the difficult but reasonable reforms of Socialism, Catholics were only too ready to consider the structural reforms promoted by the Democrats as an inadmissible pretension to the violent seizing of others' wealth. Popular excesses, in particular the June Riots, managed to frighten the great mass of Catholics, and the Christian-Democratic movement found itself engulfed in the general reaction against everything with a greater or lesser resemblance to Socialism. During the Second Empire and the beginning of the Third Republic, there will no longer be anyone but conservatives to represent Social Catholicism in

France, convinced partisans of paternalist methods and for the most part aligned with the doctrine of the Counter-revolution.

* * *

At the moment when Social Catholicism makes as it were a re-entry curve in France and practically disappears in its Christian-Democrat form for a quarter century, the torch seemed to be re-lit in Rome itself. It is in fact curious to discover in the first years of *La Civiltà cattolica*, the Roman Jesuit journal founded in 1850 in a decidedly anti-revolutionary perspective, a series of articles by the FF. Taparelli d'Azeglio, Liberatore, and Curci which indicate, by the positions they take and by their suggestions for practical reforms, a real social sensibility to the abuses engendered by the capitalist exploitation of workers.[6] They denounce both the crime against humanity of an economic system which sees in the worker only a machine for production, and the fundamental error of Socialism, which, the better to counter Liberal individualism, stifles the person by absorbing all of his individuality, his liberty, his initiative in a state collectivity which is the only authority, as it is the only proprietor.

But these progressive ideas soon passed into the background, in part due to the reactionary wave that rolled across and weighed on Europe in the 1850s, but especially, doubtless, because the evolution of events and of the Roman question in particular left the Roman milieus much more sensitive to the repercussions of Liberalism in the political and doctrinal order of things than to its stillborn social consequences.

The criticisms that the sociologists of *La Civiltà cattolica* leveled against economic Liberalism were not however completely forgotten. It has not been sufficiently pointed out that in the encyclical *Quanta cura* of 1864 and in the *Syllabus* which accompanied it, although the Pope denounces without much subtlety the illusion of that Socialism which claims to replace Providence with the State, he likewise denounces the material and pagan character of economic Liberalism, which excludes morality from the relationship between capital and labor. These admonitions did not pass entirely unnoticed,[7] but it is assuredly not this aspect of the *Syllabus* which caught the attention of the majority of its readers.

Would the Vatican Council of 1870, had it not been interrupted, have again taken up this question? We know that a draft had been written by one of the preparatory commissions, "on easing the misery of the poor and the workers."[8] But based on moral remedies, this text seems quite weak and inefficient. It bypasses, moreover, certain essential aspects and is not favorable to institutional solutions. This attitude can be explained by the mistrust of Socialism, regularly confused during this period with out-and-out Communism. For many ecclesiastics of the time, it was identified with Proudhon's cry "Property is theft," or with Fourier's theories on the community of women, and they were additionally indignant at hostility which Marxist theoreticians expressed toward the idea of religion, such that for them, Socialism appeared more like a subversive and atheistic ideology than like a collection of socioeconomic reforms. One finds an indication of this mentality in the reception given by the theological preparatory commission to Canon Gay's report on Socialism and Communism. They judged that it contained "abominations and absurdities which were beneath the dignity of the council's attention"; at best, a few councilors evinced surprise that one could envisage a condemnation "not, however, by council canons as with ordinary heresies, but by a general affirmation of vehement reprobation and contempt."[9]

In short, despite some stirrings which in other circumstances might have developed into a Catholic answer to both Liberalism and Socialism, it is not in Rome that the first synthesis of Social Catholicism adapted to the industrial society of the 19th century would be elaborated, but rather in the Germanic countries.

* * *

In Germany, even though industrial progress announced itself later than in France, Catholics were very early on sensitive to the destabilization of traditional social structures by Liberal capitalism. They were of an even more conservative mindset than French Catholics, and attached at least as much importance as the latter to the maintenance of "order." Only, unlike France, where too many Catholics merely set their sights on superficial order and the submission of workers to the existing state of affairs, the order which the German Catholics sought to restore was the traditional order, the social organicism of the *Ancien régime*, hardly democratic, of course, but which at least had the advantage of protecting the little man from the unrestrained exploitation of the wealthy.

In truth, until 1870, it is primarily the uplifting of the craftspeople and the organization of the peasants which preoccupies the majority of German Catholics seeking to "bring the Church closer to the people in order to bring the people closer to the Church." But gradually the Workers Question *per se* gained equal attention. By 1837, the Baden Catholic militant Buss was denouncing the dangers of uncontrolled industrialization and demanding, in opposition to the sacrosanct principles of economic Liberalism, an intervention by the State to regulate the workers' situation, affirming that the Church had the duty to defend them as they were deprived of official representation.[10]

In 1846, a former apprentice shoemaker turned priest, Fr. Kolping, established the first *Gesellenverein* ["companion society"]. Thanks to collaborators from among the elite and the active participation of the apprentices themselves, to whom Kolping, as in the modern J.O.C., left considerable initiative, the organization, blessed by Cardinal Geissel of Cologne, prospered rapidly and, from the Rhineland, spread its branches all across Germany and all the way into Austria and Switzerland.[11] Little by little other social organizations developed in the industrial regions of the Rhineland, which would one day lead to the founding of the *Volksverein* ["people's society"] and the *Mönchen-Gladbach* movement:[12] to the desire for the saving of souls and the easing of suffering, which was long predominant, was gradually added that of organizing the profession and furnishing a solid base of action for the workers' militantism, with a view to eventually modifying the system of labor.

In 1863, the Workers Question even formed the principal theme of Frankfort's *Katholikentag* ["Catholic Day"]. A priest there denounced a regime which "far from recognizing the man within the worker, only considers him to be a machine and even treats him worse than a machine" and, after having listened to theoretical exposés and some concrete testimony, the participants concluded by recommending immediately to Catholics that they "take up the study of the great social question that, certainly, can only be brought to an appropriate resolution in the light of Christianity."[13]

In this evolution where, increasingly, the workers problem appeared to German Catholics as a question of institutional reform more than as a simple matter of organizing assistance, an important role was played by the Bishop of Mainz, Msgr. Ketteler.[14] His role has often been misunderstood, the prelate being presented as a pioneer of Christian Democracy and as the initiator of the flourishing social works movement of contemporary Germany. But, many of these organizations, originating in the Cologne region, were born apart from his initiatives and, besides, although Ketteler, when he undertook to find practical solutions, was sometimes largely inspired by Socialist doctrines, especially in the form which Lassale had given to them, and although he even echoed some of Lassale's arguments and his complaints against capitalism,[15] he nevertheless had scant sympathy for democracy: when he stood up against the oppression of which the economically weak were victims under the social regime of his time, this Westphalian aristocrat, dreamed above all of a return to the cooperatively based society such as that known under the Holy Roman Empire in the Middle Ages. Ketteler's influence on contemporary Social Catholicism remains nevertheless considerable.

First, let us examine the ideological level, where his true genius lies. By condensing, in 1864, in *La question ouvrière et le christianisme* [*The Workers Question and Christianity*], the results of fifteen years of reflection, he intended not only to suggest certain concrete reforms, but above all to show that the solution to the workers problem could only be conceived of in terms of a general conception of the State and of society, as much in direct opposition to Liberal individualism as to modern State centralized totalitarianism. He took a vigorous stand against the solutions put forward by the capitalist bourgeoisie or by *étatiste* socialism and exalted, under the influence of the Catholic Romanticism which had marked his youth, a conception of society presented as a living organism, animated by the unity of faith and strongly hierarchical, in which professions would be organized with an aim to the smooth operation of the entire State, reduced to the role of a simple function of this great body. In so doing, he appeared as the first theoretician of this cooperatively based social organism that would constitute for more than half a century the foundation of Catholic Social doctrine.

Even on a practical level, where he was less original, one cannot minimize the support for the labor cause represented by intervention of the energetic prelate, who put all his episcopal prestige at its service. Well realizing that he must have no illusions about the time necessary for a social reform as profound as the one he envisioned, and anxious in the meantime to parry as quickly as possible by improving the workers' situation within the framework of the existing regime, he recognized the usefulness of calling on intervention from the State, which he had at first distrusted, in order to counterbalance the power of the capitalists and to obtain certain concrete results such as the augmentation of salaries, the reduction of working hours, the Sunday repose, or the abolition of child labor in factories.

Ketteler, about whom Leo XIII would say that he had been his "great predecessor," died in 1877, but his spirit did not die with him. The support which the Center Party (which encompassed the German Catholics in the Reichstag) gave to the first social legislation, can in large measure be attributed to his impetus; this legislation, introduced after 1879 and especially after 1881, gave Germany a notable lead in this domain over other countries. Furthermore, a few theologians, especially Jesuits, began to take an interest in questions of social morality, for example Fr. Cathrein in a series of articles published in the *Stimmen aus Maria Laach* [Voices from...] from 1879 to 1882, and Fr. Lehmkuhl, who, in his *Theologia moralis* (1883), devoted some pages of ideas that were novel for that period to the question of a fair salary.[16]

* * *

The ideas launched by Ketteler and his collaborators met with particular success in Austria, thanks to the Baron von Vogelsang,[17] a noble of German origin converted to Catholicism by Ketteler and retired in Vienna since 1864. He had there become editor-in-chief of the *Vaterland*, the organ of the federalist and agrarian aristocracy, extremely hostile to nascent high finance and large industry, who was in part controlled by Jews. Preoccupied not only with the workers problem but equally with the peasant question, extremely important in Central Europe, he founded a journal to encourage their study in 1879, the *Oesterreichische Monatschrift für Gesellschaftswissenschaft und Volkswissenschaft* [*Austrian Journal of Social Science and Folk Science*], which later became *Monatschrift für christliche Sozialreform*. With an intensity which would earn him the epithet "Christian Socialist," he criticizes the capitalist system born of the Revolution, and makes himself the apologist for State intervention aimed at bringing order to individualist anarchy and at liberating the means of production from its traditional social attributions. Following his teacher Ketteler, he points out the social function of property and, more than the latter, he insists on the necessity of organizing the professions, not in the Socialist manner, moreover, too étatiste for his likes, but by returning to the medieval ideal of co-operatives [guilds/corporations] adapted to the modern era.

Vogelsang succeeded in winning a group of young Austrian Catholics to his ideas, such as Fr. Schindler, who would succeed him as head of the Austrian Social School; Lueger, future mayor of Vienna, where he realized a remarkable social works program; and the Prince Charles von Löewenstein, who organized meetings of Social Christians on his property of Haid from 1883 to 1888, from which would emerge among other things the famous "theses of Haid."[18] In them, it was confirmed that the labor contract is of a completely different nature from the contract for hire, due to the moral nature of human activity; that it is necessary to obligatorily organize co-operatives combining employers and employees, whose mission would be to regulate relations between them, to develop the sense of honor in a job well done, to found professional schools, to take care of members in need, and that this co-operative organization be extended to include large industries; that the State should not intervene in the internal operations of co-operatives but must protect them from the outside by developing social legislation which, in the labor contract, would impose voluntary limitations on the contracting parties inspired by the exigencies of the common good; that salaries must assure workers and their families of a decent life and permit them to put away money against the risks of accidents and unemployment; finally that it would be useful on a political level to create a Chamber of Workers, within the framework of general representation of the economic interests.

These ideas, which to us today seem rather poorly adapted to the scale of the changes wrought by industrial society, but which were quite novel at the time outside of revolutionary circles and which ran into strong resistance on the part of the episcopate, were spread abroad thanks to an international journal, the *Correspondance de Genève*, founded and directed by a member of the Vogelsang group, the Count von Blome, himself of German origin as well, converted to Catholicism by Fr. Félix.

* * *

In comparison with what was happening in the Germanic countries, the social thought and action of French Catholics during the third quarter of the 19th century seem singularly disappointing. To be sure, an increasing number of them become aware of the social obligations implied by the Christian faith and, led by Armand de Melun and Augustin Cochin, some generous men make efforts to ameliorate the workers' condition, but their attempts, which J.B. Duroselle has made known in detail, are met with general indifference and on the whole, moreover, bear witness to a great timidity.

On the doctrinal level, the French Social Catholics have only a summary knowledge of economic science, even though it was in full flower during this period, and their numerous writings testify as much to the imprecision and inefficiency of their thought as to their good intentions. They had neither their Marx nor even their Proudhon; the theory which inspired them most was that of Le Play, whose scientific character leaves much to be desired and which, combined with a strict interpretation of the *Syllabus*, contributes to orientate them toward "counter-revolutionary" doctrine, hostile to the "rights of man" and to democratic egalitarianism.

Their actions appear as hesitant as their ideas. A certain number of captains of industry do indeed take the path of the *"patronat social,"* by creating institutions seeking the well being of their workers, and a few priests, rather rare besides, concentrate on a popular apostolate, especially among young workers. But practically nowhere does one see the idea dawn that responsibility for the Catholic social organizations being created must be conferred on the workers themselves.[19] Now, it is at this moment that the workers' movement, in France as in the rest of Europe, is evolving precisely in a direction increasingly opposed to paternalism; not surprising that the workers adopt a reticent attitude toward Catholic social initiatives and that these initiatives fail to reach the veritable workers' elite.

This is ultimately the same judgement which must be made concerning *L'Œuvre des cercles catholiques d'ouvriers* [Association of Catholic Workers' Clubs], founded Christmas 1871 by a young officer, Albert de Mun,[20] who had come in contact with the work of Ketteler during his captivity in Aix-la-Chapelle and discovered his "social vocation" at the time of the Paris Commune. In close contact with Fr. Maignen, he had attempted to reproduce throughout France associations like the one headed by the latter in Montparnasse, by adjoining to each of them a protecting committee recruited from the "ruling class," the whole being unified by a general committee residing in Paris.

Under the initiative of its indefatigable secretary general, *L'Œuvre des cercles* at first enjoyed a rapid growth, in spite of the reticence of the clergy, which, through narrow-mindedness, was troubled to see these Catholic "families" taking shape outside of the parish and under lay leadership. But in reality, despite some 35,000 adherents that it counted in 1878, *L'Œuvre* always remained marginal to the veritable workers' milieu. The extremely paternalistic orientation given to the associations by the majority of directors, despite the efforts of the founders, caused them to be avoided by the real working class, who were further shocked by the anti-revolutionary ideology which prevailed in them. The hostility to the spirit of 1789 and the nostalgia for the social order of past centuries would inevitably make *L'Œuvre* seem like a reactionary enterprise, even though, in reality, the social concerns of Albert de Mun and his group situates them far in advance not only of the Orléanists, but even of most republican leaders of the time.

In spite of its apparent failure, *L'Œuvre des cercles* would exercise a lasting influence on the development of the Social Christian movement in France by assuring wide publicity for the concrete realizations of Léon Harmel and the doctrinal program of René de La Tour du Pin.

The social action of Léon Harmel[21] is well known. Although his mistrust of State intervention led him at a certain moment to take sides with the *Patrons du Nord* [Bosses of the North] in a camp which to us today seems indeed reactionary, he was nevertheless a pioneer of Christian Democracy in his creation, at his Val-des-Bois factory, of a veritable workers' association which managed the social works of the enterprise, while awaiting to create there, after the release of the encyclical, of factory councils assuring a real participation of the workers in the professional and disciplinary management of the factory. He thus put into practice the principle he loved to repeat: "The good of the worker with him, never without him, all the more reason why never in spite of him." It is in this same spirit that he hoped to see employers' association and parallel workers' association organized within each industry, this latter association run by the workers themselves.

Harmel was a man of action. René de La Tour du Pin[22] was the group's thinker and, under the influence of *L'Œuvre des cercles*, especially after 1878, would concentrate more and more on doctrinal research aimed at elaborating a complete plan for the restoration of a co-operatively based Christian society, founded on the proclamation of the social royalty of Jesus Christ. It is he who becomes the director of the fourth section, the *Conseil des études* [Council of Studies], where he introduced a series of worthy men, notably Henri Lorin, the future founder of the *Semaines sociales* [Social Weeks], and Count de Roquefeuil, director of the journal founded in 1876, *L'Association catholique*. The studies and documents of all sorts published every month during this period seek to bring gradually a solution to all the social problems which are ever more ardently discussed among Catholics: relationship between justice and charity, basis and limits of property rights, elements of a fair salary, the credit system, and the cooperative organization of society.

The school assembled in this way around La Tour du Pin, which brings together theologians and sociologists, first affirms the priority of the duties of justice over those of charity, and stands up to certain theologians of a Liberal bent, too inclined to make of charity's virtue the unique foundation of the Christian social order. On the question of property rights, the school attempts, not without difficulty or exaggeration, to refute collectivism by foregrounding the social character of property, and by reconciling it with the needs of the common good. As for the difficult problem of a fair salary, object of innumerable controversies among theologians, La Tour du Pin and his friends suggest the great principle of the fair salary being sufficient to the needs of the worker and his family. Before Leo XIII, they insist on the necessary and personal character of work, and show that the remuneration must be adapted to the individual. Still more advanced, La Tour du Pin justifies the worker's inclusion in the benefits of the enterprise.

But he looks beyond these particular questions and seeks to elaborate a complete program of professional organization and of representation of the national interest. On this last point, he draws inspiration from the Vogelsang School, but also develops certain more original points-of-view, which have until now received too little attention.

The work which La Tour du Pin and his friends elaborated through trial and error has in fact often been treated with scorn by historians of the social movement, who saw in it only a nostalgic attempt at returning to the *Ancien Régime*. The detailed and subtle study that Fr. Talmy recently devoted to him permits us at present to bring a more nuanced judgement to his work. Assuredly, in the light of this study, La Tour du Pin appears more than ever as an "intransigent visionary," little apt at concrete projects and dominated, even as were his collaborators, by "certain ways of seeing things as in the medieval past," to the extent that their positions, on several essential points, seem incomplete and dated, and must already have appeared that way to their contemporaries: these "gentlemen farmers" saw the social problem from the point of view of great landowners, barely aware of the new problems that were being posed, with the beginning of large industries, by the question of private appropriation of the means of production. And yet, as anachronistic as he may have been, as attached to the *Ancien régime* by all the fibers of his being and his mind, La Tour du Pin appears in some ways more modern than many of his contemporaries, and more so even than certain of those who kept their distance because they thought him out of touch with his era. On the theoretical level for one: concerning the State's right to intervene in economic and social life, and especially concerning the limits on the right of private ownership, La Tour du Pin and the theoreticians he had gathered round him took positions, under the influence of the scholastic doctrines, that were diametrically opposed to the Liberalism of their times, positions which went much further than those adopted by Leo XIII in the encyclical *Rerum novarum* and which singularly resembled not only certain socialist points-of-view of the 19th century, but social concepts on their way to becoming classics of the current era.

Something still more paradoxical, it is equally on the level of practical attitudes that the "reactionary" La Tour du Pin appears to us, in certain regards, considerably more modern than one would have thought. In effect, behind the conflict that sets him against his friend Albert de Mun, Fr. Talmy shows us the dilemma, still with us today, between real Catholic action and a neutral social politics of ostensibly Christian inspiration.

Whereas Albert de Mun only sees the French Revolution Counter-Centenary movement as an opportunity to develop *L'Œuvre des cercles* by once again assuring Catholic doctrine in the realm of politics, La Tour du Pin, on the contrary, tried to make it the point of departure for a reorganization of society, for a new Christian social order. Now he envisions this social order in and of itself, and no longer from a political or a religious slant; and the tentative professional organization that he proposes—so anachronistic, let us repeat, in its concrete form—tends at bottom to assure the professional ranks their full autonomy within his order, by recognizing that it concerns a domain which, in itself, is not confessional.

It is far from being the case that all French Catholics who take an active interest in the Workers Problem, still relatively few in 1880, rally to the system advocated by the *Conseil des études* under La Tour du Pin's impulse. This system is on the contrary energetically attacked by another group of Social Catholics, known sometimes as the Belgian

School (because its master thinker, Charles Périn, was professor at the University of Louvain), sometimes as the School of Angers (because it is patronized with much commotion by Msgr. Freppel, Bishop of Angers), and which, according to Fr. Jarlot, constitutes "more precisely the School of the *Patrons du Nord* ["Bosses of the North"], notwithstanding the inclusion of a good number of Belgian thinkers and men of action."[23]

The group's theoretician, Périn,[24] was a brilliant professor of public law and political economics, whose fundamental work, *De la richesse dans les sociétés chrétiennes* [On Wealth in Christian Societies] (1861), was translated into most European languages. While he advocates the workers' association, the return to co-operatives, and a more humane labor system, he confides the execution of these wishes exclusively to private initiative and above all to the responsibility of Christian employers. In effect this ultramontane, who energetically denounces the lamentable abuses of which the labor class is victim and who teaches that moral laws must dominate the economy, remains a partisan of Economic Liberalism and denies the State any and all intervention in the workplace, seeking the solution to the Social Problem uniquely in the progress of morality and in the Christian spirit among employers and workers.

These social ideas of Liberal and paternalistic inspiration were very favorably received among Belgian Catholics,[25] who based the entire defense of their religious rights precisely on the call to freedom and the fear of promoting the nationalist tendencies of their adversaries.

The same notions were propagated in France by the *Revue catholique des institutions et du droit* [Catholic Review of Institutions and Law], organ of the Catholic Jurists Association, patronized by Msgr. Freppel, one of the French bishops who was most interested in the Social Question in the aftermath of 1870, but who, until his death in 1891, would lead an unswerving opposition to the School of La Tour du Pin. Fr. Jarlot, clearly marks the points of divergence between the two groups: "Both speak of Christian corporation, promotion of labor, devotion of the ruling classes, and corporative patrimony, but they do not call the same things by the same names. The first group is inspired by social justice, the other by charity; there, organization of the body public, here, the free association of individuals; there, obligation, and here, spontaneous devotion. The first group demands official recognition, which would make their corporation an organism of public law; the second is suspicious of the State and rejects it in the name of the liberty of labor."[26] Perhaps it is this profound mistrust of the State—which they see only as having the traits of the Jacobin State, hostile to the Church—which constitutes the essential characteristic of this second group. This mistrust also explains in large measure their opposition to the organization of a social security. According to them, the State does not have the right to oblige the worker to pay an insurance premium, which is always a lottery ticket, nor to constrain others to pay for a doctor in his place. Moreover, in their eyes, assistance to the ill or to accident victims is a work of Christian charity and the public exercise of charity traditionally belongs to the Church and not to the State.

It is just, however, in order to equitably judge this second group, to take into account R. Talmy's remark: "Compared to the bold ideas of La Tour du Pin, the social thought of the *Patrons du Nord* will doubtless appear quite insufficient, and often steeped in Liberalism. Nevertheless, on a practical level, they exhibited a dynamism which the friends of La Tour du Pin would never have."[27] But in this brief study dedicated principally to doctrinal issues, we cannot enter into details concerning concrete projects.

*   *   *

It is likewise mistrust of the State that characterizes in general the Italian Social Catholics at the beginning of Leo XIII's pontificate. And for similar reasons, like the Belgian and French Catholics, and even more than they, they find themselves at odds with a Liberal government, one which is extremely anticlerical and which claims the right to intervene in an often vexing manner in various aspects of the Church's operation, including the nomination of pastors.

Italian Catholics only woke up to the Workers Problem very slowly, and the consideration, rather general moreover, which was given to it by Cardinal Pecci, the future Leo XIII, in his famous pastorals of 1877 and 1878, still constitutes at that date an exception.[28] What is striking, in the peninsula as in France and Belgium, is that it is *not* in the politically open-minded milieus—the *transigenti*, as Catholic Liberals in Italy were called—that we should look for the pioneers of social reform, but on the contrary in those milieus in revolt against the entire democratic system born of the great revolution of the end of the 18th century. It is not only that these milieus are less concerned with the process of industrialization and thus less sensitive to the "iron laws" imposed by the exigencies of competition, but additionally, they see social action (conceived of most often, besides, from a very paternalistic perspective) as a means of rallying the popular masses, which constitute the "real nation," to their struggle against the anticlerical, timocratic bourgeoisie.

Excepting a few "snipers" from the Liberal Catholic side—for example the ex-Jesuit Curci, who in 1885 will publish a work whose programmatic title is: *Di un socialismo cristiano nella questione operaia* [On Christian Socialism in the Workers Question]—and also, not to forget, the sometimes rather audacious articles on the social problem published in the 1880's in *La Civiltà cattolica*, one must above all insist on the role played by *L'Œuvre des congrès*, organization inspired by the German *Katholikentage* [Catholic Day], which included all Catholics who were adversaries of the modern State, despoiler of the Holy See. It is from within this organism of reactionary inspiration that is born, especially after the Congress of Bergamo in 1877, an entire network of economically and socially orientated benevolent associations, bent on meeting the diverse needs of the popular classes, at least in the north and central regions of Italy, where the effects of Socialist propaganda are beginning to be felt.[29] It is likewise within the framework of *L'Œuvre des congrès* that an Italian Catholic sociology begins to be elaborated, one in which the exigencies of morality and religion must take priority over those of material interests.

The principal thinker of the group was the Professor Giuseppe Toniolo,[30] of the University of Pisa. Strongly insisting on the relationship between economics and ethics,[31] he is quite hard on the Liberal economy born of the Protestant Reformation and the French Revolution, with its materialistic and naturalistic inspiration, for which money is no longer a means but an end. At the same time, he warns just as strongly against a State Socialism, which leads to materialistic pantheism, for which society is only a collection of physical bodies obedient to an irresistible force. This system would be equivalent to the destruction of the family, of all hierarchy, of liberty, and of human responsibility. Thus did Toniolo recommend to Catholics that they not unreservedly encourage social and economic regimentation by the State, which would impede social action by the Church. The restoration of the Christian Social Order will depend, above all other factors, on free [i.e., private] associations and families.

But, despite the real merits of this Italian social movement, which takes shape during the first half of Leo XIII's pontificate and which a constellation of young historians has rescued from oblivion in the last fifteen years, one can still not exaggerate its impact and there is considerable truth in A. C. Jemolo's severe observation: "It did not add a great deal to the history of doctrines and ideas. It was in fact totally docile *vis-à-vis* the directives, indeed the simplest desires, of the Holy See; it could not be counted among those Catholic movements which succeeded in swaying the hierarchy, which was able to make then understand that the prolonging of their resistance would have for consequences the loss of many of the faithful, which managed to sensitize the Catholic masses to the new [social] problems. Although, after a certain point in time, the teaching Church in Italy manifested preoccupations of a social order, these had already been brought to attention well beforehand in other countries. In truth, in the social domain, the Italian Catholic movement was far from having been a driving force; at best, it let itself be carried along."[32] In particular, under the influence of the principal leaders of *L'Œuvre des congrès*, the Italian social movement long remained not only closed, but even sharply opposed, to the idea that a political democracy is the necessary condition for obtaining worthwhile social reforms.

It must however still be added that on the margins of *L'Œuvre des congrès*, which was especially active in the north of the peninsula as well as in Tuscany and the Bologna region, there was in Rome itself another circle of social studies, one which would have a particular influence on *Rerum novarum*. Behind its inception are found several foreign residents of Rome. In 1881, the Count von Kuefstein, an Austrian of the *Vogelsang* group who, married to a Princess Odescalchi who spent winters in Rome, and had organized a sort of circle of social studies with the aid of a Canadian priest, Fr. Villeneuve and especially that of the exiled Bishop of Geneva, (future Cardinal) Msgr. Mermillod,[33] who had long been concerned with the Workers' Problem and had had close contact, during his long stay in France, with *L'Œuvre des cercles*. This small group set up by Kuefstein with the encouragement of Leo XIII (but not, as has sometimes been written, at his behest), had as its mission, according to the testimony of its founder, "to study all social economics questions from the point of view of Catholic doctrine and to preferably concentrate on those questions concerning the workers; to look for the true [guiding] principles, [for] what value the present-day economy accords them, and how to finally make them reign in the heart of every society."[34] Notable participants were the Count von Blome, whenever he was in Rome, the learned Austrian Dominican Denifle, and also this or that Italian, including the secretary of the Congregation of Propaganda, Msgr. Domenico Jacobini,[35] a priest who was extremely zealous for Catholic action and open to modern ideas.

After the return of Mermillod to his diocese in 1883, this "Roman Committee of Social Studies" was reorganized under the direction of Msgr. Jacobini, this time at the instigation of the Pope himself, and, under the name of the "Catholic Union for the Social Studies," met regularly at the home of Prince Borghese. One could find there, besides a few foreigners, Soderini, Santucci, Vespignani, occasionally Msgr. Talamo, one of the revivalists of Thomism, and also a few Jesuits from *La Civiltà cattolica*, Fr. Querini and especially Fr. Liberatore. It is within this group that Liberatore ripened his *Principii di economia politica*, published in 1889, in which he sought a middle road between Liberalism and Socialism.

* * *

The diverse Catholic groups preoccupied with the Social Problem in Germany, in Austria, in France, and in Belgium did not remain completely unknown to one another. They were aware of each other through their respective publications and more or less occasional contact had been occurring. It is thus that in 1877, Mermillod had introduced La Tour du Pin to several disciples of Vogelsang, the two princes of Liechtenstein, and the Count von Blome in his residence of Ferney. The Roman group had likewise furnished the occasion of several meetings. It soon seemed desirable to make these meetings more regular in order to coordinate research and to make it more efficient. In October 1884, the Prince von Loewenstein, Kuefstein, La Tour du Pin, and one of his collaborators, L. Milcent, met at Fribourg with Msgr. Mermillod, in order to examine opportunities for creating an international Catholic center for social studies. Charles Périn, who was then staying in Fribourg, was invited to join them, but he declined the invitation, apparently having little desire to compromise himself by meeting with "interventionists" whose views on social questions were so different from his own. They decided it would meet every year in Fribourg under the presidency of Msgr. Mermillod, which would assure their liaison with Rome. All the members of the association would be invited, and a few others as well, on condition that they shared their ideas. Secrecy would be the rule, following the express desires of Msgr. Mermillod. On the 23ʳᵈ of October, 1883, the statutes, prepared by Kuefstein, were approved. *L'Union catholique d'études sociales* would be comprised of a limited number of titular members and national sections with corresponding membership. A council—at most three members per nation—would decide on new admissions. The bureau included Msgr. Mermillod as president, the Prince of Liechtenstein as honorary president, and Count von Blome as vice-president. Kuefstein was secretary of studies and La Tour du Pin secretary of the council. Among the most assiduous members, let us point out from Germany the Jesuit Lehmkuhl, from Italy the Count Medalago-Albani, who represented *L'Œuvre des congrès*, from France Henri Lorin, from Switzerland Gaspard Decurtins. Belgium was represented by the Duke d'Ursel, brother-in-law of Albert de Mun, and Georges Helleputte, the principal theoretician of Belgian corporatism at the time,[36] before aligning himself, after 1891, with the Christian Democrats, but he made only one appearance. Some members never showed up at all: Vogelsang, Toniolo, Fr. Liberatore.

The principal activity of the Union of Fribourg took place between 1885 and 1890: Mermillod's departure for Rome, where he was named Cardinal of the Curia, then his death two years later, would be fatal to it. It has been observed that the Union was only ever intended to reach people "professing the same principles." The founders judged in effect that it would be a waste of time to engage in endless discussions with proponents of Economic Liberalism, in their eyes the principal cause of their social ills. They planned to put their efforts toward elaborating a version, adapted to our era, of the corporatist doctrine of society which had been the glory of the Middle Ages, and it is not surprising that the works of the Union of Fribourg echo, sometimes in an expanded fashion, the theses elaborated by Haid or by the Council of Studies in Paris. Notably dealt with by the Union[37] were the corporative regime in large industries, in small businesses, and in commerce; the system of rural property and the organization of the agricultural classes; the labor system; the fair salary; mandatory workers' insurance; the credit system (the Austrians especially were concerned over usurious interest rates); the State's right to intervene in economic and social activities in order to counterbalance the power of capital and its duty to take necessary measures "in cases where normal initiatives would be powerless or insufficient."

Although, on many points, the deliberations of the Union of Fribourg did not go beyond the level of pure theory, they lead to an important concrete result in the domain of international cooperation with a view toward labor legislation. The question had been raised in the *Katholiekentag* of 1885, then in an article of the *Association catholique* in 1886. The Union's members examined it in turn and contacted the Pope. At the end of 1887, one of them, Decurtins, invited the Swiss Federal Council to establish contact with other countries possessing labor legislation in order to arrive at an accord on the protection of working children, the limitation of the labor of women, the weekly day off, and the standard workday. The German emperor, Wilhelm II, who convened the Berlin Conference, 1890, took up the idea again soon after.

* * *

We have said that Msgr. Mermillod assured relations with Rome. Regularly, reports were sent to the Pope to keep him abreast of the results of deliberations, and he became more and more interested in them, for the idea of a social encyclical was gradually ripening in his mind. At the beginning of his pontificate, he had, in the encyclical *Quod apostolici muneris* (28 December 1878), harshly condemned Socialism, confused rather quickly with anarchism and total collectivism.[38] But he had grown since then. Already in 1885, when Msgr. Jacobini, while introducing René de La Tour du Pin, explained to him how the latter was coming under attack—"Most Holy Father, these good workers are sometimes accused of socialism"—the Pope had protested: "Of socialism! It's Christianity. Our adversaries do not suspect the fundamental principles of the Christian social order. Very well! The Pope will make it known to them. Wait for my next encyclical!."[39] In October 1887, Msgr. Mermillod stated, during the Union of Fribourg's general session, that on several occasions, the Pope had dreamed of editing an encyclical, but that reasons of great prudence had obliged him to suspend this extremely delicate work, which consisted of identifying the exact point between justice and charity.[40] The next year, during an audience which Leo XIII granted to members of the Union of Fribourg present in Rome, Msgr. Mermillod made an address to the Pope that demanded his immediate pronouncement: "When the voice of your blessed paternity, resounding throughout a world that is moved by its sacerdotal jubilee, will have made known the dignity of the worker, made his rights respected, and made the workers to organize as Christians, then these, rather than being lead blindly by the enemies of Jesus Christ, will be the most faithful champions of the liberty of the Church and the independence of its chief."[41]

Among the factors during these years which came to reinforce Leo XIII in the idea that it was time to intervene officially, it is especially necessary to point out the pilgrimages to Rome by "France du travail" [Working France], organized since 1885 by Léon Harmel in order to bring the working masses closer to the Pope and to put him in direct contact with the people of the factories. Attention must likewise be given to the intervention of the Cardinal Archbishop of Baltimore in the United States, Gibbons, in 1887-88, in order to avoid a condemnation by the Holy See of the Knights of Labor, the first American workers' organization.[42] The fact that this association was not under the control of the clergy, and above all its image as a secret society which made it suspected of compromise with anarchism, had worried certain members of the hierarchy, who had alerted the Holy See. A condemnation appeared imminent, but Gibbons' firm and skilled intervention in Rome, supported by several of his American colleagues and also by the Cardinal, Archbishop of Westminster, Manning, succeeded in changing the initial judgement of the Holy See, and it concluded in August 1888 with a *Tollerari possunt* whose repercussion was great and which contributed to drawing the attention of the Catholic world to the importance of the Workers' Problem.[43]

We have just mentioned Manning. He too, although he never participated in the discussions of the corporatist doctrinaires on the continent, contributed much during these same years to the Catholic Church's orientation toward taking a firm stand on social issues. By 1877, in a very publicized conference given in the industrial city of Leeds on "The Rights and the Dignity of Labor," he had encouraged the active support of all initiatives tending to protect workers from the abuses of the capitalist system; and his intervention during the famous Dock Strike of 1889, which ended with what the public called "the Cardinal's peace," had an impact all through Europe.[44]

In the presence of all these converging phenomena, it became increasingly clear that the supreme authority of the Church had to speak out. A new flare up of the controversy between "interventionists" Catholics and "Liberal" Catholics on the occasion of the Catholic Congress of Liège finished convincing Leo XIII that he could wait no longer.

A former workers association almoner who in 1879 became Bishop of Liège, Msgr. Doutreloux,[45] aided by the professor of morals from his major seminary, Fr. Pottier,[46] one of the principal pioneers of Christian Democracy in Belgium, had gathered round him Belgian Catholics who had sympathetically followed the German social projects and the works of La Tour du Pin's *Conseil des études*, and who wished to act in a like manner. In 1886, 1887, and 1890 he organized international congresses in his episcopal city, in which social questions were widely discussed. The German and Austrian participation there was considerable, and several organizations in the congresses were in close contact with the Union of Fribourg. They strongly defended the idea of the necessity of State intervention in economic and social activities and of the legitimacy of unions charged with defending the workers demands *vis-à-vis* their employers.

These congresses, especially the third, garnered a lot of attention, and a portion of Catholic opinion reacted negatively, in the name of liberty, against what seemed to it to be excessive concessions to Socialism. Already during the proceedings of the congress itself, some opposition had made itself known. At the last minute, Fr. Pottier, after an intervention by the Bishop of Trier, had seen the reading of his report cancelled, a report in which he was demanding State intervention to establish a minimum wage; and several courageous demands proposed by the Christian Democrats had to be withdrawn, which caused the leader of the conservative Catholics, Charles Woeste, to say with joy: "The assembly remained well this side of the conclusions in the letter which Cardinal Manning had addressed to it."

Although many among the opposition had conservative or paternalistic tendencies, there were also those who, like Léon Harmel or the *Patrons du Nord*, were open-minded from a social point of view, but for tactical or doctrinal reasons were apprehensive of any and all State intervention. Lead by the Bishop of Angers, they would find themselves a few weeks later, in October 1890, at another congress organized in response to the one in Liège.[48] To prevent this conflict between Social Catholics from developing into the greatest damnation of the common good, it was essential that Rome issue precise directives. This was the encyclical *Rerum novarum*, in which Leo XIII would, on the principal points, come down on the side of the Liège School, itself the inheritor of the social thought of Ketteler and the Union of Fribourg. An important step in the history of Social Catholicism would thus be accomplished.

* * *

As to how the text of the encyclical was elaborated and gradually completed, many a hypothesis was formulated over the half-century which followed. The matter seems a good deal clearer since Msgr. Antonazzi's publication in 1957 of the various preparatory drafts conserved in the Vatican Archives.[49] At present we can determine with certainty the different steps in this long and meticulous labor from which would emerge the definitive text of the encyclical.

A first point is henceforth established: the editing of a social encyclical was already well underway several months before the meeting of the Congress of Liège in September 1890 and the controversies to which it gave rise.[50] By the beginning of July, in fact, Fr. Liberatore was submitting a first draft which the Pope had charged him with editing. Actually, Leo XIII did not write his encyclicals himself. He put forth ideas, indicated the development and the "plot," sometimes even dictated more delicate points, but he left to his secretaries the editing of his acts itself, ready thereafter to correct in detail, going so far as examining each variant, suggesting this or that correction, eliminating others of them.

Liberatore's text did not entirely satisfy Leo XIII. He found it too brief, the style mediocre, and moreover Liberatore was taking sides rather resolutely with the corporatist School. However, as Fr. Jarlot has observed, Leo XIII did not want to be the man of a single school: "If there were conflicts between Catholics, he had to put himself above them, so as to be no one's prisoner. He was in the service of the one truth. He would side with the Social Catholics against their adversaries when they were objectively right; he would abandon them when their arguments were only the theses of a School."[51]

The Pope therefore assigned the Dominican Cardinal Zigliara, one of his principal auxiliaries in the Thomist revival, to edit a new draft, at once less committed to a single direction and following a broader schema. This new text, written, like the previous one, in Italian, was submitted in September, and the Pope was apparently more satisfied with it, because he ordered his secretary to begin the Latin translation. But on October 28, when only 12 pages had been translated, the work was "suspended by superior orders." One can suppose that it is the new set of circumstances resulting from the two Congresses, Liège and Angers, which caused the Pope to have the text reworked, so as to respond better to those questions creating difficulties. Whatever the case may be, a new draft was drawn up: it substantially reiterated the preceding one, but included once more certain elements from Liberatore's initial draft. In addition, it was submitted for revision to Cardinal Mazzella, then to Liberatore himself. Msgr. Volpini completed a first Latin translation of this new text during the months of December 1890, and January 1891. The undertaking was difficult: it involved a subject matter which was not only delicate in itself, but particularly ill-suited to an appropriate expression in Latin, and it was necessary to create audacious periphrases, circumlocutions, or neologisms while still respecting the gravity of the Curia's style, and without obfuscating the clarity of thought. Despite unheard of efforts,[52] Msgr. Volpini, one of the Vatican's most renowned Latinists, was unable to satisfy the Pope, who, it is known, was extremely demanding in matters of Latin style: "Yes, he observed, all the content is there, but it is not the proper tone. We must throw all this away and do it over." It was another secretary, Msgr. Boccali, who was given the assignment. His work was finished by the middle of April, but it was further reworked, corrected, and re-corrected according to the Pope's precise instructions for almost a month. Let us note that it was only in this final stage that the solemn initial passage was perfected.

Here is not the place to analyze in detail the text of the encyclical, but it is interesting to rapidly note some of the basic modifications which the text underwent in the course of its writing.[53] Three points especially mark the opposition among Catholics who were concerned with the social problem: 1) the fair salary, 2) the professional association, and 3) the State's right to intervene.

On the first point, Liberatore's original version unhesitatingly defended the stance taken by the Austrians, the Paris *Conseil des études*, and the Liège School: a family-sustaining salary demanded by justice, whereas the disciples of Périn and of Msgr. Freppel saw in this demand an attack on the natural rights of private ownership and, while still admitting the employer's obligation to be charitable, believed that justice only held him to pay the amount established by contract, taking into account the laws of supply and demand. Zigliara, in his draft, abandoned the familial salary but maintained that the worker must be able to live on his salary[54] and that, therefore, if constrained by necessity he freely accepts a salary inadequate to assuring him an acceptable existence, he is suffering a violent injustice, and the courts must intervene. The third version, the one reviewed and corrected by Mazella and Liberatore, while maintaining the anti-liberal affirmation of a livable wage, discards the recourse of the courts: "so that too great a meddling by the public powers not lead to a *Socialism of the State*, it will be more opportune to leave its determination to corporative societies, composed of employers and workers." The definitive edition, less corporatist in its orientation, as we will see, modified the passage once more and, dropping the allusion to Socialism, envisions the possibility of intervention by the State: "For fear that...the public powers might intervene inopportunely, given especially the vagaries of circumstances, of time, and of place, it will be preferable that in principle the solution be reserved for the professional associations, of which we will speak later on, or that one have recourse to some other means of safeguarding the interests of the workers, even, if the occasion demanded, with the help and support of the State."

As far as the professional associations are concerned, although all Social Catholics were in agreement as to condemning the economic individualism issued from the Revolution of 1789, and to calling for an organization of the professions, we have already seen that they differed profoundly as to the manner in which they conceived of these new "corporations." The Theses of Haid, like the conclusions of the *Conseil des études* and of the Union of Fribourg, propose the organization of a corporative system: to stand against the Jacobean State, there must be opposing "social bodies" or intermediary bodies, and it is to the organized professions that the defense of public liberty is confided. The other school [of thought] believes on the contrary that, in the altogether novel conditions of the 19th century economy, a climate of liberty is indispensable and moreover favorable to the common good, since free market competition permits the maximum lowering of the prices of consumer goods. Thus they affirm that the economic domain must remain outside of corporative jurisdiction. A few among the Social Catholics finally realized that professional associations combining employers and workers would in fact never escape from paternalist temptations, and judged it preferable, in order to arrive at a real enfranchisement of the working class, to organize pure labor syndicates, controlled by the workers themselves, after the example of the English trade unions.

Liberatore's schema was plainly corporatist and presented corporations as the major remedy for the ills of the working class, corporations within which employers and workers must be united in such a way as to lessen the antagonism between the social classes. Zigliara renounces the "Christian social order" preached by the corporatists and falls back on the professional association. More than Liberatore, he insists on the autonomy of these associations, on there private, voluntary, and free character. In greater defiance of the State, he refuses to attribute to them a public character or a political function. For him the public order and the private order are two distinct domains, which would become confused in a corporatist system. A certain empiricism, allowing a place for variety in methods, is besides necessary to take into account diverse national temperaments and acquired customs. On the other hand, more so than in the first draft, the accent is placed on the religious objectives, which the associations must strive for, which seem to have been conceived of along the lines of the ancient brotherhoods. But although he renounces corporations in the public domain in favor of free [i.e., private] associations, Zigliara continues to promote mixed associations, that is to say, combining employers and workers.

At the last minute, the Pope introduced a modification here, small in appearance but of capital importance. To the text which said, concerning professional associations: "it is with pleasure that we see the formation of this type of association," he added, between the 10th and the 15th of May, the following words: "whether composed entirely of workers, or mixed, assembling both workers and employers." This was recognition, outside of the corporative organization, of workers' syndicalism, about which the previous drafts had not spoken. But this followed from what influences? The answer is not clear. Fr. Pottier and certain members of the Liège School were leaning this way. So, it seems, was Toniolo, whose influence was great in the Vatican, even though his role in editing the encyclical was less than some have claimed. Perhaps the Pope was also thinking about the particular situation in the Anglo-Saxon countries, England and the United States. Whatever the case, one thing seems clear from the publication of the successive versions of the encyclical:

> From Liberatore's first draft to the version by Zigliara, to Boccali's version, to the definitive text, the affirmation of a corporatist regime gradually gives way to professional associations, preferably mixed, but not at all necessarily, whose essential aim would be the spiritual good of the workers, whose immediate aim would be social peace,

by victory over class struggle and the cooperation of all, employers and employees, with a view to ameliorating the material conditions of the workers and the poor.[55]

And we can without fear of error attribute this gradual evolution to the personal will of Leo XIII who, although writing nothing with his own hand, imposed his thought everywhere and, in the end, left his mark on everything.

The progress was less remarkable concerning another much discussed question, that of the State's role in economic and social activity. Here too Liberatore, faithful to the views of the Union of Fribourg, themselves echoes of the Vogelsang and La Tour du Pin groups, attributed an extensive responsibility to the State, not only for the organization of labor, but also for controlling the constitution of monopolies or stock market speculation. Zigliara's version seems more preoccupied with anticipating objections, by introducing his conclusions with long discussions of social philosophy. Clearly he is responding to someone he hopes to convince, after having made the necessary concessions. Having sought to thoroughly delimit the State's responsibilities before the natural rights of the individual and of intermediary institutions, he introduces a long dissertation on distributive justice and legal justice. In the name of the first, the State must vigilantly insure an honest and proportional repartition of resources from which the family will benefit; in the name of the second, the State must coordinate everyone's efforts toward the formation of the common good and maintain the hierarchy of functions and powers. And as the wealth of nation results from the labor of its workers, the State undermines none of its rights but rather accomplishes its proper function by taking the former's interests in its hands. The third version dropped this dissertation on justice, but it reappeared in the second Latin version, the one effectuated by Msgr. Boccali, who introduced, obviously at the Pope's request, a good number of formal modifications, displacing several passages in order to obtain a more logical and more coherent whole, illuminating the idea or introducing some new argument to make it more precise. But in general, on this point, it is the interventionist schema of the Liège School (so-called since the congress of 1890) that received the official sanction of the Church against the excessive Liberalism of the Angers School and the *Patrons du Nord*. But the many nuances and hints increasingly introduced into the text show the prudence—and hesitancy—with which the Holy See embarked on this path. This prudence is certainly explained in part by the concern to not shock too violently the conservatives, whom almost nothing in the official teachings of the 19th-century Church had prepared, up to that time, to hear these harsh truths; also by the concern, already mentioned, to not precipitously canonize one Catholic school at the others' expense. But, in order to understand certain of Leo XIII's reservations, it is also necessary to realize the fact that, while still wanting to react in the name of scholastic tradition against an individualistic conception of society, he was very concerned with not giving legitimacy to the totalitarian aspect often presented by the doctrinaire socialism of his times.

The historian should not make value judgements and it is not his job to appreciate in itself the social doctrine proposed by Leo XIII. He can however attempt to characterize its historical significance. It seems to me that two things especially deserve mention.

In the first place, the encyclical's significance relative to the half-century of Social Catholicism preceded it. We have been able to show, despite the summary nature of this article, that Catholics of the 19th century did not remain as indifferent to the new problems posed by the economic and social changes of their times as is sometimes said. Assuredly, many of them, for a long time, only saw the problem in terms of the workers' poverty, to which they saw no other solution than charity. But nearly everywhere—more so, it must be said, in the lay world than among the clergy, and, it must also be said, most of the time spurred by the "socialist peril"—pioneers appeared rather quickly, who realized that there was also in it a question of justice, and that institutional modifications, structural reforms, were called for. At the same time, with very rare exception, these are Social Catholics who are nostalgic for traditional, predominantly rural society, who sing the praises of peasant virtues, and who reason from a pre-capitalist perspective. Combining the political and religious Revolution with the Industrial Revolution in one single aversion, they condemn the capitalist system as an absolute evil which they believe destined to fall sooner or later, and they propose replacing it with a completely different organization of society, inspired by that of the *Ancien ré-*

gime, by reinstating the corporatist system. Now, this was obviously a dead end in terms of large, modern industries. One of the merits of the encyclical *Rerum novarum* is to have been able to go beyond this pre-capitalist perspective, at least partially, and, while still keeping a good bit of what was positive in the corporatists' protests against the new bourgeois order, to aim at raising up the working class within the framework of existing economic institutions; in other words, to renounce romantic utopias and to take a realistic stand analogous to that of reformist Socialism, not hesitating to accept finally, albeit halfheartedly, the [political] leverage which the latter would use so efficiently, labor unions.

In the second place, concerning the historical significance of *Rerum novarum* relative to the subsequent workers' movement, it seems to me one can say that, even though it is undeniable that the encyclical was still far from constituting the ideal workers' charter—it suffices to be convinced of this to compare it to *Mater et magistra* and even before to *Quadragesimo anno*—it remains nevertheless true that, for the first time, workers' rights and the injustice of the entire Liberal system were solemnly proclaimed by the highest spiritual authority. This was important for the future direction of Catholics, because, despite numerous misgivings, they had to indeed admit that there was something needed changing in their attitude, and an increasing number, if still too few, began after 1891 to take steps on the path of Christian Democracy. But the importance of the position taken by Leo XIII goes beyond the Catholic milieus alone. Certainly, well before he took it, the workers' movement was already in full swing, and the credit for the initiative belongs essentially to the various Socialist movements. But, for the first time, with *Rerum novarum*, this workers' movement received the solemn sanction of one of the principal forces for order in the world, and such a sanction would contribute to remove the revolutionary, even "antisocial" character it had had until then in the eyes of the great majority of the bourgeois world. From a psychological point-of-view—and it is a point-of-view which has its importance in history—this was far from being negligible.

Notes

[1] Paris, 1951. This volume of nearly 800 pages has practically exhausted the subject. It must still however be made complete by Fr. Drouler's research, which will be mentioned below, concerning the attitude of the episcopate.

[2] B. Mirkine-Guetevtch and M. Prélot, in the preface to the cited work by Duroselle, p. XI.

[3] *L'épiscopat devant la question ouvrière en France sous la Monarchie de juillet*, in *Revue historique*, t. CCXXIX, 1963, pp. 335-362; *Des évêques parlent de la question ouvrière en France avant 1848*, in *Revue de l'action populaire*, April 1961, pp. 442-460; *Action pastorale et problèmes sociaux sous la Monarchie de juillet chez Mgr. D'Astros*, Paris, 1954, Part II; *Le cardinal de Bonald et la grève des mineurs de Rive-de-Gier en 1844*, in *Cahiers d'histoire*, t. VI, 1961, pp. 265-285.

[4] *La nonciature de Paris et les troubles socio-politiques sous la Monarchie de juillet*, in *Saggi storici intorno al papato*, Rome, 1959, pp. 401-463.

[5] Especially in his *Histoire des catholiques français au XIXe s.*, Geneva-Paris, 1947.

[6] Fr. Droulers, *Question sociale, État, Église dans la "Civilità cattolica" à ses débuts*, in *Chiesa e Stato nell'Ottocento. Miscellanea P. Pirri*, Padua, 1962, t. I, pp. 123-147.

[7] One of those who best used the encyclical as the basis for a socially-motivated Catholic action was the Alsacien deputy E. Keller in chapter XVII (pp. 279-341) of his work *L'Encyclique du 8 décembre 1864 et les principes de 1789*, Paris, 1865.

[8] Text in Mansi, *Amplissima collectio conciliorum*, t. LIII, col. 867-872; analysis in H. Rondet, *Vatican I*, Paris, 1962, pp. 209-212.

[9] Mansi, t. XLIX, col. 718. During the council, several fathers demanded a condemnation of socialism from this same negative perspective, while calling attention elsewhere to the miserable condition of the working class and the Church's obligation to deal with it (cf. E. Lio, *La Questione operaia nei "postulata" di alcuni padri del concilio Vaticano primo*, in *Osservatore romano*, 29 March 1961, p. 3).

[10] F. Schnabel, *Deutsche Geschichte im XIX. Jahrhundert*, t. IV, Fribourg-en-Brisgau, 1934, pp. 202-207.

[11] On Adolphe Kolping (1813-1865), see F. G. Schaffer, *A. Kolping*, 8th edition reedited by J. Dahl and B. Ridder, Cologne, 1961, as well as *100 Jahre Kolpingsfamilie, 1849-1949*, under the direction of D. Weber, Cologne, 1949.

[12] On the beginnings of the Volksverein and what it would represent for German Social Catholicism and the Mönchen-Gladbach movement, see E. Ritter, *Die katholische Sozialbewegung Deutschlands im 19. Jahrhundert und der Volksverein*, Cologne, 1954.

[13] G. B. Kissling, *Geschichte der deutschen Katholiekentage*, t. I, Munster, 1920, pp. 395 and 437-440.

[14] On the social activity of Ketteler (1811-1877), in addition to his biography by F. Vigener, *Ketteler. Ein deutscher Bischofsleben des 19. Jahrhundert*, Munich, 1924, see T. Brauer, *Ketteler, Der deutsche Bischof und soziale Reformer*, Hamburg, 1927, and G. Goyau, *Ketteler*, Paris, 1908 (translated excerpts from his works on political and social problems).

[15] On the influence that Lassale exercised on Ketteler, and its limits, see especially G. Jarlot, *Doctrine pontificale et histoire*, Rome, 1964, pp. 179-182. In particular p. 181: "These arguments, with their share of objectivity and their manifest exaggerations, come from Lassale. But it is the social structure, not the wealth of individuals, which is being questioned"; or p. 182: "The co-operatives of production which

Ketteler dreams of are not those of Lassale. The final objective is indeed to have the instruments of labor pass into the hands of these societies, in order to establish, within large-scale modern industries, a workers' organization comparable to those of craftspeople in the Middle Ages. But it is by no means a question of Marxist expropriation of the propriators." It is through Christian charity that Ketteler hopes to see the instruments of production gradually ratcheted away from their proprietors and transformed into the collective property of the workers.

[16] *Theologia moralis*, Freiburg-in-Breisgau, 1883, p. 708 ff. See on this subject R. Talmy, *Aux sources du catholicisme social*, Tournai-Paris, 1963, pp. 36-37.

[17] On the Baron Karl von Vogelsang (1818-1890), see J. Ch. Allmayerbeck, *Vogelsang. Von Feudalismus zur Volksbewegung*, Vienna, 1952.

[18] Their complete text is reproduced in the review *L'Association catholique*, t. XVI, 1883, pp. 358 ff.

[19] There are however several exceptions, Fr. Maignen for example, who had made contact with Kolping's associations and appears as a precursor in that he accorded to young workers a greater autonomy in the administration of the circles he had founded.

[20] On Albert de Mun (1841-1914), in addition to his memoirs, *Ma vocation sociale*, Paris, 1911, see H. Fontanille, *L'œuvre sociale d'Albert de Mun*, Paris, 1926 and a good anthology, *Albert de Mun. Introduction et choix de textes* by R. Talmy, Paris, 1964. On the *Œuvre des cercles*, see H. Rollet, *L'action sociale des catholiques en France (1871-1901)*, Paris, 1948.

[21] On Léon Harmel (1834-1915), see G. Guitton, *Léon Harmel*, Paris, 1927, 2 Vol.

[22] On René de La Tour du Pin (1834-1924), see J. Tirot, *Un précurseur, La Tour du Pin*, Paris, 1942 and especially Robert Talmy, *Aux sources du catholicisme social. L'École de La Tour du Pin*, Tournai-Paris, 1963 (by the same author, *La Tour du Pin. Introduction et choix de textes*, Paris, 1964).

[23] *Doctrine pontificale et histoire*, Rome, 1964, p. 188, n. 11. It is in 1884 that several Catholic industrialists from Tourcoing, at the behest of C. Fréron-Vrau, formed an association that was joined by a certain number of employers from the departments of the North and the Pas-de-Calais. Léon Harmel sympathized with this group on many points.

[24] On Charles Périn (1815-1905), see the entry by A. Louant in the Belgian *Biographie nationale*, t. XXX, col. 665-671, and R. Kothen, *La pensée et l'action sociale des catholiques*, Louvain, 1945, pp. 139-148.

[25] On this Belgian Social Catholicism of paternalistic inspiration, see R. Rezsohazy, *Origines et formations du catholicisme social en Belgique*, Louvain, 1958, chap. 3. On the very conservative attitude of Belgian bishops, who even in the industrial dioceses will be late in recognizing the true scope of the workers' problem, too long confused with that of pauperism, see the two chapters by A. Simon in *150 Jaar Katholieke Arbeidersbeweging in België*, Brussels, 1963-65, t. I, pp.111-142, and t. II, pp. 87-126.

[26] *Doctrine pontificale et histoire*, p. 188.

[27] *Aux sources du catholicisme social*, p. 50.

[28] It has been shown, it is true, that before 1848 there were two interventions by bishops of the Kingdom of Piedmont, Msgr. Charvaz and especially Msgr. Rendu, whose memoir addressed in 1845 to king Charles-Albert (cf. P. Guichonnet in

Rassegna storica del Risorgimento, t. XLII, 1955, pp. 305-319) is considered by Fr. Droulers as "maybe the most farsighted document coming from a bishop of this time" (*Civiltà cattolica*, 1961, vol. II, p. 355). But it must be noted that in both cases these bishops were natives of the Savoy region of the kingdom.

[29] See especially the excellent work (based for the first time on an ample archival documentation) by Angelo Gambasin, *Il movimento sociale nell'Opera dei Congressi, 1874-1904*, Rome, 1958.

[30] On Giuseppe Toniolo (1845-1918), see R. Angeli, *La doctrina sociale di G. Toniolo*, Pinerolo, 1956.

[31] Under the influence of his German teachers, but also, it is often forgotten, following the line of an authentic Italian tradition going back to the 18th century (see the intervention by L. Dalpane in *Aspetti della cultura cattolica nell' età di Leone XIII*, Rome, 1961, pp. 38-41).

[32] *L'Église et l'État en Italie du Risorgimento à nos jours*, French translation, Paris, 1955, p. 65.

[33] On Gaspard Mermillod (1824-1892), named Cardinal in 1890, see Ch. Comte, *Le cardinal Mermillod d'après sa correspondance*, Paris, 1924, and C. Massard, *L'œuvre sociale du cardinal Mermillod*, Louvain, 1914.

[34] Cited by C. Massard, *op. cit.*, pp. 82-83. The result of this group's work (sometimes designated as the "theses of Rome"), rather unoriginal, were mentioned in writing by Kuefstein and later published, in 1893, simultaneously in Paris and Vienna.

[35] On Msgr. Jacobini (1833-1900), see L. Lazzareschi, *Il cardinale Domenico Jacobini*, Rome, 1900.

[36] On the ideology and actions of Belgian corporatism, see K. Van Isacker, *Averechtse democratie. De gilden en de christelijke democratie in België, 1875-1914*, Antwerp, 1959, and for a more positive view, R. Ernotte, *Les aléas d'un idéal corporatif. G. Helleputte et la Gilde des métiers de Louvain (1878-1914)*, photocopied M.A. dissertation, Louvain, 1963.

[37] One can follow its work in detail using the unpublished minutes of the proceedings in the work of C. Massard, *L'Œuvre sociale du cardinal Mermillod: L'Union de Fribourg*, Louvain, 1914.

[38] On this encyclical, in which he lays the blame on "the sect of these men who call themselves variously and with almost barbaric names *socialists, communists*, and *nihilists*," and on the historical context in which it must be understood, see G. Jarlot, *Doctrine pontificale et histoire*, chap. II (pp. 41-59).

[39] Cited by G. Hoog, *Histoire du catholicisme social en France*, Paris, 1946, pp. 24-25.

[40] See C. Massard, *op cit.*, p. 261.

[41] *Ibid.*, p. 264.

[42] See H. J. Browne, *The Catholic Church and the Knights of Labour*, Washington, 1949.

[43] In fact, as Browne has quite demonstrated, although it cannot be said that the effect of Gibbon's intervention in Rome on the prehistory of *Rerum novarum* was negligible, one should nevertheless not exaggerate the social preoccupations of the Archbishop of Baltimore. While he may have lucidly discerned how inopportune a condemnation of the Knights of Labor would have been, discrediting as it would have the Catholic Church in the eyes of the workers by making it seem the ally of

the financial powers, Gibbons never gave positive support to their action and, unlike Manning, cannot be considered a resolute champion of the workers' cause.

[44] See P. Thureau-Dangin, *La Renaissance catholique en Angleterre*, t. III, Paris, 1906, pp. 260-271, and, for more details, E. S. Purcell, *Life of Cardinal Manning*, London, 1896, t. II, pp. 638-671 (the chap. "Manning as social reformer"). What drove Manning to become involved more and more resolutely in this direction was certainly the very sincere compassion he had always had, since the time when he was a young Anglican vicar, for the misery of the working classes. But it was also the reasoned conviction that the future of the Catholic church lay in this direction: "God grant," he wrote, in an autobiographical note, "that the people never consider us *Tories*, belonging to the party which stands in the way of the bettering of their condition, that we never appear to them to be the servants of the plutocracy instead of the guides and protectors of the poor." He saw still another advantage in this social orientation: a means of bringing English Catholics out of the isolated condition which several centuries of proscription had reduced them to, and of helping them to regain their place, beside their non-Catholic fellow citizens, in the life of the nation. Manning, unfortunately, had no imitator or successor in the English hierarchy of his time.

[45] On Victor-Joseph Doutreloux (1837-1901), the first Belgian social bishop, see P. Gérin, art. *Doutreloux*, in the *Dictionnaire d'histoire et de géographie ecclésiastiques*, t. XIV, col. 748-751, and *Les origines de la Démocratie chrétienne à Liège*, Brussels, 1958, pp. 104-119.

[46] On Antoine Pottier (1849-1923), see Canon Cardolle, *Un précurseur, un docteur, un pionnier social: Mgr. Pottier*, Brussels, 1951, and P. Gérin, *op. cit.*, pp. 119-128.

[47] See P. Gérin, *op. cit.*, in particular pp. 87-101, and R Rezoshazy, *Origines et formation du catholicisme social en Belgique*, pp. 103-108.

[48] See E. Terrien, *Mgr. Freppel*, 2nd ed., t. II, Paris, 1936, pp. 603-607, and G. Guitton, *L. Harmel*, t. I, pp. 134 ff. and t. II, pp. 50 ff.

[49] Giovanni Antonazzi, *L'enciclica Rerum novarum, testo autentico e redazioni preparatorie dai documenti originali*, Rome, 1957.

[50] It can be reasonably conjectured that the decisive impetus came from the meeting in Berlin, at the beginning of 1890, of an International Conference on labor legislation. As the French ambassador to the Vatican observed: "Not without some reason, the Pope believes himself justified in maintaining that, in our time, the Church became concerned, well before the emperor of Germany, in the fate of the working classes... I have reason to believe that Leo XIII will not stop there, and that before long the Social Question will be, on his part, the subject of one of those encyclicals which in its entirety is destined to one day mark in history the high philosophical tendencies of the present pontificate" (dispatch of 27 February 1890, Archives du Ministère des Affaires étrangères de Paris, *Rome*, vol. 1099).

[51] *Doctrine pontificale et histoire*, pp. 204-205.

[52] This can especially seen by looking at plates 8 through 10 of the Antonazzi's cited work, which reproduce the pages devoted to capitalism. They are full of cross-outs, of corrections in every corner, and of variants between the lines.

[53] See G. Jarlot, *Doctrine pontificale et histoire*, chap. VII (pp. 202-225), and for greater detail, *L'encyclique Rerum novarum devant le problème du juste salaire*, in *La Vie économique et sociale*, t. XXX, 1959, pp. 11 ff. and *Les avant-projets de Rerum*

novarum et les anciennes corporations, in *Nouvelle Revue théologique*, t. LXXXI, 1959, pp. 60-77.

[54] The famous definition: "the sober and honest worker" will only appear in the final version. "This change introduced at the last minute was evidently the wish of Leo XIII, because of the polemics which were then circulating" (G. Jarlot, *op. cit.*, p. 211).

[55] *Op. cit.*, p. 215.

Social Christianity
XIIIe Congrès International Des
Sciences Historiques
Moscow, 16—23 August 1970

The topic at hand is particularly vast, as it covers not only the social activity and thinking of the various Christian churches, which unfolded more or less independently, but additionally, I have been asked to not to limit it to the period between the two wars, but to take it up from its beginning, which is around the middle of the 19th century. There is therefore no question, in the few pages dedicated to each report, of sketching even summarily the bibliographic record, and we must be content with a certain number of methodological reflections likely to furnish material for a discussion which will bring forth, we hope, enlightening observations.

It is important to begin by specifying a bit what we are talking about. And first of all a word on vocabulary, put into very precise terms by Fr. Paul Droulers and with which I agree wholeheartedly: "In the speech of Germany, as well as in that of France, and afterwards of all the other countries, since the beginning of our century and even for more than a hundred years, when one talks about the workers question, the term *social* is employed antithetically to that of *charity* (alms giving, relief work, philanthropy), and it designates along with the rejection of economic liberalism, the call for legislative interventionism by the State, and for institutions created in the name of *justice*, very expressly. History therefore cannot accept the precisely contrary interpretation which was proposed fewer than ten years ago by an historian, then a beginner: that which would label Social Catholics (for lack of a better term) conservatives embracing economic liberalism and pure charity. A question of terminology, no doubt, but one not without importance, for words contribute to clarify problems, or to compound them."[1] While it would be rather a vain hope to try and fix a precise date for the appearance of that tendency which substitutes, in place of charitable activities, efforts at structural reform destined to improve the social situation of the workers, one can at least generally situate its first steps in the second quarter of the 19ᵗʰ century, but the movement will only really gain strength during the last decades of the century.

In the second place, even when carefully distinguishing between charitable activity and "social" activity, one cannot lump together any and every social activity of Christians into the historical phenomenon known as "Social Christianity," because a certain number of Christians, especially in Protestant countries, became individually involved in socialist movements or in other social activities of a secular nature. The term "Social Christianity" must be reserved for the *organized, and therefore collective,* efforts of Christians aimed at bringing a contribution, *inspired by Christian principles,* to the solution of what has been called the "social question," that is to say the situation of the working classes in modern capitalist societies. Even restricted in this way, the topic to be explored remains considerable, and cannot be limited to just social organizations in the strict sense—such as unions, benevolent societies, social schools—and it is equally necessary to include activities of a cultural sort—for example certain popular education enterprises or even a movement like Msgr. Cardijn's Young Christian Workers (J.O.C.), which from its inception had objectives that were simultaneously religious, educational, and social—and also an entire political sector, because the effort towards a democratization of political institutions is intimately tied to social reforms, and, moreover, most of the religious parties were in fact from the beginning of the 20ᵗʰ century more and more tightly linked with Christian social organizations. Under these conditions, the study of the diverse embodiments of Social Christianity over the last century constitutes an essential theme not only for historians of the Church[2], but equally a theme which naturally the attention of specialists in social history and political history (not to mention the general history of civilization). As B. Mirkine-Guetzévich and M. Prélot noted in their preface to J.B. Durocelle's essay on *Les débuts du catholicisme social en France* ("The Beginnings of Social Catholicism in France"), which appeared in the collection "Les grandes forces politiques"[3] ("Great Political Forces"): "Spiritual forces have always exercised considerable political influence, but this one, at certain times and in certain places, took on some very diverse aspects. Now a sacred character is attributed to the powers themselves, now the ecclesiastic authorities act directly upon these powers, now [religious] beliefs engender a powerful [public] opinion. The modern era has nearly eliminated this first tendency in passing from sacred power to the power of reason; it has gotten further and further away from the second, discredited under the label of *clericalism*; on the other hand, it has seen considerable growth in religion's civic influence as a shaper of public opinion." Given these conditions, one understands why scientific works relative to our topic have multiplied in the last few years, and this interest is especially confirmed by the increasing attention given to the history of Social Catholicism by certain occidental Marxists.[4] It is therefore all the more surprising that to observe (according to, among others, surveys taken by the Schulbuchinstitut of Braunschweig) that in the area of middle-school textbooks, Social Christianity is habitually only mentioned in a few rare paragraphs, most often rather superficial ones. The gap between the level of research and the level of public dissemination of knowledge is seen here yet again, perhaps aggravated in the present case by the weight of certain anticlerical prejudices.

* * *

I had hoped, given the diversity of the phenomenon, that the preparation of this report would be jointly entrusted to a Catholic and a Protestant; but this hope was unfortunately not realized. One will have to excuse the particularly incomplete character of the following notes concerning the non-Catholic denominations.

Even if one can identify a few isolated voices among continental Catholics[5] which testify to an awareness, before 1848, of the new problems posed to the working classes by the Industrial Revolution—in its triple aspect of mechanization, urbanization, and economic liberalism—it is undeniable that it is in Great Britain, in Anglican and especially non-conformist circles, that there appeared, around the middle of the century, the first efforts organized for the purpose of

reacting in the name of Christian principles against the exploitation of the weak by the strong, and of reacting not by promoting a
return to the "good old days," rural and patriarchal, as was long the
case in France and in Germany, but by seeking to reform industrial
capitalism, accepted with realism as a *fait accompli*, and rendering it
more humane—and more Christian—thanks to appropriate organizations of the new sort and eventually to the intervention of the public
powers. A good overview had been sketched 40 years ago by Gilbert
Clive Binyon: *The Christian Movement in England. An introduction
to the study of its history* (London, 1931). The subject was taken up
again more recently by an Australian historian, K. S. Inglis, in the
last chapter of his book *Churches and the Working Class in Victorian
England* (London, 1963), which sums up in 70 pages (pp. 250-321)
the attitude of the different Churches (Anglican, non-conformist, and
Catholic) concerning social reforms, and by Dr. Mayor: *The Churches
and the Labour Movement* (London, 1967), focused on the relations
between the Churches and the social and political movements of the
workers.[6] But these observations are effectively limited to the period
prior to 1914 and synthesizing scientific essay for the last half-century
would be desirable.

One aspect of this history has been studied in particular: the words
and the deeds of the first "Christian Socialists," the theologian F. D.
Maurice and his two associates, J.M. Ludlow, a man of action especially concerned with creating a current of cooperative associations,
and C. Kingsley, a talented orator and writer. Impressed by the French
Revolution of 1848, they, instead of going along with the reactionary wave which then unfurled across Europe, tried to persuade their
compatriots that the essential task of the moment was to Christianize
the socialist movement and to "win over to the reign of Christ the
new industrial world," by a transformation of liberal society's social
and mental structures, and simultaneously by a spiritual education
of the working masses. C. E. Raven's old work, *Christian Socialism,
1848-1854* (London, 1920), which was long the authority, has been
revisited with a wider base of documentation by the Danish historian
Torben Christensen: *Origin and History of Christian Socialism, 1848-
1954* (Aarhaus, 1962). As for the central figure of the movement,
Maurice, he has been the object of several studies, in particular by

Alec C. Vidler. After having shown Maurice to be, in *The Theology of F. D. Maurice* (London, 1948), not only a terrific "awakener," but one of the most profound theologians and spiritual guides of the last century in England, Vidler reedited his lectures, complementing them with the first study of the relations between Maurice and Coleridge, Carlyle, Hare Eskine, Hughes, and the exegetist Westcott, who would succeed him in the role of Christian Socialism's British prophet (*F. D. Maurice and Company*, London, 1966).

In the short term, the movement launched by Maurice was rather a failure, but it would make several comebacks at the end of the century, notably with Stewart Headlam's Guild of St. Matthew, then with the Christian Social Union founded in Oxford in 1889 by a few progressive theologians. Forty years after publication of D. O. Wagner's work, *The Church of England and Social Reform since 1854* (London, 1930), a comprehensive study, not limited to the established Church, has just been consecrated by an American, P. Jones, to *The Christian Socialist Revival, 1877-1914. Religion, Class, and Social Conscience in Late-Victorian England* (Princeton, 1968). Doubtless, new bibliographic studies as well as systematic investigation of periodicals could shed more light on the subject.

Among the points which deserve consideration, let us identify two: one, were the tractarians of the Oxford Movement, preoccupied with intra-ecclesiastical questions, as closed to the workers' problems as claims Desmond Brown in his book, focused on the social contribution of the Anglican Church, *The Idea of the Victorian Church. A Study of the Church of England, 1833-1889* (Montreal, 1968)? And what should be made of Inglis' hypothesis, according to which the evangelical tendency, by foregrounding the question of individual salvation, impeded social awareness? J. D. Bollen, in Sidney's *Journal of Religious History* (t. III, 1964, p. 99), has advanced several theories which invite the nuancing of such a claim. Furthermore, it is certain that much remains to be done for the study of how the Churches' social positions in Great Britain spread throughout the British Empire.[7]

Whereas in England, social awareness awakened rather quickly in men of the Church, which heightened the tension between socialism and religion, Protestant Germany long depended on individual initiatives of a questionable nature, notably on the part of industrialists touched by the *Erweckungsbewegung* [Awakening-Movement], and even the initiatives of J. H. Wichern, the director of the Interior Mission, hardly went beyond this. Christian Socialism in particular reached only a few isolated individuals or very tiny fractions of the Churches. This slow progress of Christian Socialism seems explainable by factors both sociological and theological: on the one hand, the close ties between the Throne and the altar, between Protestantism and the bourgeoisie; on the other, the reticence of Lutheranism *vis-à-vis* the temporal actions of Christians as such, the doctrine of the two kingdoms having petrified to the point of affirming the "absolute *Eigengesetzlichkeit*" of politics and economics.

One of the first to react and to follow the path of Socialism was the Pietismist Johann Christoph Blumhardt, who energetically defended the idea that the kingdom of God is not purely interior and who saw in Socialism an instrument created by God to partially assure its realization. His biography, often re-edited, written by F. Zündel in 1880, the very year of his death, has yet not been replaced.

It is only toward the end of the century that we see the appearance of officially taken positions. In 1884, the central committee of the Interior Mission publishes a report, rather timid moreover, entitled: *Die Aufgaben der Kirche und ihrer inneren Mission gegenüber den wirtschaftlichen und gesellschaftlichen Kampfen der Gegenwart* [The Role of the Church and its Interior Mission regarding the Economic and Social Struggles of the Modern Era]. And six years later, certain personalities, including the royal chaplain A. Stoecker and the celebrated theologian Harnack, found the *Evangelisch-sozial Kongress*, which retained a strong academic bent. Although its positions were far from revolutionary, they seemed nevertheless too advanced to Stoecker, who left in 1896 and the next year, along with L. Weber, founded the more conservative *Freie Kirchliche-soziale Konferenz*, seeking to act in a more practical fashion while remaining on ecclesiastical ground, in the manner of Wichern. The difficulties, which Friedrich Naumann encountered in his efforts at understanding with regard to the Socialist movement and democratic tendencies, are likewise characteristic of the atmosphere that prevailed in German Protestantism at the time of Wilhelm II. It is in Switzerland, around Hermann Kutter and Leonard

Ragaz, that there formed in the beginning of the 20th century, under the name of *Religiös-sozialen*, a group of Christian Socialists which gave birth in 1910 to the *Internationale Bund Religiöser Sozialisten*, resolutely accepting Socialism as expression of God's will in this world. The movement wound up having some success in between-the-wars Germany, through E. Heimann and P. Tillich, while the ties between the *Kirchliche-soziale Bund* and the Interior Mission were strengthened under the common presidency of R. Seeberg.

One sees hardly any comprehensive works recently dealing with the history of these different movements. The works of G. Soecknick, *Religiöser Sozialismus der neueren Zeit unter Besondere Berücksichtigung Deutschlands* [Religious Socialism of the New Age with Particular Consideration of Germany] (1926) and of Emil Fuchs, *Von Naumann zu den religiosen Sozialisten, 1894-1929* [From Naumann to the Religious Socialists] (1929), and that of W. Frank, *Hofprediger A. Stoecker und die christlich-soziale Bewegung* [Royal Chaplain]. A. Stoecker and the Christian Social Movement (1928) are more than 40 years old, and H. Eger's book on the *Evangelisch-sozial Kongress* (1930) is hardly more recent. Moreover, we are still waiting for a good critical review of the activity of the *Gesamtverband der evangelischen Arbeitervereine Deutschlands*, [Collective Union of German Christian Workers' Societies] founded in 1890, in a decidedly anti-socialist spirit, and the same for the *Internationale Arbeitsgemeinschaft evangelischer Arbeitnehmerverbänder* [International Guild of Christian Workers], founded in Dusseldorf in 1928. Doubtless a certain number of monographs, and especially biographies,[8] should be undertaken to begin with, and it is to be hoped without delay in order to avoid the loss of numerous documents and to take advantage of the oral histories which it is still possible to collect. Also very useful would be the systematic exploitation, if possible in collaboration between historians and sociologists, of periodical publications such as the *Verhandlungen des Evangelischsoziales Kongresses* (since 1890), *Evangelisch-sozial* (1904-1922 and 1924-1941), the *Verhandlungsberichte und Hefte der Kirchlich-sozialen Bundes* (1897-1932) or the *Kirchliche-soziale Blätter* (1898-1934), not just to expose the positions taken but to try to explain them in the context of their times, the pressures on the ecclesiastic and lay personalities and the evolution of attitudes in matters religious and profane.

If the current state of the German bibliography is somewhat disappointing, this is not the case for the third important center of Social Protestantism, the United States, where in particular the movement designated by the name of Social Gospel, born from the conjunction of industrial society's problems and the Puritan idea of "God's Kingdom in America" (Niebuhr) transposed onto the terrain of liberal theology, has been the object of numerous studies, including several remarkable ones, notably, to speak only of the comprehensive studies, the works of C. H. Hopkins, *The Rise of the Social Gospel in American Protestantism, 1865-1915* (New Haven, 1940), P. Carter, *The Decline and Revival of the Social Gospel, 1920-1940* (Ithaca, 1956), and H. S. May, *Protestant Churches and Industrial America* (New York, 1949). This last author, who distinguishes three fundamental tendencies from the beginning (conservative, limited to pursuing an improvement in living conditions; progressive, envisaging certain structural reforms; and radical, seeking a synthesis of Marxism and Christianity), further insists on the fact that the social preoccupations of American Protestantism over the last century are not limited to the Social Gospel movement, which only represents one particularly noticeable phase. Equally to be taken into account, given the social pessimism inherited from the Puritan tradition, of the revivalist enthusiasm of the Evangelists in the second half of the 19th century, which is at the root of numerous social emancipation movements; and, after the golden age of Liberalism, adaptations to the repeated reactions of the fundamentalists, then of the neo-orthodox, resulting in a moderately pessimist and conservative theology joined to a faith which was moderately progressive insofar as social actions.

The existence of an already rather large number of good books does not mean that historians have hardly any more possibilities for research. Account must be taken of the extreme complexity of American Protestantism, and of the great independence often enjoyed by local communities, which has as a consequence profound differences within a same denomination, particularly in social matters, and thus solidifying the local as tightly as possible: the monographic studies, although less stimulating than the great syntheses, are a condition *sine qua non* of the latter.

Before finishing up with Social Protestantism, a last sector must be brought to the attention of historians: the activities and the social ideas of the Ecumenical Movement. They have always held a special place, from the Life and Work conference in Stockholm in 1925 to the recent 1966 Geneva conference on the theme "Church and Society." But it seems that so far the subject has retained greater interest among theologians and sociologists than among historians. Indeed, not only are these historians disposed of numerous archives which would permit them to illuminate the evolution of different viewpoints, but above all, this research would make for instructive confrontations between the positions of the various Protestant Churches in social matters, whose study has up until now been pursued within a strictly national framework.

*   *   *

When tackling the history of Social Catholicism, one risks running into the opposite problem: aware of the extremely centralized nature of contemporary Catholicism, one can be tempted to more or less identify the history of Social Catholicism with that of Rome's positions, while neglecting the very important part played by local initiative, often of quite divergent sorts. In social matters, as in many other domains, an encyclical is generally the culmination of a maturation which has for the most part taken place in the entire Catholic world, and at the same time a point of departure for new doctrinal exploration and new practical applications which can be very different from one country to another and even within a single country.

The thing is very clear in the case of the first social encyclical, *Rerun novarum*, published in 1891 by Leo XIII. It appears more and more to have been the result of reflection and practical endeavours which had been pursued by the entire Church for some twenty years:[10] in Germany, under the impetus of Msgr. Ketteler, amidst the *Volksverein* of München-Gladbach; in Austria, around the Baron von Vogelsang, the Prince von Loewenstein and the Haid Group; in France, with

Albert de Mun, leader of the *Œuvre des cercles catholiques ouvriers* [Organization of Catholic Workers Groups], with Léon Harmel, model Christian employer of his time, and especially with René de la Tour du Pin, the group's thinker; in Italy, with Professor Toniolo and the *Opera dei Congressi*, but above all with a circle of social studies which brought together a number of foreigners living in Rome; in Belgium, where clashed partisans and adversaries of corporatism and State intervention in economic and social life; in Switzerland, with the Union of Fribourg presided over by Msgr. Mermillod; to which must be added the impression made in Rome by the intervention of Cardinal Gibbons, Archbishop of Baltimore, in favor of the workers organization Knights of Labor, and by the support of Cardinal Manning, Archbishop of Westminster, for the London dock workers' strike of 1889. All these factors are becoming rather well known, in themselves and in their impact on the Holy See. Of particular note among recent works, those by E. Ritter, *Die Katholische Sozialbewegung Deutschlands im 19. Jht und der Volkverein* (Cologne, 1954), by J. C. Allmayerbeck, *Vogelsang. Von Feudalismus zur Volksbewegung* (Vienna, 1952), by G. Silberbauer, *Osterreichs Katholiken und die Arbeiterfrage* (Gratz, 1966), whose first section benefited from unpublished dissertations written at the University of Vienna, by H. Rollet, *L'action sociale des catholiques en France, 1871-1901* (Paris, 1948), by R. Talmy, *Aux sources du catholicisme social. L'École de La Tour du Pin* (Tournai-Paris, 1963), by A. Gambasin, *Il movimento sociale nell'Opera dei Congressi, 1874-1904* (Rome, 1958), which was for the first time able to use ample archival documentation, by R. Rezsohazy, *Origine et formation du catholicisme social en Belgique* (Louvain, 1958), by P. Gérin, *Les origines de la démocratie chrétienne à Liège* (Brussels, 1958), by K. Van Isacker, *Averechtse demokratie, De gilden en de christelijke demokratie in Belgie, 1875-1914* (Antwerp, 1959), and by H. J. Browne, *The Catholic Church and the Knights of Labor* (Washington, 1949). This last work shows how a systematic study based on primary sources can contribute to a "demythification" of certain figures. It seems in effect that Gibbons, however lucidly he may have discerned how much a condemnation of the Knights of Labor would have discredited the Church among the working classes, never positively supported their actions, and, unlike Manning, he cannot be considered, contrary to a widespread cliché, as a champion of the workers' cause. Likewise, Talmy's work, based on a detailed study of private papers and the publications of the group of sociologists gathered around La Tour du Pin bent on elaborating a plan for the restoration of a cooperatively-based Christian society, shows that in spite of the anachronistic aspect of certain of their positions, they were in reality more modern on certain essential points than many Christian Democrats before 1914, notably, taking positions on the limits of property rights, and the State's right to intervene in economic life, which are singularly close to certain socialist points of view

Although the encyclical *Rerum novarum* is the result of multiple initiatives that developed outside of Rome, it nevertheless remains the work of Leo XIII. On the way his text took shape, many hypotheses have been proposed. Things are at present a good deal more clear thanks to Msgr. Antonazzi's publication of the various preparatory versions preserved in the Vatican archives (*L'enciclica "Rerum novarum," testo autentico e redazioni preparatorie dai documenti originali*, Rome, 1957). One finds there notably the manner in which, from the first draft written by Fr. Liberatore to the new version done by P. Zigliara and finally to the definitive text, minutely reviewed by the Pope, the idea of a corporative system gradually gives way to that of professional associations, envisaging as aforetimes, if possible, the involvement of both employers and workers, but not as a necessary condition, which officially opened the door to the formula of the future, the workers union. On the other hand, if the initial option in favor of State intervention in economic and social life was maintained against the excessive liberalism of the School of Angers and the *Patrons du Nord*, the numerous nuances and hints introduced progressively into the text indicate well enough with what prudence and hesitation the Holy See took this path.

This last remark leads us to the always-disputed question of the historical significance of the encyclical *Rerum novarum*. Praised in many Catholic quarters as "the workers' charter," it is considered by others to be an essentially anti-socialist document, all in all one whose inspiration was rather reactionary, and one whose influence was in any case small in the workers emancipation movement. One must consider that not only was the encyclical written several decades after

Marx's *Manifesto*, but also that it resorts to an abstract argumentation, without analysis of the real situation created by the development of capitalism, that it contains many moralizing observations and that it remains imprecise on most of the concrete questions which were posed during the period. Not to mention the hope of finding for the Church, in the popular masses on their way to obtaining universal suffrage, a counterbalance to the anti-clerical politics so often practiced by the bourgeois secular state. There are however other, more positive aspects. In the first place, while most social Catholics of the preceding decades had been nostalgic for the traditional, preponderantly rural society, reacting against bourgeois society from a pre-capitalist perspective and advocating the return to a more-or-less modernized version of the traditional guild system (which was a dead-end at the level of the great modern industries), Leo XIII had the great merit of disengaging himself from these romantic utopias and taking his place alongside the realists, on [philosophical] ground analogous to that of reformist socialism, seeking the uplifting of the working class within the framework of existing institutions, including labor unions, whose legitimacy is recognized, even if it is half-heartedly. In the second place, it was not something unimportant that for the first time the rights of workers and the injustice of the entire liberal system were solemnly proclaimed by the highest spiritual authority. Catholics were quite forced to admit, despite numerous reservations, that a change was needed, and the most open-minded began to follow the path of Christian democracy. But the importance of Leo XIII's stance went far beyond Catholic circles. Assuredly, well before *Rerum novarum*, the labor movement was up and running, and the credit for the initiative goes essentially to the socialists. But for the first time this labor movement received the solemn sanction of one of the principal forces of order in the world, and such a sanction was bound to help remove the revolutionary label which it had till then worn in the eyes of the great majority of the middle class. From the psychological point of view — and it is a point-of-view which has its historical importance — this was far from being trivial. The first official guidepost of Social Catholicism was thenceforward planted. The movement, launched with the Pope's blessing, would not be stopped, in spite of some setbacks at the end of the pontificate[11] and especially under Pius X.

Although the scientific study of this last pontificate has barely been attempted, we are beginning to see the complex reasons for the reactionary social positions taken by this Pope who was otherwise very sensitive to the poverty of the workers. Native of the devout Venetian countryside, where the influence of the clergy in public life remained preponderant, he could not understand the tendency of many Christian Democrats to minimize the moral aspect of social questions in favor of material demands, and especially to demand a more autonomous posture for their actions *vis-à-vis* the hierarchy. This last consideration seems to have been overriding, but we must add the compromise of certain Christian Democrats with modern ism, especially in the Italian group led by Fr. Murri,[12] or, as in France, with governments openly hostile to the Church. The pontifical mistrust was maintained and reinforced by lay and ecclesiastic pressure groups, who, convinced that they were defending the true tradition of the Church, which they identified with Pope Pius IX's anathemas against the "modern world," tried to confirm the Pope in the idea that Christian Democracy, if it were not strictly controlled by ecclesiastic authority, risked sinking into naturalism and even becoming the Trojan Horse of atheist socialism. The encyclical of 24 September 1912, on Christian Syndicalism expresses this state of mind, although with a certain number of nuances in which one recognizes Roman diplomacy.

It is in Germany that we find the epicenter of the conflict between Christian Democrats and "Catholic fundamentalists," but it is in France where, over the course of the last few years, we have seen appear the most important and most original works on the subject. Two theses which unite the political and social aspects of the problem, that are a bit clustered but extremely well-documented, that of Jeanne Caron on *Le Sillon et la Démocratie chrétienne, 1894-1910* (Paris, 1967) and that of Jean-Marie Mayeur, *Un prêtre démocrate, l'abbé Lemire* (Paris, 1968), a model biography which attempts to shed light on the relations between the personality being studied and the groups and movements of which he was a part or with which he was confronted, and which offers the additional advantage of putting its finger on the diversity of positions which were in reality covered by the label "Christian Democrat."[13] Next, Emile Poulat's publication of the famous secret dossier *Sapinière*, which concerns "social modernism" much more than doctrinal modernism, publication accompanied by an annotation whose disconcerting erudition considerably enriches our knowledge of the men and events in the two camps, and preceded by an introduction which sheds a lot of light on the attitudes of the fundamentalists and on the true relationship of the powers in Rome, both of which are too often presented in simplistic terms (*Intégrisme et catholicisme intégral. Un réseau secret international anti-moderniste*, Paris, 1969). Finally, Fr. Paul Droulers' work, *Politique sociale et christianisme. Le P. Desbuquois et l' "Action populaire." Débuts. Syndicalisme et intégristes, 1903-1918* (Paris, 1969), a monograph in which the author was deliberately content with studying a very limited sector of the Social Catholic apostolate in France under Pius X, without even pretending to trace the complete history of *Action populaire*—the history of *Semaines sociales* especially has yet to be written—but which, through a man who was at one of the principal crossroads, permits a glimpse from a new perspective at a certain underside of the fundamentalist campaign.

These works, and still others which it is not possible to cite here, have considerably increased our knowledge, but they also pose various problems that historians' future research must attempt to clarify: the exact degree of Pius X's personal responsibility in the fundamentalist campaign against Christian Democracy, which seems to be greater than has been stated; the divergent ways in which the men involved in Catholic social action understood the demands of submission to pontifical authority in these matters; the respective importance which these men attributed to the two ends of Christian social activity, one religious and moral, the other socioeconomic, or even political, and the nature of the spiritual engagement (which many recent historians have a tendency to lose sight of) given by a certain number of them to their temporal actions; the diverse sociological circles in which the principal tendencies of Social Catholicism were elaborated and developed during that period; the reasons for which the fundamentalist campaign against the Christian unions intensified after the Spring of 1912 (should we see in this a consequence of the rise of Socialism all over Europe?); and above all—Mr. Poulat insisted strongly on this point[14]—to what extent is the cleavage which separates Social Catholics and fundamentalist Catholics under Pius X a continuation of the divisions in the Catholic ranks provoked in relation to the encyclical *Rerum novarum?* It appears in effect that more than a few of the fundamentalist adversaries of Christian Democracy had been, under Leo XIII, social Catholics clearly opposed to the School of Angers, and from this springs the question of explaining in what context and for what motives a confrontation had developed within an ideological milieu with a common origin, one side aligning itself more and more with social and political democracy, the others with the conservatives, although they were persuaded to remain faithful to their original orientation, based on the restoration of the "Social Reign of Jesus Christ."

A related question likewise demands framing: to what degree did the paternalistic phase of Social Catholicism—the phase of Catholic organizations *for* workers run by pious respectable persons, for which were substituted, more or less rapidly depending on the country, Catholic workers organizations run by those workers—delay the flowering of Christian Democracy, or did it, on the contrary, efficiently prepare the way for it, both by facilitating the transition of the ruling classes—to whom it gave awareness of the true scope of the workers problem—and by furnishing troops who were already organized for the first Christian unions and other autonomous workers' organizations?[15]

The answer to most of these questions requires the pursuit of monographic studies on a regional level. Such works have multiplied in the last few years and one can easily make the point thanks to the collective work published under the direction of the late Canon F. H. Scholl: *150 ans de mouvement ouvrier chrétien en Europe de l'Ouest, 1789-1939* [150 years of the Christian Workers Movement in Western Europe],[16] at least for Western Europe.[17] But much remains to be done at the biographical level, and in terms of the different organizatiions,[18] in terms of the international contacts and perhaps even more in terms of ideas (the study of sermons, of catechisms, of theological manuals, of mass-distribution brochures, of periodical publications, especially utilizing the methodology of content analysis in order to pick out the evolutions and the shifts of emphasis). And, in spite of several partial syntheses whose merit we in no way wish to diminish, there is likewise a good deal which remains to be done to bring together the results of these diverse types of monographic inquiries: in particular the role of certain personalities in the development of certain organizations and of certain movements, or further still the influence of ideas on action (or the absence of action: the shame of "theologizing" instead of looking at the concrete and acting [on it], among many Catholics, especially in the Latin countries, doubtless explains their frequent ineffectiveness in social matters, as much as, if not more, than their conservative reflexes).

For the period between the wars, and *a fortiori* for the pontificate of Pius XII (1939-1958), the serious work (superficial publications of an apologetic or even polemic nature are not lacking), is even less advanced, although a certain number of beacons have already been lit, either by historians—often in studies whose point of departure goes back to the 19th century, such as the works created by Roland Ruffieux on Catholic social action in the francophone regions of Switzerland[19]—or else by sociologists, who too often have a tendency to neglect the evolution of a question, but whose contribution is nonetheless very useful, as proven for example by the thesis of P. A. Dendoven on the Flemmish branch of the J. O. C.[20] or, in a completely different field, the works of J.Y. Calvez and J. Perrin or (with the care of better marking the steps) of R. L. Camp on pontifical thought in social matters.[21]

Rather than attempt an inventory which would risk turning into a prize list, let us simply point out several desirable lines of research. First, insofar as the positions taken by the Holy See are concerned. Assuredly, the abnormally long delay in the opening of the Vatican Archives—which contrasts painfully with the policy followed by the Ecumenical Council of Churches—does not facilitate an objective study, but it is still possible to significantly overcome the obstacles. Experience shows that, although the Archives remain inaccessible even now for the pontificates of Leo XIII and Pius X, it has been possible, thanks to diocesan archives and private papers, not to mention diplomatic archives, to glimpse many important things, and sometimes even things about which the Roman Archives would hardly instruct us at all. It is therefore important that we try at present to identify these sources and to complement them with interviews of still-living witnesses, especially in order to reveal what influences were exerted at decisive moments and the various councilors who advised the Popes in social matters. Likewise, in order to see beyond the contents of the pontifical documents the intentions which clarify them and permit their exact interpretation, one could begin today to situate each of these documents in its historical context, in a certain state of the Church and the world, in relation to the theological, sociological, and economic forces at play.[22] As for the content of the documents itself, thus illuminated, we will especially ask in what measure it represents an original contribution going beyond an attempt at compromise between Liberalism and Marxism, as well as in what measure the different Popes who succeeded one another attempted to make the standard fundamentalist doctrinal line they followed more profound, or if they limited themselves to giving occasional responses to particular problems with which they were presented.

A central question, which needs elucidating, is what motivated the persistent sympathies of the Catholic milieus for the corporatist formulas, and also the exact reach of these sympathies, whose extent we have a tendency to exaggerate today. A systematic study through the Social Christian press of the reception given to the encyclical *Quadragesimo anno* (and especially of a certain characteristic silence) would doubtless be rather significant; in any case, this is what is suggested by the Belgian example.

Although until the beginning of the 20th century, the influence of Social Catholicism in the political life of European states remained relatively weak, this is not the case under the pontificates of Pius XI and Pius XII, during which, under various names, it assumed an important, sometimes even exclusive, part in the direction of affairs. This phenomenon has already been studied, partially at least, in its external manifestations, but the question of its interpretation remains intact: is it a case of a new avatar of traditional clericalism and of a new effort to reconstruct Christianity in a modern political framework? Is it a case of an original formula, inspired by the Christian ideal, but whose numerous traits are in no way postulated by the principles of Catholic morality and spring rather from an effort to reconcile a certain number of positive values in Liberalism and Marxism? Or is it not a case, more simply, of a sort of historical accident with no tomorrow, made possible by the retreat of Liberalism and the great schism between socialists and communists? The historian certainly has something to say in this debate, even if it primarily concerns the politicians.

In studies conducted on a regional level, one theme worthy of attention is the question of knowing in what measure, at what moment, and under what influences the Catholic social movements, born of an anti-socialist perspective and more preoccupied with improving existing conditions than with promoting profound structural reform, evolved in the direction of a rapprochement or at least an active collaboration with Marxist organizations, and of questioning the very basis of the capitalist system. One angle among others from which this research could be conducted seems to be the study of the *Semaines sociales*, which, whatever name is given to them, have maintained themselves regularly in numerous countries over the last decades: the nature and the numbers of the participants, the deals which took place over the elaboration of the program and the choice of orators, even the content of the lessons and the echoes in the press are so many clues to be exploited.

Three more suggestions to conclude. First, the advantage there would be in giving priority to studies in all genres relative to the last half century, in order to conserve the maximum of the still-extant documentation in a domain in which—experience has already sufficiently demonstrated—private papers are not saved for very long, and also in order to record before it is too late the oral testaments which permit not only to supplement in part the frequent lack of written documentation but also to rediscover something of the atmosphere and the concrete concerns of the preceding generation, a very important psychological element if one wants to try to understand the past and especially the reasons for certain choices, certain successes or certain failures.

Second, the usefulness there would be in multiplying comparisons beyond national boundaries, in order to better shed light on both the differences which result from the diversity of historical or local situations, and on the similarities which reveal the influence and more importantly the fundamental unity of the Social Catholic movement. This internationalization of perspective, whose usefulness is undeniable from the beginning of the movement (think for example of the *Sozialaristokratismus* phenomenon or of the ultramontane origin of most European Social Catholic movements) is especially important for the more recent past, as a consequence of the multiplication of contacts and the widening of perspectives. It is evident that it must include in its field of vision not only Europe but the entire world, and in particular the Third World, for which scientific historical studies in the sector which interests us are still practically nonexistent.

Finally, the study of Social Catholicism must further widen its perspectives. It has until now most often taken place in isolation, without sufficiently taking into account concomitant Socialist endeavors and without much concern either for the parallel development of Social Christianity in the reformed milieus. To ignore the study of the Socialist movement is a fundamental methodological error, which compromises many monographs and many syntheses, sometimes extremely valuable for the facts they make known but skewed at their base by this lack of perspective. As for the social action and ideas of the non-Roman Churches, doubtless the effective contacts between the two worlds were practically nil until recently, which makes the absence of comparison less damaging insofar as the reconstitution of facts, but a direct comparison would permit better revelation of reciprocal originalities and better understanding of the degree to which the social actions and ideas of Catholics were influenced by their ecclesiological options, which appears to be very illuminating at the level of interpretation, which constitutes the historian's ultimate objective.

Notes

[1] In *Revue d'Histoire ecclésiastique*, LIII, 1968, p. 1019.

[2] "Nicht mit Unrecht ist der Zusammenstoss zwischen Christentum und Sozialismus als das kirchengeschichtliche Ereignis des ausgesenden 19. Und Beginnenden 20 Jhs. bezeichnet worden" (*Die Religion in Geschichte und Gegenwart*, 3rd ed., VI, p. 180, citing E. Thurneysen, *Sozialismus und Christentum*, in *Zwischen den Zeiten*, I, 1923, pp. 58-80).

[3] Paris, 1951, p. VII.

[4] Two examples among others: the work of Giorgio Candeloro, *Il movimento cattolico in Italia*, Rome, 1955, and that of Pierre Joye and Rosine Lewin, *L'Église et le mouvement ouvrier en Belgique*. Bruxelles, 1967.

[5] J.B. Duroselle found the first example of it in an article by Lamennais dated 1822.

[6] Worth noting, the regret of a survey taker: "Dr. Mayor's useful survey has two main weaknesses. First, it makes very little use of recent writing on the history of the labour movement: only seven books in his bibliography have appeared since 1958. Second, the analysis is not sufficiently searching to illuminate some of the central problems in what is still a difficult area both of religious and of social history." (A. Briggs, in *Journal of Ecclesiastical History*, XXIX, 1968, pp. 135-136).

[7] An example: the article by H. Roth, *The Labour Churches in New Zealand*, in *International Review of Social History*, IV, 1959, pp. 361-366.

[8] Attention is called to M. Mattmüller, *L. Ragaz und der religiöser Sozialismus*, Zolliton, 1957.

[9] The title of Robert Handy's book, *The Social Gospel in America*, should foster no illusions: it is an anthology, moreover a very well-conceived one, of briefly commented extracts by three particularly representative authors: W. Gladden, one of the precursors, R. Ely, an economist who was very concerned with the ethical approach to problems, W. Rauschenbuch, the most brilliant theologian of the group. Two of them are the subject of detailed biographies: J. H. Dorn, *W. Gladden, Prophet of the Social Gospel* (Columbus, 1967), and R. Müller, *W. Rauschenbuch* (Leiden, 1957).

[10] To speak only of the immediate and direct influences. For one cannot completely set aside groundwork that had already been laid here and there over the course of two-thirds of a century, especially in Germany (the centenary of the death of Kolping in 1965, saw several publications, but they hardly say anything new and we still await the critical edition of his autobiographical manuscripts and of his numerous articles published in journals which have become very rare today; on the other hand, the role of the Catholic Bavarian precursor von Buss from before 1848 has been given better treatment by R. Lange, *F. J. von Buss und die soziale Frage seiner Zeit*, Freiburg-in-Breisgau (1955), and in France, the extremely well-documented work by J.B. Duroselle, *Les débuts du catholicisme social en France, 1822-1870*, Paris, 1951, has practically exhausted the subject, with all the same several complementary observations brought by Fr. Paul Droulers concerning the episcopate: *Action pastorale et problèmes sociaux sous la Monarchie de Juillet chez Mgr d'Astros*, Paris, 1954, and various articles published in *Revue d'histoire moderne et contemporaine*, IV, 1957, *Cahiers d'histoire*, VI, 1961 and IX, 1964, *Revue de l'Action populaire*, no. 147, 1961, *Revue historique*, CCXXIX, 1963, *Mouvement social*, no. 57, 1966).

[11] One cannot exaggerate, however. Fr. G. Martina (*La prima redazione dell'enciclica "Graves de communi,"* in *Revista di storia della Chiesa in Italia*, XVI, 1962, pp. 492-507), has shown by comparing the first draft edited by Cardinal Cavagnis to the definitive version, that the orientation of the former was even more conservative, and he attributes the change of emphasis in favor of moderately reformist aspirations to the intervention of the Pope.

[12] While awaiting the great comprehensive study which is still lacking, numerous publications, including several based on unpublished papers, have begun in the last dozen years or so to revive this long-neglected sector of Italian historiography, but the differences in interpretation remain profound.

[13] As with the variety of motives which inspired the adversaries of the Christian Democrats: some approved their willingness to open up to modern aspirations, but found them too advanced in the social areas; others blamed their political choices even as they praised their social program; still others, more or less in political and social agreement, feared questioning the place of the hierarchy's authority in the Church. Too many hasty syntheses neglect these important nuances.

[14] See especially his discussion with Fr. Droulers in *Archives de sociologie des religions*, no. 28, 1969, pp. 131-152.

[15] In examining this question of paternalism, which occupies an important place in the Social Christianity of the 19th century and beginning of the 20th, it is important to avoid anachronisms and, rather than summarily condemning it in the name of current points of view, to try to understand it in terms of the mental schemas of the time and also in terms of the circumstances of a time when the majority of workers were still illiterate.

[16] Published in a Dutch edition (1961), Italian (1962), Spanish (1964), French and German editions (1966).

[17] Included is: Germany, Austria, Belgium, Spain, France, Great Britain, Holland, Portugal, and Switzerland. But one cannot lose sight of the fact that, since before 1914, social concerns had been manifested among Catholics in many other regions of the world: in the Slavic provinces of the Austro-Hungarian monarchy, where the rise of Social Christians at the expense of bourgeois parties, principal representatives of nationalism, prefigured a swelling of ethnic tensions at the beginning of the 20th century (cf. J. Lukaszewski in *Revue d'histoire moderne et contemporaine*, XV, 1968, pp. 491-492); in the United States for which a good comprehensive study is still lacking; in certain Latin American countries, such as Uruguay or Chile, but the work of research has scarcely begun; and even in Australia, where the decisive action of the Archbishop of Sidney, in close contact with the Labor Party, has just been made subject of a good study (Patrick Ford, *Cardinal Moran and the A. L. P. A study in the encounter between Moran and Socialism, 1890-1907; its effects upon the Australian Labor Party, the foundation of Catholic social thought and action in modern Australia* (Melbourne-London, 1966).

[18] Mutualities, unions, socially active political groups, but also training centers. We hope for more works such as that of Bruno Malinverni, *La Scuola sociale cattolica di Bergamo* (Rome, 1960).

[19] B. Prongue, *Le mouvement chrétien social dans le Jura bernois, 1891-1961*, Fribourg, 1968; R. Ruffieux, *Le mouvement chrétien social en Suisse romande 1891-1949*, Fribourg, 1969 (this work, written with the help of a team of students, shows the fruitfulness of this method of the future, which offers the advantage of in-depth research without excessive compartmentalization).

[20] *Ontstaan, structuur en werking van de Vlaamse K. A. J. Een soziografisch overzicht*, Antwerp-Brussels, 1968.

[21] J.-Y. Calvez and J. Perrin, *Église et société économique. L'enseignement social des papes de Léon XIII à Pie XII, 1878-1958*, Paris, 1959; Richard L. Camp, *The Papal Ideology of Social Reform. A Study in Historical Development, 1879-1967* (Leiden, 1969).

[22] This is what Fr. Georges Jarlot had attempted for the earlier period, *Doctrine pontificale et histoire. L'enseignement social de Léon XIII, Pie X et Benoit XV vu dans son ambiance historique, 1878-1922* (Rome, 1964). But the historian must take into account the remark by H. Desroches (in *Archives de sociologie des religions*, no. 20, 1965, p.186): it is not enough to expose the objective contexts in which the pontifical documents were written, because "from the establishment of this summary retrospective, in 1964, we do not know what the author or authors of the encyclical knew or ignored, and still less how they knew it and why they were unaware of it." The research of one of my students, concerning what Belgian Catholics at the end of the 19th century knew about socialism when they were trying to refute it, is revealing in this regard and invites historians of Social Christianity to give a much larger place to the history of attitudes of minds.

[23] The favorable welcome given to the corporatist idea in the early stages of Social Catholicism is easily understood, even if we can see clearly today the romantic chimera that this represented: it had the merit of furnishing a concept of labor with roots in the Christian past and which, in advance of paternalism, sought to give workers a certain share of responsibility alongside employers. But the problem is to know for what reasons—theological (reaction against "class struggle"), economic (pursuit of an organically anti-liberal order), political (affinities with fascist regimes)—numerous Catholics, including a good part of the Roman milieus, long continued to promote this plan and—not least important—to specify the exact idea that they placed in it.

The Beginnings of Social Catholicism
1978

Between 1848, the year when Marx published the Communist *Manifesto*, and 1891, the year when Leo XIII published the encyclical *Rerum novarum*, nearly half a century elapsed. The two dates have often been contrasted to show how belatedly, by comparison with the socialist movement, the Church became aware of the working class question. In reality the picture was one of greater nuances, although it is undeniable that the Church, in this particular field, allowed herself to be outdistanced by socialism. Thus despite the wave of reaction following 1848, Marx succeeded in setting up the First International as early as 1864 and had soon awakened the industrial proletariat to a common hope, whereas the majority of Catholics, and the majority of Catholics in authority, were to remain blind for most of the century to the necessity for 'structural reform' and to continue to regard attempts to improve the lot of the working classes by means of institutional change as perilously close to revolution. This was due, it may be remarked, not so much to lack of generosity or ignorance of the wretched condition of the workers as to sheer incomprehension of the new problems posed by the industrial revolution. But the picture would be grossly oversimplified if we were to overlook the existence alongside the rest of a keener-sighted minority of laymen, priests and bishops who were awakened quite early to a genuine social concern by their realization that the working class question was a matter not merely of charity but of social justice.

In connection with these efforts which prepared the way for the encyclical *Rerum novarum* we should first mention an aspect that used to be overlooked. Contrary to what might be expected, the socially aware Catholics of the late Pius IX and early Leo XIII period were not to be found in the circles most appreciative of political democracy—the liberal Catholics of France and Belgium, the Italian *transigenti*—but among liberalism's most decided opponents, on the face of it 'reactionary' figures, as from many points of view indeed they were. Although apparently disconcerting, on a closer look the phenomenon becomes easier to explain. In the first place, many of these early pioneers of social Catholicism belonged by birth to the landed aristocracy. Less involved than liberal Catholics in business affairs, they were therefore less sensitive to the famous imperative of the 'iron law' of competition. But above all the socially aware Catholics of the period 1860 to 1890 regarded social action—conceived most of the time in a highly paternalistic perspective—as a means of rallying the mass of the people to their cause, that is to say, to their struggle against the anti-clerical bourgeois oligarchy, which they detested on two counts: first for being anti-clerical, second for presuming to substitute the power of money for the old social sanctions. This at once makes it clear why the projects of socially aware Catholics were so often inspired by a nostalgic vision of returning to the patriarchal and corporative past rather than by a desire for realistic accommodation by the new and irreversible situation created by the industrial revolution.

The link between anti-liberalism and social concern was established very early in the *Civiltà cattolica,* as in assertions such as Fr. Taparelli's in 1852 that the guilds, suppressed by the French Revolution, belonged to the natural law, and Pius IX took care in the encyclical *Quanta cura* to denounce not only the delusion of socialism, with its claim to replace Providence by the State, but also the pagan character of economic liberalism, with its exclusion of moral considerations from the relations between capital and labor.

These ideas inspired many of the originators of the Italian Catholic Movement, who in a still largely unindustrialized country were concerned above all with the deplorable situation of the peasantry. Under the wing of the *Opera dei Congressi,* the leaders of which were fanatically hostile to the liberal State, there grew up following the congress at Bergamo in 1877 a whole network of voluntary organizations, concentrated particularly in the north - where the effects of social propaganda were beginning to bite - the purpose of which was to grapple with the social and economic needs of the lower classes. It was likewise within the *Opera* that a start was made in Italy on working out a 'sociology,' as it was termed at the time, in which the stress was more on the demands of morality and religion than on material interests, the chief exponent of which was Professor Giuseppe Toniolo. This Italian social movement taking shape during the first half of Leo XIII's pontificate, and which a galaxy of young historians has rescued from oblivion over the past twenty years, had only limited effect, not only because it was content with a pale imitation of what was being done in neighboring countries, but also because under the influence of the leading men in the Opera dei Congressi it for so long balked at the idea that political democracy was a necessary condition for obtaining worthwhile social reform.

French social Catholicism, while much more original in its thinking, long suffered from the same limitation. Under the Second Empire the relatively few who engaged in good works and who were troubled by working-class poverty were inspired for the most part by the theories of Le Play,[1] which in combination with their narrow interpretation of the *Syllabus* helped to steer them, with very few exceptions, towards a doctrine of 'counter-revolution,' hostile to the rights of man and to egalitarian democracy. After the shocks administered by the Commune there were certainly signs of a change on the way, but there was to be very little alteration in basic attitudes until the very eve of *Rerum novarum*. Almost nowhere did the idea dawn that the workers themselves should be entrusted with responsibility for running the Catholic social organizations created for their benefit. Yet this was precisely the moment when in France, as throughout Europe, the working-class movement was developing an increasing resistance to paternalism. It is thus hardly surprising that the workers were wary in their attitude towards social enterprises launched by Catholics, or that the latter failed to make an impact on the true working-class elite. A case in point is the *Œuvre des Cercles catholiques ouvriers*, founded at Christmas 1871, by a young army officer, Albert de Mun. The movement's hostility towards the principles of 1789 and its nostalgia for the social order of an earlier age inevitably made it appear reactionary, although in social concern Albert de Mun and his group were in reality far in advance not merely of the Orleanists but also of most the republican leaders of their day. Although apparently a failure, the *Œuvre des Cercles* was to exert a lasting influence on the development of the Christian social movement in France, having served to bring before a wider public the concrete achievements of a model Christian employer, Léon Harmel, and the theoretical program evolved by René de La Tour du Pin in his *Conseil des Études*.

This latter group, especially active in the 1880s, was composed of sociologists and theologians working together to design a Christian social order on the basis of a return to the corporative or guild principle. Anachronistic some of their theories might be, but as Abbé Talmy has now shown us, on several essential points their thinking was more advanced than that of many pre-1914 Christian democrats. As a result of rediscovering Scholastic teachings, for example, they took up positions on the limitation on the right to private property and on the State's right to intervene in economic affairs which were not far removed from certain socialist opinions. But by no means all French Catholics interested in the working class question subscribed to such daring views. Quite the contrary, there was another school in which these views were vigorously opposed. This was the school alluded to by contemporaries sometimes as 'the school of Angers,' on account of Bishop Freppel's vocal patronage of it, and sometimes as 'the Belgian school,' on account of the intellectual lead given to it by Charles Périn,[2] brilliant teacher of political economy at the university of Louvain and author of a treatise *De la richesse dans les sociétés chrétiennes* which was translated into most European languages. Now Périn was a doughty fighter against liberalism on the political and ideological fronts, but although he was vigorous in his exposure of the exploitation of the workers by the new bourgeoisie and made no secret of his opinion that in economic matters the moral law ought to prevail, he refused to countenance any intervention by the State, expecting the resolution of social problems to come from private initiatives and the spread of the Christian spirit among employers.

These views found great favor among Belgian Catholics, for their whole defence of their religious rights rested precisely on this principle of freedom and they had no wish to encourage the Statist tendencies of their opponents.[3] In France these views were propagated by the *Revue catholique des institutions et du droit,* the journal of the association of Catholic lawyers, and a number of Catholic factory owners in the north tried to put them into practice. In 1884, on the initiative of C. Féron-Vrau, these employers formed an association. But although prolific in concrete achievement, this association was patently paternalistic in inspiration and dominated by a profound distrust of the State, reading into it all the features of the Jacobin State, notorious oppressor of the Church.

In Germany industrial development was of more recent origin. But it was German Catholics, paradoxically enough, who initiated the more realistic social movement, open to the idea of trade unionism and prepared for the limitation of economic freedom by social legislation, which was to find its first official expression in the encyclical of Leo XIII. This social dimension to German Catholicism, which was not to be fobbed off with works of pure benevolence, as happened all too easily in France, enabled the Church to maintain close links with the masses and to count on their support in the struggle with the radical bourgeoisie at the time of the *Kulturkampf*. It is true that, down to 1870, German Catholics who tried to carry out the 1848 precept of bringing 'the Church to the people and the people to the Church' concerned themselves mostly with the betterment of craft workers and the organization of the peasantry. But attention gradually came to focus equally on the working class question proper. Organizations sprang up, most of all in the industrial regions of the Rhineland which, in addition to serving the traditional primary objectives, the saving of souls and the relief of poverty, made it their business to provide workers with a solid base from which to press their claims for improved working conditions.

If the working class question appeared increasingly to German Catholics a field demanding institutional reform rather than the mere organization of relief, the change was due in large measure to the dynamic lead given by Msgr. Ketteler, Bishop of Mainz. Those who regard Ketteler as a pioneer of Christian democracy have frequently misrepresented his role. When Ketteler, the Westphalian aristocrat, protested at the sufferings inflicted on the poor by the social system of his day, the ideal he had in mind was a return to the corporative social organization of the medieval German empire. This does not detract from his importance as an influence on the social Catholicism of the nineteenth century, to which he made an especially valuable contribution through his book *Die Arbeiterfrage und das Christentum*, 1864, which was the fruit of fifteen years' reflection. Not content with proposing various concrete reforms, he endeavored to show that the solution of the working class question could be envisaged only in relation to a general concept of society which eliminated both the individualism of the liberals and the totalitarian claims of the modern centralized State. In this book Ketteler in effect advanced for the first time the theory of the corporatively based social organism which was to be the staple of Catholic social doctrine for the next half-century and more; and on more than one occasion during the last quarter of the nineteenth century it was to conflict more obviously with the individualist ideal of economic liberalism than with the socialist ideal, whatever practical suspicions and theoretical objections there might be of the latter.

This was certainly the case with the Austrian school under its leader Baron K. von Vogelsang. By birth a German aristocrat, Vogelsang was converted to Catholicism by Ketteler and in 1864 removed to Vienna, where he became editor-in-chief of the *Vaterland,* the organ of the federalist Austrian landed aristocracy and very hostile to the newly emerging great banking and industrial concerns, many of which were under Jewish control. In 1879, Vogelsang founded the periodical which was to become the celebrated *Monatschrift für christliche Sozialreform.* He used it to mount an attack, inspired by Ketteler's ideas, on the capitalist regime which had come out of the Revolution, criticizing it with such vehemence that he was later to acquire the label 'Christian socialist,' and defending the idea of State intervention as the remedy for the disorders stemming from anarchical individualism. Vogelsang converted to his views a group of young Austrian Catholics, among them the Abbé Schindler, who succeeded him as leader of the Austrian school, Karl Lueger, future burgomaster of Vienna and responsible for an ambitious program of social reform, and Prince Charles von Löwenstein, who was host on his Haid estate between 1883 and 1888 to a series of conferences from which emerged, among other things, the celebrated 'Haid Proposals.'

These proposals strike us today as hardly adequate in scale to the vastness of the change in industrial society, but at the time they came as a great novelty to anyone outside revolutionary circles and were met with strong disapproval from the bishops. They were made known to a wider public through an international review, the *Correspondance de*

Genève, which was founded and edited by von Blome, a member of Vogelsang's group and, like Vogelsang, a German convert.

The various groups of Catholics preoccupied with the working class question in Germany, Austria, France, Belgium and Italy had not remained in complete ignorance of one another. They were kept informed of each other's activities by the exchange of literature and also through occasional encounters, of a more or less casual nature. Many of these meetings took place in Rome, at the winter residence of an Austrian ally of Vogelsang's, Count von Küfstein, whose informal study circle for the investigation of social questions, had the blessing of Leo XIII although the pope had not, as is sometimes said, taken the initiative in setting it up. It soon seemed desirable to make these contacts more regular, and to this end a Catholic union of social studies was formed (the *Union catholique d'études sociales*) which from 1884, met annually at Fribourg in Switzerland under the presidency of Bishop Mermillod, its aim being to work out a version of the corporatist theory of society adapted to the needs of the modern world. The result of the deliberations was kept secret but regular reports were sent to the pope, whose interest in the subject was becoming keener. Although he had not taken up the suggestion, emanating from France in 1881, of inviting the European governments to Rome to work out an international code of labor—hardly a realistic proposition in the prevailing diplomatic climate—the idea of an encyclical on the social question had for some time been maturing in his mind.

He was finally convinced that the time had come for him to intervene officially by a number of external happenings, of which we should mention in particular: the pilgrimages to Rome organized by Léon Harmel for French workers (the first was in 1885), which had the aim of bringing the laboring masses closer to the pope and of bringing the pope into direct contact with the factory worker; the intervention in 1887-88 of Cardinal Gibbons, archbishop of Baltimore, on behalf of the Knights of Labor, America's earliest labor organization, which was threatened with condemnation by the Holy Office, some American bishops having complained that it smacked too much of a secret society and was likely to be involved with anarchism; Cardinal Manning's support for the workers in the London dock strike, the fame of which spread throughout Europe;[4] and lastly a new flare-up, in 1890, of the controversy between 'interventionist' Catholics and the Angers School, which was sparked off by a congress organized by Msgr. Doutreloux at Liège.

With so many convergent streams, it was becoming increasingly clear that the supreme authority must speak. When it did so, through the encyclical *Rerum novarum* (15 May 1891), Leo XIII was to decide the principal points at issue in favor of the Liège school, which was in the direct line of descent from the social thinking of Ketteler and the Fribourg union. In this respect, therefore, the encyclical marks the completion of an important stage in the history of social Catholicism.

The encyclical *Rerum novarum,* as we have seen, was the product of numerous initiatives which had no connection with Rome, and this demonstrates once again the importance of laymen in the down-to-earth existence of the Catholic Church. That is not to say that the encyclical was not equally the work of Leo XIII. We are reasonably well informed about how the text took shape, thanks to the publication of the various preliminary drafts.[5] We can for example trace through the three successive versions - Fr. Liberatore's initial draft, its revision by Fr. Zigliara and the definitive text, meticulously gone through by the pope—the gradual supersession of the idea of a corporative regime by that of the trade association, envisaged as composed ideally but by no means necessarily of both workers and employers, which left the door officially open to the formula of the future, the all-labor union. On the other hand, while the initial decision to reject the excessive liberalism of the Angers school in favor of State intervention in social and economic affairs survives intact, the many nuances and muted notes introduced into the later drafts are sufficient indication of the circumspection and hesitation with which the Holy See committed itself to this path. Besides, to understand some of the hesitations of Leo XIII who, while he wrote not a single line, imposed his thinking on the text at every turn and left his mark unmistakably on the whole, we must take equally into account that for all his desire to react, on the authority of the Scholastic tradition, against an individualist conception of society and property, he was very anxious to give no pledges to socialist doctrine under the totalitarian aspects it so often presented in his time.

The encyclical *Rerum novarum,* apt to be extolled in Catholic circles between the wars as 'the workers' charter,' was regarded in other quarters as fundamentally anti-socialist, if anything somewhat reactionary and in any case of little real moment in the history of the workers' struggle for emancipation. There is no denying that, as well as being somewhat tardy, the encyclical resorts to abstract argument, and makes no analysis of the actual situation created by the development of capitalism; or that it is much taken up with ethical considerations and remains vague on most of the practical problems of its day. Nor can there be any doubt that the encyclical was partly inspired by fears of seeing Catholic workers increasingly attracted to socialism. But there are more positive aspects. In the first place, there was merit in Leo XIII's disengagement from the utopian dreams of the preceding decades, in which the majority of socially minded Catholics had been led by their yearnings for the preponderantly rural society of a former age to criticize bourgeois society from a pre-capitalist standpoint and to advocate a return in some more-or-less updated version to the corporatism of the *Ancien régime,* which for large-scale industry was certainly a blind alley. Leo XIII had the realism to place himself on ground closer to that of reformist socialism and to seek improvement for the working class within the framework of existing institutions, among them the workers' union, the legitimacy of which was recognized, even if with some reluctance. Next, it was not to be dismissed lightly that the highest spiritual authority had made solemn proclamation of the rights of workers and the injustices of the liberal system taken as a whole. While there is no denying that the workers' movement was under way well before *Rerum novarum* or that the credit for launching it belongs in essence to the socialists, this was the first time it had received a stamp of approval from any of the great forces of order in the world. This was a great advance in helping to remove the revolutionary connotation the movement had held so far in the eyes of the great majority of the bourgeoisie. From the psychological point of view this was certainly not negligible. As for Catholics, while they would continue to many years to feel misgivings, they had to admit that some change was indeed called for; and if there were many who still clung to some form of corporatism as a solution, the more forward-looking were already committing themselves to the path of Christian democracy.

But the path of Christian democracy did not prove easy, and that for two reasons. First, many who accepted that, from now on, institutional changes were necessary in order to improve the lot of the workers were nevertheless determined that changes should be made in conformity with the old maxim 'for the people but not by the people,' or at least under the strict supervision of clerical authorities. Such in particular was the view of Pius X. Certainly he wanted to see an improvement in people's living conditions—he had given proof of his concern by establishing a chair of economic and social science in his seminary—and many of his pronouncements testified to his heartfelt wish that Christian charity should lose nothing of its social dimension. But he all along envisaged social action in the strictly paternalistic and clerical perspective he shared with his Venetian contemporaries. Second, it was not entirely clear what was actually meant by Christian democracy. The expression had originated in Belgium and then won gradual acceptance elsewhere. But if its purpose was to distinguish 'Christian' democracy from the 'false' democracy of the radicals and individualists, opinions differed as to the exact bearing of the Christian reference. Were Christian democrats to form themselves into a confessional party with the ultimate aim of re-establishing a Christian State on popular foundations, or was it enough simply to accept from Christian motives part of the liberal heritage, namely the secular State as the means whereby believers and unbelievers could work together to obtain greater social justice? Here again Pius X left no doubt as to his views: there could be no abandonment of the ideal of a return to an integrally Catholic social order, which had been the goal of papal policy since the French Revolution. In these circumstances it is not surprising that many Christian democrat leaders regarded the pontificate of Pius X as their sojourn in the wilderness. But the historian should also take note of a point made by Fr. Jarlot:

> If after the First World War Catholic labor organizations, both agricultural and industrial, had reached the point of forming national and international federations, it was because the ground was prepared, in Germany, Holland, Belgium, France, Spain, Italy and

other countries, under the pontificate of Pius X. The seed sown by
Leo XIII sprouted under Pius X and under Pius XI was to come
to full flower.

It is not possible to follow here the ups and downs of the movement
in the different countries, where its characteristics varied greatly according to the local circumstances. In some countries it had the open
support of the hierarchy, as in Australia, where Cardinal Moran was
quite unabashed in declaring his sympathy with "Christian socialism,"[6] in others the incentive came from enterprising priests working
in populous parishes, for example Alfons Ariëns in the Netherlands,
who was inspired by German example to found, in 1889, the first
Catholic association intended exclusively for the workers and two
years later the first Catholic trade union for factory employees.[7] In
other countries, by contrast, the movement had to contend with the
distrust of a clergy whose sensitivity to social problems had been
blunted by too close an involvement with the ruling class, as for example in Spain;[8] or it ran into opposition from neo-corporatists, as
in Austria, where L. Kunschak, who in 1892, bravely set up the first
Christian trade unions, had great difficulty in bringing the grievances
of the working class movement to the notice of the *Christlich-soziale
Volkspartei*, which was geared to the interests of the petty bourgeoisie.
All that can be attempted in any detail here is to sketch the situation
in four countries where the internal controversies had repercussions
well beyond the national boundaries.

First Belgium, where the paternalists had been very much in com-
mand and were to remain in control of most of the charity-oriented
organizations down to 1914. The creation in February 1891, a few
months before the issue of *Rerum novarum,* of the *Ligue démocratique
belge*, marked an important turning-point and the change of emphasis
became still more noticeable when A. Verhagen took over the presidency
from J. Helleputte in 1895 and succeeded in breaking away from the
corporatist perspectives of his predecessor. Operating as a pressure
group, the *Ligue* enabled Christian democracy to make its voice heard
in parliament and to secure, in face of furious opposition, the voting
of several important reforms for the benefit of labor. Although its
direction remained in all essentials the monopoly of the non-working

class, the *Ligue* came out as early as 1892 in favor of the trade-union formula which excluded employers and from 1901, after a slow start, this type of union gradually won acceptance, thanks in particular to the sterling work and qualities of Fr. Rutten, O.P. By contrast, the Abbé Daens's attempt at a truly democratic Flemish 'Christian Labor party' (founded 1893) was wrecked after a few years by the intrigues of Charles Woeste's conservative group and by the disquiet venture aroused in the bishops, who were very anxious to keep the Catholic party united in face of anti-clericalist attacks.[9] A similar fate overtook the Abbé Pottier, between 1886 and 1895 one of the leading representatives of Liège Christian democracy, who was obliged to stay more and more in the background until in the end, after the death of Msgr. Doutreloux, he was forced by conservative pressure to leave the country. But the conservatives were soon to change their tune. Pius X surprised them by recognizing the autonomy of the *Ligue démocratique belge* within its own sphere, on condition it did nothing to jeopardise the unity of the ruling Catholic party, and he stated explicitly that the severe admonitions addressed to Murri's Christian democrat group did not apply to them. "In Belgium," he pointed out, "you have good democrats; you Belgian Catholics, whether conservative or democrat, are all in harmony with your bishops."[10] As to the bishops, while some continued very guarded in their attitude towards the Christian democrats, this was not the case with the new archbishop of Malines, Cardinal Mercier, who was roundly to assert: "When socialism strives for a more just distribution of public wealth, socialism is right."[11] Mercier showed open support for the Christian democrats on more than one occasion, and it was partly thanks to him that the Fifth Catholic Congress of Malines, held in 1909 despite the tenacious opposition of Woeste, was a triumph for their group. In 1907, moreover, two of their number had become members of the government, which helped to speed up the voting of several measures for the benefit of labor. In short, on the eve of the First World War, Belgian Christian democracy already contained in essence the ingredients that would characterize it for the next half-century. It had become a vital factor in the Catholic party, and through the trade-unions, the mutual insurance societies, the co-operatives and the various other kinds of association it was acquiring an increasingly important place in the working, economic, cultural and religious life of the country.

In Germany as in Belgium, the start of Leo XIII's pontificate found the socially-minded Catholics divided into two opposing schools. The first, whose most prominent representative was Baron von Hertling, saw a serious danger in the ever-growing power of the State. But the other, the adherents of which tended to be chiefly of the younger generation, was not dismayed at the prospect of some degree of State Socialism and looked in the works of Fr. Hitze (1851-1921) its leader, to "a wide-ranging and thorough-going legislative program, implemented by the strong arm of the State" as "the sole means of achieving the re-ordering of society."[12] Nevertheless, as in Belgium, there was great concern not to jeopardise the political unity of the Catholics, especially while the consequences of the *Kulturkampf* were still making themselves felt, and it is significant that Windthorst, whose views were in sympathy with Hertling's, figured along with Hitze as one of the founders in 1890 of the *Volksverein*. It was a disciple of Hitze's, A. Pieper, who for the next quarter of a century directed the *Volksverein* from its headquarters at München-Gladbach. Although the *Volksverein* had sections for middle class and agricultural workers, its main effort was concentrated on the urban working class. Here it was useful in injecting new life into some of the older clubs and associations which, after a period of great activity in the 1850s and 1860s, had tended during the Bismarck era to fall into abeyance. But its chief contribution was in encouraging the formation of trade unions. And the question of trade-unions lay at the heart of an increasingly bitter controversy which rocked the German Catholic world in the last decade before 1914.

After a shaky beginning in 1890, 'Christian' trade unions (that is unions comprising Catholic and Protestant workers) had begun to be developed in the Rhineland and Westphalia, with the encouragement of most Catholic politicians in the west of the country. In 1900 a federation had been formed, the *Gesamtband christlichen Gewerkschaften Deutschlands*, which in 1909, acquired in Adam Stegerwald an extremely energetic secretary general. Cardinal Fischer, Archbishop of Cologne, welcomed the trend and on several occasions defended it to the Holy See. But a section of the clergy and bishops, with Msgr.

Kopp, Archbishop of Breslau, and Msgr. Korum, Bishop of Trier, at
their head, was opposed on principle to the formula of interconfessional unions, especially since the latter showed themselves disposed
to collaborate quite closely with the socialists. They favored instead
the setting up of unions for specific trades within the framework of
existing Catholic organizations and they tried, it may be said without
much success, to implant in the west and south of the country branches
of a Catholic working people's organization, the *Verband Katholischer
Arbeitervereins Nord und Ostdeutschlands*, which had been set up in
1897 with its headquarters in Berlin. The conflict between the two
schools, 'of Cologne' and 'of Berlin,' broke out in 1904 into a headed
pamphlet warfare and gave rise to a number of unpleasant incidents.
But in addition to highlighting the interconfessional issue, the conflict
presented Catholics with some fundamental choices: the possibility
of returning to the corporative type of economic and social regime
or the necessity of being content to mitigate the capitalist system by
social reform; the legitimacy of strikes as a weapon in the struggle to
improve the condition of the working classes; and most fundamental
of all, the question how to judge whether Catholic labor organizations
were to be placed under the control of the Church or indeed whether,
laymen being responsible for their secular activities, the clergy were to
restrict themselves to giving advice on the moral aspects. The conflict
reached its climax at the end of Pius X's pontificate, exacerbated by
the integrist counter-offensive.

In France, socially concerned Catholics of the paternalist type by
no means disappeared from the scene following the publication of
Rerum novarum. With increasing assistance from the clergy, whose
part had hitherto been small, the paternalists continued to display
their devotion and ingenuity in the creation of a great range of clubs
and associations. These were designed principally for peasants and
skilled workers, but the ordinary factory worker was not completely
overlooked and at the same time efforts continued, though with no
real success, to set up industrial unions of the mixed type (comprising
workers and employers). The employers banded together as the *Patrons
du Nord* stuck doggedly to their positions. They used all their resources
to oppose the formation of Christian unions composed exclusively of
workers and they came out strongly against Léon Harmel, who was

trying to promote the interventionist view defended by the Liège school and approved by the encyclical. In 1895 they agreed to bow to the decision of Leo XIII but their deep-seated opposition continued. The solemn audience Pius X granted to the *Patrons du Nord* in 1904 was to appear to contemporaries, with good reason, as a vindication, from which they profited all the more when the abolition of the State's subsidies to the Church in the following year substantially increased the influence of such generous benefactors with the clergy. But it did nothing to improve their impact on the workers. As one of the leaders of the *Patrons du Nord* remarked in 1913, "for the past twenty years we have simply been marking time."

But noticeably gathering strength after 1891, was another stream which M. Montuclard in deference to the abortive effort of 1848, calls the 'second wave' of Christian democracy in France. This movement, incidentally much more complex than appears from Montuclard's thought-provoking but over-schematic sociologist's account, arose out of various largely uncoordinated initiatives whose convergence, achieved in face of the considerable doctrinal confusion prevailing at the outset, was an event of some significance. It was characterized by its acceptance at one and the same time of liberal values, which the pioneers of social Catholicism had spurned, and of the goal of a socially orientated Christian democracy, to which liberal Catholics remained antipathetic. Owing its initial impetus to Léon Harmel's propaganda inside the *Œuvre des Cercles*, from which it was soon to cut loose, the movement took firmer shape as the more clearsighted came to recognize the impotence of organizations of the traditional type and the need to adept the formula of the workers' union. But fired by Belgian example it soon transformed itself into a party committed to political action and in particular to *ralliement* to the Republic. Apart from a sprinkling of militant working-class Catholics and of some enthusiastic laymen with a *petitbourgeois* background, the main movers were the visionary young priests[13] known as the *abbés démocrates:* Gayraud, Six, Dabry, Naudet and boldest and most eloquent of all Lemire, the figure soon most closely identified with the movement. It occupied the front of the stage for some years, above all in northern and north-eastern France and later also in the Lyons region,[14] receiving open encouragement from the pope and basking briefly in episcopal favor. But from 1898 it was to fall into a rapid decline, so much so that after 1900 only a few isolated survivors remained. The miscarriage of the movement is not to be explained solely by circumstances such as the conservatives' opposition to a program of social reform which today appears very modest, or the failure of the policy of *ralliement,* or the lack of leaders capable of persuading a number of headstrong individuals to work together, or even the competition of Marc Sangnier's supremely energetic *Sillon*,[15] the first movement of its kind in France to possess the popular touch. What has also to be borne in mind is that the *abbés démocrates* were very soon seen to be raising a series of important questions, some of them even more fundamental than those at the base of the German controversy over trade unionism: the place of the Christian in a secularised society,[16] recognition of the Christian values implicit in secular activity, even the question of 'democratising' the government of the Church. For to demands for a new social and political order—the exact opposite of the hierarchical ideal (but which nevertheless continued to harp on peasant virtues and other equally traditionalist themes)—were added aspirations towards a general religious renewal, covering morals, the spiritual life, the pastoral ministry and ecclesiology,[17] which many of the bishops, for whom Msgr. Isoard and Msgr. Turinaz acted as spokesmen, found disturbing. The indiscretion of young priests and seminarists in appearing to confuse love of the poor with contempt for the upper classes and in whom the priest seemed too often obscured by the social and political activist, and on top of that the savage attacks of the integrist press, which identified Christian democracy indiscriminately with modernism, in the end made the position of the *abbés démocrates* untenable and a number of them eventually incurred the Church's censure, Naudet and Dabry in 1908, Lemire in 1914.

Between the two extremes, those determined not to abandon paternalism or the corporative ideal, and those determined to reconcile French Catholicism, in spite of itself, to democracy pushed to its ultimate conclusions, there developed slowly and with difficulty, but nevertheless steadily, a centrist stream which followed the cautious line laid down in *Rerum novarum.* To it belonged the parliamentary Catholics of Albert de Mun's group, who were instrumental in working out some of the earliest proposals for social legislation, and likewise the moving spirits in the A.C.J.F. This movement was originally counter-revolutionary in its ethos but, under the presidency of Henri Bazire, had become increasingly involved in social questions, encouraging its members to collaborate in setting up not only workers' reading-rooms, agricultural insurance agencies and workers' savings banks but also trade unions proper (the theme of the A.C.J.F. conference in 1903) and aid for strikers, not hesitating to entertain the idea of co-operation with socialist reformers. Also connected with this moderately progressive stream were newer bodies, founded in the early years of the 20th century: the *Union d'études des catholiques sociaux* (1901), in the description of H. Rollet a kind of 'legislation workshop'; the *Semaines sociales* (1904), a kind of itinerant university which visited a different town each year and offered its 'students'—a fairly mixed bunch—a wealth of fresh insights into the great social questions of the day (omitting, however, to deal with the strictly economic aspects). It was due to the tact of the organizers, two prominent bourgeois from Paris, Henri Lorin and Adéodat Boissard, and a modest clerk from Lyons, Marius Gonin, that despite sundry alarms the *Semaines sociales* never fell foul of the ecclesiastical authorities, although its enemies were almost the same as those of the *Sillon*.[18] Mention must equally be made of the Jesuits' *Action populaire*, founded in 1903 by Fr. H. Leroy and directed from 1905 by Fr. G. Desbuquois, the purpose of which was to 'help others to act,' by bringing interested people together and providing them with sound and stimulating advice in the form of lectures, literature and counseling, and by spreading knowledge of all 'genuinely Catholic undertakings,' that is undertakings which conformed to the general directives contained in papal documents (no protection, as it turned out, against suspicions and denunciations on the part of the integrists); and of the *Secrétariats sociaux*, also concerned to disseminate views and stimulate action, founded by Gonin in the late nineteenth century but initially confined to the Lyon region, only spreading to France as a whole when the A.C.J.F. started to take a hand in 1910. Finally, although the results were much more modest than in Belgium or Germany, we should note at the level of organized labor the appearance of the first Christian trade unions. The movement goes back to the foundation in Paris in 1887, on the initiative of the Brothers of the Christian Schools, of a clerical workers' union, the *Syndicat des employés du commerce et de l'industrie,* which became the driving force; having called together the first inter-union Christian congress in 1904, this union took the lead in 1912 in forming the *Fédération française des syndicats d'employés,* but it did not succeed in taking root in major industry.

The record, in short, shows a number of interesting initiatives, a ripening of Catholic social doctrine (subjected in some of its most delicate areas to bold speculation, when perhaps what was needed was more systematic exploration), a gradual breakthrough, effected in conditions much less favorable than under Leo XIII, but all of it the work of a group which, down to 1914, was to remain very limited in numbers and almost entirely devoid of episcopal support, a picture in contrast with the one found in neighbouring countries.

In Italy, for example the social question had become a major preoccupation of the highly authoritative *Opera dei Congressi,*[19] the intransigence of which was in no way identified with the social conservatism of the liberal bourgeoisie. On the contrary, liberalism, the ideology of the bourgeois society engendered by the Revolution, was regarded in *Opera* circles as the root of all the social evils, the emergence of socialism included. The second and by far the most active section of the *Opera,* which in 1887 had changed its name from the original title 'Charity and Catholic Economy' to 'Christian Social Economy,' could count on the co-operation of a substantial number of the clergy, who tended to be closer to the people than their counterparts in France, and on backing from a section of the Catholic press, with in the van Don Albertario's *Osservatore cattolico,* the paper largely responsible for awakening Catholic opinion in Italy to the social problem, a problem which in a country still so little industrialized revolved chiefly round the condition of the peasantry. The Italian Catholic social movement was also fortunate in having at hand one or two experienced practitioners, for example Don Luigi Cerutti, who between 1893 and 1898 covered first the Veneto and then the whole of northern Italy with a network of agricultural credit banks (there were 893 in 1898) and N. Rezzara, who turned the province of Bergamo into an exceptionally lively center of Christian social action. It is true that most of the leading men in the *Opera dei Congressi* long remained paternalistic in their outlook and that control of the organizations intended for peasants and workers (the network was now spreading from the north into other regions, notably into Sicily) remained almost invariably in the hands of clergy or lay notables. But during the 1890's, things started to change.

In December 1889, Toniolo had helped to found at Padua the *Unione cattolica per gli studi sociali* and had provided it, in 1893, with a serious journal, the *Rivista internationale di scienze sociali*, to disseminate its views. The Union made its presence felt in various ways, by setting up study circles specializing in social questions, soon to be found in most of the principal cities of Italy, by founding chairs of social economy in a number of seminaries, by organizing two social congresses, one at Genoa in 1892 and the other at Padua in 1896, and by drawing up, in 1894, the 'Programme of Milan,' which was an endeavour to translate into practical terms—with an undeniable boldness considering the period—the principles enunciated in *Rerum novarum*.[20] However, the official title of the program was symptomatic of the defensive mentality which prompted this burst of social activity: 'Catholic program to counteract socialism.' Moreover, in his pursuit of a chimerical vision of uniting all Catholics round a 'democratic' program directed in the best neo-Guelf tradition by the pope, a program which, to avoid argument, had to remain vague and abstract, Toniolo was bound to finish up by emptying Christian democracy of its content.[21] But younger Catholics, fired by foreign example, were reacting in increasing numbers against this attitude, which they saw as hindering the natural ripening of the movement into a force for change and popular emancipation, acting in the parliamentary sphere along the lines pioneered by French and Belgian Christian democrats. But a development of this nature was not acceptable to the Holy See, which was convinced that the ruling on political absention must be maintained so long as the Roman question remained unsettled; and the leaders of the *Opera dei Congressi*, whose conservatism had become even more pronounced after the events in Milan in 1898, when the government had suppressed socialism and the Catholic movement at one fell swoop, were twice as anxious as the Holy See to discourage the new tendencies.

The views in question had been nurtured by an avid study of *Rerum novarum*, which in Italy had impressed most deeply by its anti-liberal perspectives. Around 1900 they were in evidence from north to south of the peninsula, but in forms that varied greatly with the local circumstances. Some people, opposed to economic and social liberalism though they might be, remained strongly under the influence of the traditionalist inheritance which had fed the ideology of the intransigents. They therefore exalted the virtues of the land and of local autonomy, continued to expand the network of Catholic friendly societies, rural co-operatives and farmers' credit banks and in some cases still clung to the corporatist ideal. Others, stimulated by the presence of active socialist cells, set about organizing unions exclusively for the workers and came forward with demands for labor legislation, a ministry of labor and a system of social insurance. The former, especially when they were northerners, believed with Filippo Meda[22] that it was preferable, in order to have a chance to implement their social program, to place themselves on constitutional ground; and they did not refuse, when the time came, to collaborate with the conservative democracy of Giolitti. The latter, much more radically inclined, refused to have any dealings with the bourgeois State, although they were just as conscious as the rest of the need to campaign in the political arena. This was the case with Don Sturzo, in Sicily, and still more with Romolo Murri (1870-1944), a priest born in the Marches who attracted a great following among students and seminarists. It was above all round Murri and his review *Cultura sociale*, founded 1898, that the opposition of progressive young Christian democrats inside the *Opera dei Congressi* polarised for a few years, gathering to itself support from a growing number of the younger clergy. This last development was displeasing to the majority of bishops, who were hostile to the movement not only on political and social grounds, but precisely because they feared to see their authority undermined by a transposition of democratic principles to the internal government of the Church.

Leo XIII, who was both conscious of the need for a wider viewpoint than that of the conservatives and very anxious to keep Catholic forces united, sought with his encyclical *Graves de communi* (18 January 1901) to direct the exuberance of the Christian democrats into safer channels.[23] While recognizing the legitimacy of the expression 'Christian democracy'; which from certain Catholic quarters, notably the *Civiltà cattolica*, was under heavy attack, the pope, adopting the socio-ethical standpoint of Toniolo, defined the term in a very restrictive sense:

"In present circumstances it must be employed only in a completely non-political sense and taken as implying no more than Christian action for the people's good." While this was a far cry from the *Abbés democrates* slogan 'for the people and by the people,' at least it did not close the door to further activity of a moderately reforming type.[24]

Although the prevailing climate of their formative years had left Italian Christian democrats with nostalgic yearnings for a single confessional movement, uniting all Catholics, and with a greater submissiveness to clerical direction in temporal matters than was common among their foreign counterparts, the more progressive among them refused to be subdued by this application of the brake, which some took to be back-pedalling. And the young guard were still not satisfied when in October 1902, Leo XIII met some of their objections by making a change in the leadership of the *Opera dei Congressi*, which gave it a less conservative and elderly tone. Even within the group favoring social reform there was a widening split between the moderates who supported Meda's line and the extremists who had rallied to Murri's banner. The change of pontificate increased the tension, for Pius X was even more hostile than his predecessor to Murri's aspirations to freedom from the hierarchy's control in social and political affairs, even though—perhaps chiefly because—Murri was anxious to see the clergy undertaking to direct Catholics in these secular domains; for his program remained faithful to its origins in retaining some markedly clerical features. The open rupture came in November 1905, when Murri and his allies, incensed by the obvious drawing together of the official Catholic movement and the moderate liberals, broke away to form their own *Lega democratica nazionale*. But the latter, repudiated by the Vatican and cold-shouldered by the socialists, failed to make an impact; and by the time Murri was excommunicated in the context of the anti-modernist reaction in 1909, he had long since been deserted by most of those who had helped him launch the movement.

The majority of socially concerned Catholics took refuge in the *Unione economico-sociale*, which replaced the second or social and economic section of the *Opera dei Congressi* when the latter was dissolved by Pius X. But the atmosphere was not particularly encouraging and, aside from one or two interesting projects, for example the foundation at Bergamo in 1910 of a school for training Catholic social workers,[25] there was little to show in the way of positive achievement. Hence the launching before long of a new challenge from the left, as when Miglioli and Don Cecconcelli protested at the meeting of the congress in Modena in 1910 against the continuing suspicion in which unions composed exclusively of workers were held by those in authority.

This matter of trade unions was about to rear its head again over the next few years, and in a context much wider than that of Italy. The enemies of Christian democracy were spurred on by the encyclical *Pascendi* to denounce it as one of the heads of the modernist hydra, 'social modernism' and 'political modernism' appearing in their eyes a consequence of modernism in religion. The proponents of 'integral Catholicism' claimed that the social question was above all else "a moral and hence a religious question, which only Catholic teaching strictly in accordance with Rome will resolve."[26] From 1909, they became increasingly savage in their attacks on socially committed Catholics who, for the sake of greater effectiveness, departed from the model hitherto accepted in Christian civilized countries and organized the defense of the working classes on a neutral 'trades' basis, thus permitting collaboration with non-Catholics, or who, while keeping the confessional label, defined trade unions in terms of their economic and social function, without placing in the forefront their moral and religious goal. The conflict broke out in different parts of Western Europe at much the same time: in Italy, as we have just seen; in France, where the attack concentrated on the *Action populaire* of the Jesuits;[27] in Belgium, where the inquisitors of the *Sapiniere* more than once took Fr. Rutten to task;[28] in Holland, where Fr. Poels, brilliantly successful organizer of the workers' movement in Limburg, was denounced by the integrists of the 'Leyden school.'[29] But the epicenter of the storm lay in Germany.

We have already seen how at the beginning of the twentieth century an ideological cleavage set the 'Berlin' school, loyal to the old tradition of associations exclusively for Catholic workers, at loggerheads with the rapidly expanding 'Cologne' school (with a membership in 1914 of close on one-and-a-half million, against the ten thousand odd of the Berlin school), which worked on the formula of inter-confessionalism and de-clericalization. Pius X, whose sympathies were clearly with the former but who had to take into account the strength of the latter, and the fact that it had support from the great majority of the episcopate, tried to halt the increasingly bitter controversy by publishing in September 1912 an encyclical on trade unions[30] in which he approved without reserve the Berlin formula, but accepted that others might be tolerated in order to avoid a greater evil. Far from relieving tension, the Pope's intervention only made for greater confusion and the controversy was resumed with redoubled vigour, not merely in Germany where both sides claimed the victory, but equally in France, with a resumption of integrist attacks on Christian democracy,[31] and a little later in Rome, where in February 1914 the *Civiltà cattolica* published what was clearly an inspired article which seemed to be testing the ground for the issue of a new and sterner papal document, intended to warn the Christian trade-union movement against a trend carrying it further and further from the social ideology, which so far as Pius X was concerned (though certain historical apologists have since tried to deny it) was the only one truly in keeping with Catholic orthodoxy. People who understood that on this point the Pope was prisoner of an outdated 'model' (in the sociological sense) and who were anxious for no further delay in the Church's adaptation to the changes in modern society, were at pains to avert the impending blow. Their task was made easier by the fact that an international federation of Christian trade unions had come into existence a few years earlier.[32] Discreet intervention on the part of Cardinals Maffi and Mercier, the general of the Jesuits (who was a German), Toniolo, Harmel, and others, persuaded the Pope to stay his hand. In this 'last great battle of the pontificate' (Poulat), the Christian democrats had at length scored a success over their integrist opponents.

Notes

[1] On Frédéric Le Play (1806-82), social economist and founder of the *Société internationale des Hautes Études d'Économie Sociale*, see J. B. Duroselle, *Les Débuts du catholicisme social en France*, pp. 672-84 and D. Herbertson, *Fréderic Le Play*, Ledbury, 1952.

[2] See the article on him by A. Louant, *Biographie nationale* (of Belgium), XXX, cols. 665-71.

[3] On this paternalist form of Belgian social Catholicism see R. Rezsohazy, *Origines et formation du catholicisme social en Belgique*, ch. 3. On the highly conservative attitude of the Belgian bishops, who even in the industrial dioceses were to be very slow to grasp the true dimensions of the working class question, regarding it for too long merely as identical with the problem of recovering lost ground, see

the two chapters by Msgr. A. Simon in *150 Jaar Katholieke Arbeidersbeweging in Belgie* (Brussels 1963-5), I, 111-42, and II, pp. 187-226.

[4] See E. S. Purcell, *Life of Cardinal Manning* (London 1896), II, 638-71. Manning's contribution in the social field is brought out by V. A. McClelland, *Cardinal Manning, his public life and influence, 1865-1892,* London, 1962.

[5] G. Antonazzi, *L'enciclica Rerum novarum, testo autentico e redazioni preparatorie dai documenti originali,* Rome, 1957.

[6] Cf. P. Ford, *Cardinal Moran and the A.L.P. A Study in the Encounter between Moran and Socialism, 1890-1907,* Melbourne-London 1966. In England by contrast, Manning's successors, Cardinal Vaughan and more particularly Cardinal Bourne, were very reserved in their attitude towards the working class movement and so far as the majority of Catholics was concerned, the social encyclicals long remained a dead letter, despite the tentative efforts of V. McNabb, O.P. and C. Platen, S.J., founders in 1909 of the Catholic Social Guild on the model of the Fabian Society.

[7] On the great work done by Ariëns from his parish base at Enschede in Twente see G. Brom, *A. Ariëns,* 2 vols, Amsterdam 1941. Although the Dutch episcopate long continued to be paternalistic in its attitude, Ariens had support from the archbishop of Utrecht. In the succeeding decade the Catholic working-class movement, having started in the north, spread gradually south. Mention should also be made of J. F. Vlekke, one of the few factory employers of the period to progress beyond a paternalistic relationship between management and workers (cf. F. Van der Ven, *J. F. Vlekke, 1849-1903, ein pionier der socials ondernemingspolitiek* in *Noord-Brabant,* Tilburg, 1947).

[8] Some efforts were made, especially in the rural sector (where syndicates set up by priests with a view to organising agricultural credit came together in 1912, to form the *Confederació national catolico-agraria*) but also in the factory sector. In 1880 one pioneer, the Valencian A. Vicent, S.J. (1837-1912), started to set up workers' circles but the *Consejo national de las corporaciones catolicas de obreros* escaped his influence and developed in a conservative direction. A few of his disciples tried without much success to promote Christian trade unionism proper: Professor S. Aznar, founder in 1910 of the review *Renovación social,* two Dominicans, Gerard and Gafo, above all G. Palau, S.J., founder of *Ación social popular* at Barcelona, were eventually obliged to emigrate to the Argentine.

[9] In 1898-99, Daens severed his connections with the bishopric of Ghent and drew closer to the socialists. He was to be condemned by Pius X in 1905. On this whole affair, in itself of minor importance but highly sympomatic, see H. J. Elias, *Priester Daens en de Christene Volkspartij,* Aalst 1940; K. Van Isacker, *Het Daensisme,* Antwerp 1959; L. Wils, *Het Daensisme,* Louvain 1969.

[10] Letter from Baron d'Erp, quoted in *Rivista di storia della Chiesa in Italia,* XII (1958), 240, n. 70.

[11] Speech of 5 July 1909, printed in his *Œuvres pastorales,* XI (Brussels 1912), pp. 324-25.

[12] F. Hitze, *Kapital und Arbeit* (Paderborn 1881), p. 120.

[13] Worth noting is the comment of R. Cornilleau, *De Waldeck-Rousseau à Poincaré,* Paris 1926, p. 43: "What the Christian democrats lacked was a Jaures, that is a lay leader to act as the brains and voice of the party. Their movement looked altogether too churchy, not to say clerical."

[14] See for example J.-M. Mayeur, *Les Congrès nationaux de la "Démocratie chrétienne" à Lyon (1896, 1897, 1898)*, in *Revue d'histoire moderne et contemporaine*, IX (1962), pp. 171-206.

[15] On the origins of the Sillon, see ch. 3, pp. 48-51, and for further details the first two sections of the thesis by J. Caron *Le Sillon et la Démocratie chrétienne, 1894-1910*, Paris, 1967.

[16] On this point, however, the Christian democrats were themselves divided. Only a minority resigned themselves to accepting the society born from the Revolution in which the Christian has to be content with acting as a leavening agent through participation in nonconfessional institutions. Many dreamed by contrast of a new Christendom, popular but also clerical in character, fruit of an alliance between the Church and the people on the model of medieval society as depicted by the Romantic historians but departing from the model in comprising a network of Christian institutions contained within a democratic framework and based on universal suffrage (or on a variant of it: the family vote, as tried out in Belgium, representation by trades, as suggested in La Tour de Pin's program).

[17] Montuclard even claims to detect "beneath identical professions of orthodoxy and loyalty profound divergences which set Christian democrat thinking in total opposition to that of Catholics at the end of the nineteenth century" (*Une crise de la pensée catholique à la fin du XIXᵉ siècle*, in *Annales de la Faculté des lettres d'Aix*, XLIV (1968), pp. 33-65).

[18] The idea was to be imitated in Spain as early as 1906, in Italy from 1907. There were also 'social weeks' in Germany, but these were of a different type, being limited to a small number of specialists.

[19] On this see *The Church in a Secularized Society*, Paulist Press, 1978, chapter 7, pp. 139-41.

[20] The program called not only for the revival of trade associations and the abolition of usury but also for agricultural workers to have a share in the improvement of large estates, and factory workers in the profits and even in the capital. It was not easily accepted by the *Opera dei Congressi*.

[21] See for example the Christian democrat reaction to Toniolo's famous lecture of 1897 (cf. F. Fonzi, *L'epistolario di G. Toniolo*, in *Quaderni di cultura e storia sociale*, III (1954), pp. 22-32).

[22] For the career of this Milanese layman (1869-1939) who, having left militant *intransigentismo* along with Fr. Albertario, became the first Italian Catholic to enter the government, see G. De Rosa, *F. Meda e l'età liberale*, Florence, 1959.

[23] *A.S.S.*, XXI (1901), pp. 3-20.

[24] As regards the last point, it is instructive to compare the first draft by Cardinal Cavagnis with the final text, the tone of which is noticeably less conservative, although it still stresses the difference between the Christian social program and a socialist program (cf. G. Martina, in *Rivista di storia della Chiesa in Italia*, XVI (1962), pp. 492-507).

[25] Founded by Count Medolago Albani with the aim of giving doctrinal training to militants and chaplains engaged in Catholic Action. Cf. B. Malinverni, *La Scuola sociale cattolica di Bergamo*, Rome, 1960.

[26] Foreword to the first issue (7 December 1912) of the *Correspondance catholique* of Ghent, organ of the *Sodalitium Pianum* (*Sapinière*) in Belgium.

[27] Many details, often from unpublished material, are given by P. Droulers, *Politique sociale et christianisme. Le P. Desbuquois et l'Action populaire. Syndicalisme et intégristes (1903-1918)*, Paris, 1969.

[28] See among others É. Poulat, *Integrisme et Catholicisme intégral* (Paris, 1969), pp. 284-7.

[29] See Colsen, *Poels* (Roermond, 1955), pp. 514-37.

[30] *Singulars quadam, A.A.S.*, IV (1912), pp. 657-62.

[31] A public letter addressed by Cardinal Merry del Val to Albert de Mun, 7 January 1913 (see R. Talmy, *Le Syndicalisme chrétien*, pp. 122-4), constituted an initial victory for the integrists, but the succeeding months brought some relaxation in the tension.

[32] The way having been prepared in the late nineteenth century by the drawing together of the Dutch and Belgian federations and later of the German textile federation, the International Federation of Christian Trade Unions had been set up at Zurich in 1908. There was also regular contact between the leading newspapers with Christian democrat leanings.

Development of the Social Teaching of the Church in Europe from Leo XIII to Pius XI
1984

It is quite a challenge to cover such a vast topic in half an hour—40 years in many countries, the impact inside the Church, on secular society, and on the other Christian Churches—but, at the risk of being superficial, it is not without its usefulness to broach this subject parallel to the exposés on the teaching of the present *Magisterium* in social matters.

The subject is particularly complex.[1] In the first place, there is geographic pluralism, which is explained both by the different national traditions in the domains of ideas and social organization, and by the very different social conditions, depending on whether one is dealing with societies of an industrial type, as in Western Europe, or with essentially rural societies, as in Central Europe and in certain Mediterranean regions (these last also posing problems of social justice, although of a sort different from those which belong to the factory proletariat).

In the second place, one must take into account the changes which have occurred during the forty years being considered; changes inevitable not only due to the direction taken by each pontificate—what differences there are between the perspectives of Leo XIII, of Pius X, or of Pius XI—but for other reasons as well. First, the intrinsic discoveries within the Catholic Social Movement. In effect, the more one delves into the exigencies of Christian social justice in the light of Holy Scripture and of social philosophy, the more one discovers the complexity of the problem, or rather problems. Fr. Cottier spoke concerning Paul VI's teaching, about "new reflections arising from new questions." One could multiply the examples for the period 1891-1931. I will only site three: the question of the familial salary, which was not even broached in *Rerum novarum*; the question of "the autonomy of the temporal," a claim considered before 1914 as part of "social modernism"[2] and which little by little cleared a path for itself between the wars to become, since Vatican II, a banality; the evolution of ideas in Catholic milieus concerning the right of private property (from the defense of private property against a communist-style socialism, to a gradual recognition of the necessity to increase collective ownership in reaction against the excesses of unregulated capitalism). However, it is not only the ideas of Catholic sociologists that have evolved; it is the economic and social reality itself that has profoundly changed in forty years, which has obliged the nuancing and sometimes the modification of initially-taken positions (because, unless dealing with pure abstractions having no real impact, one always takes a position relative to something and, most often, against something). The capitalism in small and mid-sized enterprises of the second half of the 19th century, in which the management generally had the possibility of maintaining "human" relations with the workers, has evolved during the first half of the 20th century toward what Pius XI called "hypercapitalism"—a capitalism centered on a few oligopolies and multinational corporations, and in which relations between the executives at the top and the tens of thousands of salaried employees dispersed across several continents become impossible, and in which financial games increasingly take priority in the decision-making of executive boards.[3] Socialism, for its part, likewise evolved a great deal between the foundation of the First International and the end of the 20th century. From its revolutionary beginnings, of which the Paris Commune of 1870-71 was the symbol for Leo XIII's contemporaries, it gradually changed into "social-democratic" reformism, denounced with disgust by the communists, and then even became, more and more, a workers' humanism, separated from all anti-religious ideology, which explains why an increasing number of Christians look sympathetically on the idea of reconciliation and even collaboration.

Faced with such a complex and varied subject—and one in addition rather poorly explored in a number of areas, especially the period between the wars—it will be necessary to stick to a few general considerations and to a few suggestions for research. The First World War can serve as a guidepost: in general, it marked the watershed between the

Liberal Europe of the 19th century and the Labor Unionist Europe of the 20th; moreover, within the Catholic Church, it coincides with the end of the pontificate of Pius X, which, in this domain as in others, marks the end of an era.[4]

Under Leo XIII and Pius X

A preliminary remark is called for: one must avoid overly contrasting Leo XIII, the social Pope, with Pius X, the reactionary Pope who condemned the *Democrazia cristiana* of R. Murri and the *Sillon* of Marc Sangnier and who was one step away, in 1913, from condemning the Christian unions. First, because we cannot forget that if Leo XIII is the Pope of *Rerum novarum*, he is also the author of the encyclical *Graves de communi*, which, concerning Christian Democracy, marks an undeniable step backwards. But above all, because the historian must observe that, although Pius X was personally very reticent *vis-à-vis* Social Catholicism's evolution toward Christian Democracy, many things were accomplished under his pontificate which reinforced what had been begun under Leo XIII and prepared the way for what would be realized under Pius XI. Assuredly, Pius X always retained, as far as he was concerned, the strictly paternalist and clerical perspective that was that of Venetian Catholics of his time, headed by the elderly Paganuzzi. For him, there could be no question of renouncing the ideal of a thoroughly Christian social order. But if, under these conditions, the progressive Social Catholics of the century's first fifteen years, who had a "sense of history," had the impression that for them this pontificate constituted the "crossing of the desert," the historian, across the distance of time, must observe, along with Fr. Jarlot, that "if, in the aftermath of the First World War, labor, agricultural, and professional Catholic organizations were able to federate on a national and international scale, it is because they were first planted under the reign of Pius X in Germany, Holland, Belgium, France, Italy, and elsewhere. The seeds sown by Leo XIII germinated under Pius X and would flourish under Pius XI."[5]

There is no question, let me repeat, of following, even very briefly, the vicissitudes of the Catholic Social Movement in the different countries, where it took on very varied forms according to local circumstances. Sometimes openly supported by the hierarchy, as in Australia,[6] where

Cardinal Moran, Archbishop of Sydney, does not hesitate to present himself as a representative of "Christian Socialism."[7] Sometimes fostered and encouraged by enterprising vicars from working-class parishes, such as Fr. Alfons Ariëns in the Netherlands.[8] Sometimes on the contrary the object of suspicion of a clergy but little sensitive to the problem, as a result of its too-close relations with the ruling classes, as in Spain,[9] or again the object of objections by the theoreticians of neo-corporatism, as in Austria, where the courageous founder of the first Christian unions (beginning in 1892), Leopold Kunschak, had great difficulty in making the demands of the workers movement understood at the core of the People's Christian Social Party, which was however called *christlich-sozial*, but which was in fact focused on the petite bourgeoisie.[10] I will limit myself to rapidly evoking the evolution of the situation in four countries whose internal conflicts awakened echoes beyond their borders.

First, Belgium,[11] where the expression "Christian Democracy" seems to have been born. The men of charity having paternalist leanings retain the leadership of most social benevolent organizations until the First World War. But in 1891, on the eve of the publication of *Rerum novarum*, the *Belgian Democratic League* had been founded and the shift in direction would be accentuated by the substitution, as president, of Arthur Verhaegen for the corporatist Georges Helleputte. The *League* rather quickly became an effective pressure group, which will obtain some of the first social laws, and it slowly acclimates people to the formula of syndicates made up entirely of workers, which begin to develop during the decade which precedes the War, thanks to the actions of the Dominican leader Rutten. Outflanked for a moment on the left by Fr. Daens, the object of opposition from certain bishops (in particular the Bishop of Liège, Msgr. Rutten), but supported by the new Archbishop of Malines, Msgr. Mercier, the *League* makes its debut in government in 1907 (two ministers), which accelerates the passage of several legislative measures in favor of the workers. In short, on the eve of the First War, Christian Democracy has become an essential component of the Belgian Catholic Party and, in the form of unions, mutual societies, cooperatives, etc., in continuous expansion, it is increasingly present in the professional, economic, cultural, and religious life of the country.

A question can be posed when considering the support lent to the movement by Cardinal Mercier: did the Thomist renaissance, the Catholic University of Louvain Higher Institute of Philosophy being one of its most active centers, exercise an influence on Social Catholicism? Without going into details, [12] it can be noted that Simon Deploige, one of Mercier's chief collaborators, was preoccupied with integrating the recent findings of sociology into the Thomist synthesis, whether in the second section of the circles of study at the Higher Institute of Philosophy ("Section on Social Philosophy," which deals with subjects such as trade-unions, mandatory workers' insurance, the representation of economic and social interests in Parliament), or in the *Revue sociale catholique*, founded in 1897, along with the *Revue néo-scolastique*; and that he worked in close collaboration with Professor V. Brants of the School of Political and Social Sciences, a friend of Toniolo, author of a book on *L'économie politique au moyen âge* [The Political Economy of the Middle-Ages] (1895), in which he highlighted the modernity of scholastic doctrines concerning property, profit, etc., and in charge of a course of *Économie sociale dans ses rapports avec la question ouvrière* [Social Economics in Relation to the Workers Question].

In Germany, [13] two schools of thought collide around 1890 within the Catholic Social Movement. Whereas some, whose leader is the Baron von Hertling, manifest very clear reservations regarding State intervention in economic and social life, others, on the contrary, believe along with their leader Fr. Hitze, that "only an ample and profound body of law, only the omnipotent hand of the State can restore order to society." However, extremely concerned with maintaining intact the unity of Catholics against their adversaries—the *Kulturkampf* is not far off—the two tendencies coexist peacefully within the *Volksverein* (founded in 1890 and headed by Pieper, a disciple of Fr. Hitze), which at the same time extends to agricultural workers, the middle class, and factory workers, and which notably develops workers' unions. The formula preferred by the *Volksverein* is that of "mixed" syndicates (that is to say, combining Catholics and Protestants) emphasizing the demands of the professions and giving rather great responsibility to the lay leadership (the clergy only intervening in the role of councilors for moral aspects). This results in new tensions after 1900, because op-posed to these tendencies preached by the men of München-Gladbach of a new social and political order opposed to the hierarchical vision of society dear to the traditionalists, and the Christian's place in a secularized society.

Between the two extremes is seen the gradual development and affirmation of, on the eve of the First War, a centrist current, following the line, relatively traditional but open-minded, traced by *Rerum novarum*: the A.C.J.F. with H. Bazire; the *Semaines sociales de France* [Social Weeks], founded in 1904 by two powerful bourgeois, H. Lorin and A. Boissard, and by a minor employee from Lyons, M. Gonin, a sort of university itinerant who, during a week of reflection and of exchanging views, proposes a sometimes rather new instruction on the great social questions at the level of the family, the profession, or the city, but unfortunately while neglecting economic aspects; the *Action populaire* of the Jesuits, founded in 1903 and to which, beginning in 1905, Fr. Desbuquois will give a decisive impetus, an "intellectual center putting its doctrinal studies, its practical documentation, and its technical competence at the service of all" (R. Kothen); finally, the syndicates of workers and employees, whose development is certainly modest when compared with those of Germany or Belgium, but which at least lay the groundwork for an organization that will grow between the two wars.

In Italy, [16] a country where industry only "takes off" at the end of the 19th century, the efforts were relatively timid compared to the three aforementioned countries, but there was nevertheless between 1890 and 1914, within the framework of the *Opera dei Congressi* [Work of the Congresses], a whole series of worthwhile initiatives that the regional and local monographs published over the last three decades have increasingly brought to light. The second section of the *Opera*, which in 1887 had changed its original name of "Catholic Charity and Economics" to "Christian Social Economics," was able to count on the collaboration of a notable portion of the clergy, which was often closer to the common people than in France, and on the support of a portion of the Catholic press, foremost being the *Osservatore cattolico* of Don Albertario, [17] who did much to awaken Italian Catholic opinion to the social problem. Italian Social Catholicism also had the good fortune to be disposed of several experienced practitioners, such as Fr. Cerutti, [18] the propagator of the rural insurance funds in the Venice (center of the *Volksverein*) is that, more conservative, of the inheritors of the *Arbeitervereine* from the middle of the 19th century, who promote strictly professional unions, which in the end are primarily religious and whose activities are watched over and directed by ecclesiastics. Between the two schools of thought, the hierarchy is divided. The majority of bishops, under the leadership of the Archbishop of Cologne, supports the first (called *Kölner Richtung*), while the Bishops of Wroclaw (Breslau) and of Trier, openly encouraged by the Holy See, support the second (called *Berliner Richtung*). [14]

Let us point out further that, parallel to these organizational problems which take on an aspect of extreme bitterness between 1910 and 1914, a work of more serene reflection, exploring the exigencies of justice in social matters, develops in several theological centers, notably among the Jesuits (especially Fr. Pesch, to whom we will return in the second part of this exposé).

In France, [15] an analogous conflict is found on the eve of 1900. On one side, the paternalist group *Patrons du Nord* [Industrialists of the North Department], hostile to State intervention in economic and social affairs (accepted, however, by Léon Harmel) and opposed to the creation of Christian workers unions, on icy terms with Leo XIII, this group would again find an audience in Rome under Pius X. On the other side, what Fr. Montuclard has called the "Second Christian Democracy" (the first being that of 1848, with the *Ère nouvelle* [New Era]), which accepts the values of political Liberalism (including the rallying to the republic), rejected by the pioneers of Social Catholicism, but which desires at the same time to construct a social democracy of Christian inspiration, to which Liberal Catholics are allergic. On this common ground of political and social democracy, nuances and even rather divergent currents must indeed be distinguished. Let us stop at recalling the *abbés démocrates* [Democratic Priests] of the 1890's (Naudet, Lemire, etc.), soon compromised by the imprudent actions of young priests who seemed more like social militants than religious apostles, and, in the first decade of the 20th century, the *Sillon* of Marc Sangnier. Under Pius X they will be denounced by the fundamentalist press as a particularly dangerous variety of modernists. However, they did point out, maladroitly, some real problems, even more basic than those discussed in Germany in the same period: the constitution years, supported by a growing fraction of the young clergy in spite of the reservations held by the majority of the episcopate, which was hostile to the movement not only for social and political reasons, but also because it feared seeing its authority called into question by a transposition of democratic principles inside the Church.

Leo XIII, who was at the same time aware of the necessity to go beyond the conservatives' restricted point-of-view and very carefully to maintain the unity of the Catholic forces, tried in vain to channel the energies of Christian Democrats with his encyclical *Graves de communi* of 18 January 1901. This holding action did not calm the impatience of the most progressive and the change of the pontificate further accentuated tensions, because Pius X was even more hostile than his predecessor to Murri's pretensions to assume the hierarchy's control of social and political matters, even—and doubtless especially—if the former, whose program from its inception retained very clerical characteristics, hoped to see the clergy take charge of Catholics in these profane domains. To cut short this groundswell, the new Pope decided in 1905 to dissolve the *Opera dei Congressi* and to reorganize Catholic efforts in the social arena, under the direction of ecclesiastic authority, in the *Unione economico-sociale*, but in spite of several interesting initiatives, such as the founding in 1910 of the Catholic Social School of Bergamo, [22] the concrete realizations were rather modest. And very soon a new opposition from the left was reborn, which was felt noticeably during the Congress of Modena in 1910, in the protestations of Miglioli and Don Cecconcelli against the suspicions, on the part of official instances, of which the workers unions remained the object.

It is important to note that the briefly discussed diverse national developments did not transpire in closed vessels; there were frequent contacts between Social Catholics beyond their frontiers. To give a single example, let us cite the Belgo-Italian relationship. Toniolo was in contact with Victor Brants, with the Bishop of Liège, Msgr. Doutreloux, the most "social" of the Belgian bishops at the time, with Cardinal Mercier, and in Italy they closely followed the Liège social experiments of Fr. Pottier.

One can further observe, beyond the diversity of the situations and solutions, which are explained largely by the diversity of national region and the whole of Northern Italy (there will already be 893 in 1898), and of seeing the formation in the province of Bergamo, under N. Rezzara, a particularly active center of Christian social action. It is true that the outlook of most of the *Opera's* leadership long remained paternalistic, and that the administration of organizations intended for workers or peasants (which from the North spread progressively toward other regions and especially to Sicily) was almost always in the hands of the clergy or of the ruling class. However, during the 1890s, a change was brewing.

In December 1889, the *Unione cattolica per gli studi sociali* [Catholic Union for Social Studies] had been founded, headed by Toniolo,[19] who, in 1893, will give them a quality doctrinal organ, the *Revista internazionale di scienze sociali* [International Review of Social Studies]. The *Unione* was known especially for creating circles of social studies, which sprang up rapidly in the major cities of Italy, and for chairs of social economics in several seminaries, for the meeting of two "social congresses" in Genoa in 1892, and in Padua in 1896, and for the creation in 1894 of the "Program of Milan," which sought to put into practice, with "an undeniably bold vision for the times" (M. Vaussard), the principles enunciated in *Rerum novarum*.[20] The official title of this program is still symptomatic of the defensive mentality that inspired this social action: "Program of Catholics confronting Socialism." In addition, Toniolo, in pursuit of a chimerical unity of all Catholics in a program of "democracy" directed by the Pope in the best "neo-Guelfe" tradition, a program which would remain fatally vague and abstract to avoid conflicts between ideologies, inevitably resulted in emptying its content of the concept of Christian Democracy by focusing all its efforts on the cooperation of social classes within the Catholic organizations, thereby minimizing the tension between employees and capitalists in modern industrial society. However, stimulated by foreign example, increasing numbers of young people reacted against this way of seeing things, which impeded the movement's normal maturation into an effective force for popular freedom and for progress, acting on the political level like the Christian Democrats of France and Belgium. It is notably under the influence of a dynamic young priest, Romolo Murri,[21] that the opposition of Progressive Christian Democrats within the *Opera dei Congressi* will polarize over several the Jesuits and the Dominicans); studies on the content of textbooks used in seminaries at the time (to what degree do they include the progress in doctrine and in pontifical documents?); studies on the influence exerted by the Young Christian Workers (J.O.C.) on the evolution not only of social strategy, but also of the very concept of Christian reflection on social matters.[24]

In the current state, still quite incomplete, of our knowledge, we already glimpse the great diversity of perspectives and teachings, just as marked as for the preceding period. Limiting ourselves to the strictly doctrinal aspect of things, a superficial glance suffices to observe this diversity in the teachings of Don Sturzo (who especially emphasizes the importance of the intermediary public bodies); Jacques Maritain, (whose influence in Latin America is known); Jacques Leclercq in volume IV of his *Leçons de droit naturel* [Lessons of Natural Law]; the group from *Catholic Worker* in the United States, led among others by Dorothy Day (reacting vigorously against the materialist principles which it denounces at the base of the socio-economic capitalist system); the Austrian School of Johannes Ude and Anton Orel,[25] whose radical condemnation of the capitalist system, as intrinsically flawed, will be in its turn condemned by the episcopate in a collective letter of Spring 1932; the Circle of German Jesuits in Königswinter, in which the effort of elaborating a conception of society as far removed from liberalism as from socialism, inaugurated at the end of the 19th century by Fathers Cathrein and Heinrich Pesch, is pursued between the wars by Oswald von Nell-Breuning and Gustav Gundlach.[26]

It is precisely this ever more vivid awareness of the multitude of directions taken by social studies research in the Catholic Church, and of the problem there was in plumbing these new questions pell-mell, which was at the origin of the *International Union of Social Studies of Malines*. The idea was put forward by two veterans from before the war, the Belgian Georges Helleputte and the Frenchman Eugène Duthoit, president of *Semaines sociales* [Social Weeks], who proposed the idea to Cardinal Mercier, crowned with international glory after the First War. Upon reflection, the latter accepted and entrusted the secretariat general to one of his former students, Maurice Defourny, professor of political economics at the University of Louvain. The *Union* had three objectives: to study social problems from the perspective of Catholic political circumstances (for example, the incidence of the problem of rallying to the Republic in France, of the Roman Question in Italy), a certain number of common traits. Hence, the lasting attachment to paternalism ("*for* the people but not *by* the people"), encouraged by the encyclical *Graves de Communi* (which defined Christian Democracy "*actio benefica in populum*"). Hence, the gradual integration into the Christian Democratic program of the Liberal Catholic heritage, respective of the realization that the utilization of modern freedoms in the framework of political democracy was in fact the necessary condition of the march toward social democracy (the demand for universal suffrage in Belgium, the pleading for a reintegration of Catholics into the political and social life of France and Italy). One can also observe more or less everywhere how much the Christian Democrats remain influenced by their ultramontane roots. Even Murri remains profoundly marked by the theocratic and fundamentalist program of the early *Movimento cattolico*. Similarly, the weight of scholastic education often leads to difficulty in assimilating the problematic schema of the modern social movement, all the more in that around 1900, many of the leaders and inspirers of Christian Democracy were priests, who only with great difficulty let go of the intellectual orientation acquired at the seminary. A last common trait is due precisely to this preponderance of ecclesiastics in the movement; namely, the frequent difficulties between "progressive" priests and their bishops in the social arena: Fr. Daens in Belgium, the "Democratic Priests" in France, Murri in Italy... to cite only a few leaders.

Between the Wars

Presenting a synthesis of the social teachings of the Church at the various levels—pontifical *magisterium*, episcopal *magisterium*, theological reflection, popularization for the Christian common folk—for the decade before the encyclical *Quadragesimo anno* is even harder than for the preceding period, because we can dispose of far fewer preliminary works, not to speak of syntheses, which are almost entirely lacking.[23] Many monographs would be necessary, especially studies of certain major journals and their eventual evolutions (thus the *Cité chrétienne* of Jacques Leclercq in Belgium, or a comparison between the "social" articles in *Études* and the *Vie intellectuelle*, run respectively in France by morality; to transmit concrete directives and resolutions approved in common after deliberations to the public at large and specifically to men of charitable action; and eventually, to create a bureau of social consultations, which would play a role analogous on the international level to that played by the Jesuits' *Action populaire* in France.

Instead of a synthesis, which it would be premature to undertake and which, in any case, would demand much more time from us than we dispose of, it seemed to me useful to present briefly a few of the grand themes that ripened during the two decades between the Wars and whose gradual elaboration it would be profitable to follow by exposing the points of consensus and of divergence. I have chosen some ten of them.

First, the dilemma of Corporatism-Syndicalism. It had been wildly discussed during the pontificate of Pius X, [27] who, in 1913, was one step away from condemning Christian unions.[28] Certain fundamentalist Catholics, to whom the quasi-official *Civiltà cattolica* brought its decided support, believed the two terms were incompatible because the idea of labor unions was based on the concept of class struggle, which seemed radically opposed to the notion of Christian charity. The energetic reaction of several bishops, especially in Germany, but as well Cardinal Mercier, then the death of Pius X, warded off the danger, and after the War, there was no more question of condemning Christian syndicalism. Still, the idea of corporatism remained quite alive in certain Social Christian milieus, especially in Austria, where it inspired the politics of Chancellor Dollfuss. While Catholic sociologists exhibited strong reservations regarding State corporatism, as was conceived in fascist Italy, they nevertheless followed Salazar's Portuguese experiment with lively interest. It would be interesting, among other things, to investigate country by country the reactions of Catholic specialists on these questions to those passages in *Quadragesimo anno* which exhibit sympathy for a corporatist organization of society.[29]

Another theme much in favor between the Wars: the relationship between the Individual and Society. Catholic sociologists had to find a balance between the defense of the human individual's rights—to which Pius XI showed himself increasingly sensitive as he became obliged to react against totalitarian regimes on the right and on the left—and the rights necessitated by the common good against the persistence in the minds of many, even within the Church, of the Liberal conception of society.

Another division along the same lines: the affirmation, on the one hand, of the role which the State must play in regulating economic and social life, and the affirmation, otherwise, of the principle of "subsidiarity," which implies that the State should not monopolize all tasks, but on the contrary, should delegate as many as possible to the intermediary public bodies, seeking a middle road between the State's absorption of the economy and the economy's absorption of the State.

In mentioning the discussions that revolved around the rights of ownership, I will limit myself to doing so *apropos* of the question, already timely a half-century ago, of nationalization. We can refer to Professor Vallarché's communication on this topic.

By about 1930, no one was still talking about "theology of terrestrial realities," but under the combined influences of Marxist ideas, Jocism [J.O.C. - Young Christian Workers], and of the Great Depression with its millions of unemployed, an interest arose in the Christian notion of work—to probe the doctrinal foundations of the right to work, for example.

Among the topics worth reflecting on, let us also note the question of salary, concerning which one no longer stops at exploring the question of the familial salary and the concrete means of realizing it, but takes an equal interest in the workers' sharing in the profits and benefits of an enterprise (not yet in its management); the question of a fair price, an old problem but presented in new terms due to a new economic reality—inflation; and the question of reforming the capitalist system, brought up again both by the encyclical *Quadragesimo anno* and by the growing audience Marxist critics were finding to be against "capitalist alienation."

The increasing role played by Marxism, both in everyday social life and in the reflection of intellectuals, led Christian thinkers to explore the question of class struggle's legitimacy. It had once been summarily denounced as contrary to the Christian doctrine of charity, and insistence had above all been placed on common interests between employers and employees existing within the enterprise, united in the same boat, and on the particular necessity for Christians to do everything to lessen tensions among the brothers of Jesus Christ. However, the economic and social realities of modern industrial society made it increasingly obvious that there was also, inevitably between capitalists and workers, divergent interests. If reservations remain great concerning violent struggle, it is increasingly recognized that there are, by the very givens of the situation, permanent tensions, a structural opposition of the interests involved; more concretely, that the tensions are not the result of this or that bad employer but that there is necessarily divergence of interests between management on one side and labor on the other. Here too, one can suppose that the Young Christian Workers contributed to leading Catholic thinkers to a more realistic view of the problem by having the Church officially recognize the profound sociological reality of differentiated "social milieus," recognition which is basic to specialized Catholic action.[30]

I will be a little longer in one last case: the efforts of Catholic sociologists with a view to defining the very notion of "social justice."[31] The 20th century having begun, everyone agrees on the fact that the workers question involves not only charity, but justice as well. However, theologians and philosophers continue to argue over whether it is a matter of subjective obligations of justice (dependent on commutative or, strictly speaking, distributive justice) or if it is a matter of objective norms of justice ruling these diverse subjective obligations and being dependent on a specific category, social justice. It will be necessary to wait for *Quadragesimo anno* before seeing this last term appear in a document coming from the *magisterium*, and it is besides relatively recent in the vocabulary of theology and of traditional moral philosophy. St. Thomas spoke only of legal justice or general justice. Why has it been judged necessary to create a new term rather than to adopt the expressions of St. Thomas? Fr. Pesch and the Jesuits of *Stimmen aus Maria Laach* were at first satisfied with them, but the expression "legal justice" seemed unfortunate in that it appeared to favor the opinion that one only needed to observe the positive laws enacted by the State. Some proposed, therefore, the new term "social justice," but it immediately ran into violent opposition, notably from Charles Périn, who reproached it not only for being "a neologism which hides the vagueness of the idea," but what is worse, for being the Trojan Horse of Socialism. The new term was especially diffused by

French Social Catholics in the years 1880-90, and by 1900, A. Pottier was writing in his *De justitia et jure*: *"Justitia legalis...vocatur quoque socialis, praesertim in usu loquendi odierno."* An important step was taken by the little article published in 1895 by Fr. de la Bégassière and diffused later as a brochure, titled *The Notion of Social Justice*, which inspired Fr. Charles Antoine to redo the corresponding paragraph of his *Course in Social Economics*, widely diffused at the time and frequently reissued just after the First War. Fr. de la Bégassière clearly distinguished social justice from any ideology related to the "leveling socialism" denounced by Périn, as well as from the various subjective obligations coming from distributive or commutative justice. He presented a concept of objective social justice that was very close to the legal or general justice of St. Thomas, whose ideas helped him to define clearly the notion designated by the new term. Social justice, he wrote, is nothing less than "that justice whose object is the social good and the common good of all." In his wake, Fr. Pesch, from 1905, was introducing the German world to the expression *Soziale Gerechtigheit*, which was taken up by the majority of German authors and especially by Fr. O. von Nell-Breuning, one of the inspirers of the encyclical *Quadragesimo anno*. Basically, what we are talking about here is the rediscovery of a long-forgotten aspect of traditional Thomist doctrine, but henceforward presented under the veil of a new expression, one which is better suited to an era in which law ("legal" justice) is spoken of less, and sociology ("social" justice) is spoken of more. The term thus presented and perfected nevertheless continued to encounter certain objections. So it is that Fr. Vermeersch, at the beginning of 1931, was still writing in an article on *Justice in Rerum novarum*: "We have not talked about social justice, of which such use is made in books on social morals. The reader may be surprised by this. Our reason is simple: unless we are going to identify social justice with general justice, there is no *special* virtue that could merit this name."[32] But precisely, it was simply a matter of a new name, which was proposed for greater clarity to designate the old general justice. The encyclical *Quadragesimo anno*, which used the expression, would officially give it the stamp of approval.

I would like before finishing to make a last observation. One of the traits which characterizes Catholic Social Teachings during the pontificate of Pius XI is the slow awakening to the necessary distinction between the moral aspect of the Social Question, which belongs to philosophy and theology, and its technical aspect, which belongs to independent disciplines, economics, and sociology. This distinction, well illuminated by Fr. Höffe in his report *De Rerum novarum à 80° anno*, first appears timidly, then, over the course of the 1930's, increasingly clearer. At first, there had often been a tendency to mix the two aspects, the "social doctrine of the Church" not only to enunciate principles but also equally to furnish solutions, even recipes. The temptation in this direction was great in that this "social doctrine" was often elaborated and diffused by ecclesiastics engaged in social action. Then, after the First War, the role of laymen increased and an increasingly important role in the reflection on these matters was taken by organisms under lay administration, such as the German *Volksverein*. It was normal then that a clearer distinction be made between, on the one hand, the elaboration of doctrine, setting principles which would inspire solutions, and, on the other, the elaboration of these solutions, which often vary according to the contingencies of time and place, and which call on the expertise of economists and social science specialists for their concrete realization. It is only after the Second War that there comes a full awareness of the distinction between these two levels (that especially explains the variety of practical options coming out of a single faith and a single fundamental teaching), but the first signs of this direction were already clearly seen by the 1930s.

Notes

1 To borrow a remark by Pierre Letamendia at the beginning of his little volume in the collection *QUE SAIS-JE* on *La démocratie chrétienne*: "Christian Democracy will never have *one* thinker having established in a clear and definitive way a complete doctrinal system. This characteristic can alter the coherence of the doctrine, but on the other hand, it thus avoids dogmatism and facilitates indispensable evolutions" (Paris, 1977, p. 25).

2 Christian Democracy at the time of Leo XIII—and this is the perspective which continues to be held against R. Murri or Marc Sangnier under Pius X—basically sought to reconstitute an ersatz Christianity by substituting, for the outdated alliance between the Throne and the Altar, an "alliance of the People and the Altar" against the Liberal and anticlerical bourgeoisie: using more modern and more popular means, it was still the same ideal of a "Christian society informed by the

Church" which was being pursued (see on this subject the illuminating work by É. Poulat, *Église contre bourgeoisie. Introduction au devenir du catholicisme social* [Church against Bourgeoisie. Introduction to the Evolution of Social Catholicism], Tournai-Paris, 1977).

³ It is important to observe that whatever the new moral problems raised by this evolution, it is that in part the ineluctable result of the evolution of industrial society itself, which demands an increasing concentration, both for technological reasons and for commercial-technical reasons.

⁴ Which, moreover, does not exclude that, in certain domains, this pontificate constituted a new beginning, which has led me to title the pages dedicated to this Pope in the *Handbuch der Kirchengeschicte* [Handbook of Church History] under the direction of Msgr. Jedin, "*ein konsevativer Reformpapst*" [A conservative reform pope] (t. VI, Freiburg-en-Breisgau, 1973, pp. 391-405).

⁵ Georges Jarlot, *Doctrine pontificale et histoire. L'enseignement social de Léon XIII, Pie X et Benoît XV vu dans son ambiance historique* [The Social Teachings of Leo XIII, Pius X, and Benedict XV viewed in their Historical Context], Rome, 1964, pp. 13-14.

⁶ Should we add: or like in the United States? Cardinal Gibbons' intervention on behalf of the "Knights of Labor," which succeeded in avoiding an imminent condemnation by Rome of these Christian labor unions, is well known and has often been invoked as an example of the support which the official American Church gave to the workers' demands. But in reality, Henry Browne's work (*The Catholic Church and the Knights of Labor*, Washington, 1949) has shown that this intervention was situated in a very particular context and that, on the whole, Gibbons' social stance, like that of the other American bishops, was rather conservative.

⁷ See P. Ford, *Cardinal Moran and the A.L.P. A study in the encounter between Moran and socialism, 1890-1907*, Melbourne, 1966.

⁸ See G. Brom, *A. Ariëns*, Amsterdam, 1941, 2 vol. Although the Dutch episcopate long retained its paternalist outlook, Ariëns could count on the support of the Archbishop of Utrecht.

⁹ See J. Tussel Gomez, *Historia de la democracia cristiana en España*, t. I, Madrid, 1974.

¹⁰ See especially G. Silberhamer, *Österreichs Katholiken und die Arbeiterfrage* [Austrian Catholics and the Workers Question], Graz, 1966; A. Wandruska, *Il cattolicesimo politico e sociale nell'Austria-Ungheria degli anni 1870-1914* [Political and Social Catholicism in Austria-Hungary in the years...], in *Il cattolicesimo politico e sociale in Italia e Germania dal 1870 al 1914*, Bologna, 1977, pp. 151-77.

¹¹ See especially R. Rezsohazy, *Origines et formation du catholicisme social en Belgique*, Louvain, 1958, and *150 Jaar Katholieke Arbeidersbeweging in België* [150 Years of the Catholic Workers Movement in Belgium], edited by S. H. Scholl, t. II, Brussels, 1965.

¹² See some precise details in my contribution to the round table organized during the Fermo colloquium of 1970 on the theme: *Ritorno al tomismo e tradizione democratico-cristiana* [Return to Thomism and Christian-Democratic Tradition], in *Romolo Murri nella storia politica e religiosa del suo tempo* [R.M. in the Political and Religious History of his Time], edited by G. Rossini, Rome, 1972, pp. 414-27.

[13] See especially: K.H. Brüls, *Geschichte der katholisch-sozialen Bewegung in Deutschland* [History of the Social Catholic Movement in Germany], Munster, 1958; J. Joos, *Katholische Arbeiterbewegung* [Catholic Workers Movement], Cologne, 1963; and E. Ritter, *Die katholische soziale Bewegung Deutschlands im 19. Jh und der Volksverein* [The German Catholic Social Movement in the 19th century and the Volksverein], Cologne, 1954.

[14] On the controversy relative to the Christian syndicates, see E. Deuerlein, *Der Gewerkschaftsstreit* [The Labor Union Quarrel], in *Theologische Quartalschrift*, CXXXIX, 1959, pp. 40-81.

[15] See especially: H. Rollet, *L'action sociale des catholiques en France (1871-1914)*, Paris, 1947-1958, 2 vol.; R. Talmy, *Le syndicalisme chrétien en France (1871-1930). Difficultés et controverses*, Paris, 1966; M. Montuclard, *Conscience religieuse et Démocratie. La deuxième Démocratie chrétienne en France, 1891-1902*, Paris, 1965; J.M. Mayeur, *Un prêtre démocrate, l'abbé Lemire*, Tournai-Paris, 1968; P. Droulers, *Politique sociale et christianisme. Le P. Desbuquois et l'Action populaire, 1903-1918*, Paris, 1969 (cf. É. Poulat, in *Archives de sociologie des religions*, n° 29, 1969, pp. 131-147; and M. Launay, in *Revue d'histoire moderne et contemporaine*, XXI, 1974, pp. 623-30).

[16] See especially: A. Gambasin, *Il movimento sociale nell'Opera dei Congressi (1874-1904)*, Rome, 1958; G. Are, *I cattolici e la questione sociale in Italia (1894-1904)*, Milan, 1963 (anthology); L. Bedeschi, *I Pionieri della D. C.: 1896-1906*, Milan, 1966; as well as two veterans' eye-witness accounts: D. Secco Suardo, *Da Leone XIII a Pio X*, Rome, 1967; and G. Valente, *Aspetti e momenti dell'Azione sociale dei cattolici in Italia (1892-1926)*, edited by F. Malgeri, Rome, 1968 (both published in *La Collana di storia del Movimento cattolico*).

[17] See lastly C. Snider, *L'episcopato del cardinale Andrea Ferrari*, t. I, *Gli ultimi anni dell'Ottocento, 1891-1903*, Vicence, 1981, chapters XII to XV (pp. 447-700).

[18] Cf. S. Tramontin, *La figura e l'opera sociale di Luigi Cerutti*, Brescia, 1968.

[19] A scientific biography of Giuseppe Toniolo is still lacking. See, in the meantime, R. Angeli, *La dottrina sociale di G. Toniolo*, Pignerol, 1956, and P. Pecorari, *Ketteler e Toniolo, Topologie sociali del movimento cattolico in Europa*, Rome, 1977, in particular pp. 49-73.

[20] See C. Snider, *op. cit.*, t. I, pp. 500-\15.

[21] See especially: Acts of the Congress of Fermo (1970), cited in note 12; S. Zoppi, *R. Murri e la prima democrazia cristiana*, Florence, 1968; C. Lorusso, *R. Murri dalla Democrazia cristiana al Partito radicale*, Bari, 1981.

[22] Cf. B. Malinverni, *La scuola sociale cattolica di Bergamo (1910-1932)*, Rome, 1960.

[23] Not totally, however. See for example G. Jarlot, *Action pontificale et Histoire*, t. II, *Pie XI. Doctrine et action*, Rome, 1973 (in which an abundant bibliography is found), or further from a more systematic perspective, J.-Y. Calvez et J. Perrin, *Église et Société économique. L'enseignement social des papes de Léon XIII à Pie XII*, Paris, 1959.

[24] Two examples: to what extent did Cardijn's imperative to "See, judge, act" lead to the sociological point-of-view (promoted at Louvain by men like Brants or Msgr. Deploige) being given preference over abstract theories, *a priori*, which were preferred by many neo-scholastic thinkers? And to what extent did the perspective

which the J.O.C. introduced to Catholic Action not contribute to substituting an authentic democratic point-of-view for one based on social hierarchies, which was still often seen in Social Catholics before 1914?

[25] See for example, by the first, *Eigentum, Kapitalismus, Christentum* (1930), and by the second, *Oeconomia perennis* (1930).

[26] We know that the encyclical *Quadragesimo anno* was characterized, with the exaggeration inherent in all sayings of this type, as "*ein grandioses Plagiat an Gundlach,*" Fr. Nell-Breuning serving as intermediary.

[27] Note that the passages in the encyclical *Rerum novarum* relative to workers' associations (called *collegia* or *sodalitia*) were interpreted by some as promoting the corporative system and by others as promoting the development of labor unions.

[28] Cf. É. Poulat, *La dernière bataille du pontificat de Pie X,* in *Rivista di storia della Chiesa in Italia,* XXV, 1971, pp. 83-107.

[29] See as a prime example concerning Belgium, where the reservations were great, the pages by S.H. School in: *150 Jaar Katholieke Arbeidersbeweging in België,* t. III, Brussels, 1966, pp. 274-80.

[30] This did not happen moreover without difficulties. When, in the beginning of the 1920's, Fr. Cardijn preached the formula, which would circle the globe with Pius XI's benediction, of a specifically working-class Catholic Action; it attracted virulent criticism from supporters of a general Catholic Action, gathering together young people from different social milieus within parochial teams. The founder of the J.O.C., wrote Canon Brohée to Cardinal Mercier, introduced "an idea which is not Christian and which is socialist, the idea of *class*" (cf. M. Walckiers, *Sources inédites relatives aux débuts de la J.O.C., 1919-1925,* Louvain-Paris, 1970, p. 26; see, in the same vein, pp. 37, 42, 52). He and his adjutant, Fr. Picard, will go so far as to reproach Cardijn of "tearing the mystical body of Christ."

[31] Cf. J.-Y. Calvez and J. Perrin, *Église et Société économique. L'enseignement social des papes de Léon XIII à Pie XII,* Paris, 1959, Appendix 1, "L'expression *Justice sociale* avant *Quadragesimo anno,*" pp. 543-57, where useful references will be found.

[32] He wrote further: "Social justice is an imprecise expression which designates a goal rather than a virtue, a goal to which various virtues contribute" (the goal in question being social peace).

The Encyclical *Rerum novarum*: Culmination of a Slow Maturation 1991

We have here a work which is appearing near the end of the Rerum novarum *centennial: after so many publications dealing with the two encyclicals of Leo XlII and of John-Paul II, can this one find a lasting originality, as the Pontifical Council "Justice and Peace" thinks it can?*

First of all, presenting the two complete pontifical documents together permits us to better understand that which unites and distinguishes them. In fact, because of the acceleration of history, it is not one hundred years but several centuries which separate the two monumental works; if we do not take the trouble to explore the first as well as we do the second, we cannot honestly celebrate this centenary and truly measure its full importance.

Roger Aubert and Michel Schooyans help us to retrace the prehistory of Rerum novarum *and to penetrate its posterity. The sharply focused perspectives of these two highly qualified observers lead us to a vivid understanding of a Church anxious to insert the ever-new Gospel of salvation into the social fabric of humanity. The light shed by these two studies is stimulating: looking back, an encyclical's audacity is not the result of spontaneous generation, but must be sown; looking ahead, an encyclical's fecundity depends on faithful attention, and must be cultivated.*

Social education in the Church is not a still-life, it is a work-site open day and night to which all are called: in the center, there is an idea of the human person, unique in his identity, diverse in his vocation, fiercely demanding in his dignity. When the hundred candles, blown out on Rerum novarum, *are everywhere extinguished, every man will be able to take up his journey reinvigorated by the words of Leo XIII, recalled by John-Paul II in* Centesimus annus *(n. 56): "Let each undertake without delay the part assigned to him, for fear that in deferring the remedy we render incurable a malady already so grave. As for the Church, her actions will not be found wanting in any circumstances" (RN, n. 45).*

Roger Cardinal Etchegaray

The first "social" encyclical, which was published in May 1891 by Leo XIII, was, to use an expression of Jean-Marie Mayeur recently taken up by Rene Rémond at the international colloquium on the encyclical organized by the French School of Rome, a "foundation text": it in fact constituted a point of departure for later reflection by Catholic theologians and sociologists, and at the same time for the more-and-more decisive action of the Christian Democrats anxious to react against the "undeserved poverty" of the working class. And this explains why, a unique case in the history of pontifical documents, the Holy See desired on several occasions to officially celebrate its anniversary: *Quadragesimo anno, Octogesima adveniens, Centesimus annus*. Still, as is often the case with pontifical documents, this encyclical was also situated in a continuum: not only did it inscribe itself as a new element in the overall project to restore a Christian society that Leo XIII had elaborated bit by bit from the beginning of his pontificate, but it moreover consecrated a series of initiatives, both doctrinal and practical, taken more or less everywhere, over the course of the two preceding decades, by the ecclesiastical community—bishops, priests, and clergy, but also laity — animated by the desire to translate the evangelical message into the daily life of the society of their times.

With rare exceptions, the leadership of both ecclesiastics and laity took a long time to become aware of the problems posed to Christian reflection by the Industrial Revolution, which progressively substituted for traditional rural society an increasingly urban world, built around factories and capitalist institutions, and in which the living conditions of the working masses had changed profoundly. To be sure, recent research has shown that, from the 1820s on, there was no lack of generous men of the Church and laity who were moved by the poverty of the industrial proletariat and who tried to bring about change. At the very heart of Catholicism, in the quasi-official journal of the Roman Jesuits, *La Civiltà cattolica,* one finds, in the early 1850s, a real sensitivity to the abuses engendered by the capitalist exploitation of the workers.[2] While condemning — without nuances, moreover — the tendency of socialism at the time to stuff people into a state-run collectivity, these first "social Catholics" denounced just as sharply the new Liberal-inspired economic theories, which seemed to reduce man to a machine for production. One proposition in the *Syllabus* even echoed this preoccupation.[3] But most among them face the problem from a "counter-revolutionary" perspective, hostile toward democratic egalitarianism. Almost nowhere does the idea dawn that it would be necessary to confer the responsibility for Catholic social services to the workers for whom they were created, whereas it is precisely in the aftermath of 1870 that, all over Europe, the workers' movement evolves in a direction more and more opposed to paternalism.

Whatever may have been the merits of certain French Liberal Catholics between 1830 and 1848,[4] it is not in this direction that one should look for the origins of social Catholicism as it developed in the second half of the 19th century. The philosophy of Lamennais, a bit later that of Ozanam and his group, doubtless announced a social Catholicism resolutely open to the democratic evolution of the modern world. But these tentative steps did not survive the conservative reaction which followed the revolution of 1848, and although these Liberal Catholics did much in the way of private charity, they saw less and less hope of changing the existing economic and social order.

The veritable precursors of modern social Catholicism, such as will find first expression in the encyclical *Rerum novarum,* are really to be found among liberalism's most determined adversaries, who at first glance seem to be "reactionaries" and who in fact *were* from several points of view. This phenomenon, disconcerting on the surface, can be understood however as soon as one takes a closer look. First of all, many of these pioneers of social Catholicism sprang from the landed aristocracy, less involved in business than the Liberal Catholics and thus less sensitive to the famous imperative of the "law of bronze" concerning the demands of economic competition. But above all the social Catholic of the years 1860 to 1890 saw in social action a means of rallying the masses to their struggle against the anti-clerical bourgeois oligarchy, whom they hated doubly: because they were anti-clerical, and because they would substitute the power of money for traditional social authority.[5]

So it is in Italy, it is in the bosom of the *Opera dei Congressi,*[6] whose leaders were fanatically hostile to the Liberal State, that a few thinkers, principal among them the professor Toniolo,[7] began to call attention to the pagan character of economic liberalism and to the necessity of taking into account the demands of morality (and therefore of religion) in relations between capital and labor.; and in France, Albert de Mun[8] and above all René de la Tour du Pin,[9] proclaiming that the French

Revolution had only brought workers an illusory freedom and in reality subjugated isolated individuals to the power of money, extolled the return to the corporative society of the *Ancien regime* and held in honor once more certain scholastic doctrines on the state's right to intervene in economic and social life.

This is far from saying, however, that all French Catholics who took an interest in the workers problem rallied round these audacious views. The latter were on the contrary resisted with great vigor by a different group of Social Catholics, in this period sometimes referred to as the School of Angers, because it was patronized with fanfare by Msgr. Frepel, sometimes as the Belgian School, because it had for master thinker a brilliant professor of political economics from the University of Louvain, Charles Perin,[10] whose work *De la richesse dons les sociétés chrétiennes (1861)* was translated into most European languages. But, this champion in the struggle against ideological and political liberalism, though he may energetically denounce the exploitation of the workers by the new bourgeois class and teach that moral laws must govern the economy, denies the State any right to intervene in the matter, expecting a solution to the social question to come exclusively from private initiative and from the growth of Christian spirit among employers.

Paradoxically, it is Germany, where industrial progress had been slower, that sees the rise of the most realistic Social Catholic movement, one favoring limitations on economic liberty through social legislation. There too, the problem posed by the often lamentable situation of the proletariat began as and long remained a question of charity and not of justice, of aid rather than of structural reforms. But a distinct change occurred in the years 1860-1870. One man played an especially important role in this evolution: Msgr. Ketteler, Bishop of Mainz.[11] This role has sometimes been downplayed and, in fact, it is true that, when this descendant of an old Westphalian aristocratic family took up arms against the individualism of his time, source of oppression for the economically weak, he dreamed primarily of a return to the corporatively structured society known to the old German Empire of the Middle Ages; one must therefore avoid presenting Ketteler without nuances as the premier representative of Christian Democracy, as she is known today. His influence on contemporary

Social Catholicism remains nevertheless considerable, especially *via* his work *Die Arbeiterfrage und das Christentum* (1864), fruit of fifteen years' reflection, in which he did not limit himself to suggesting a few concrete reforms, but attempted above all to show that the solution to the worker problem was only thinkable in terms of a general vision of society, in direct opposition to Liberal indiviualism as much as to the totalitarianism of the modern centralized State. He appears here as the first theoretician of corporatively-based social organicism, which will constitute for more than half a century the foundation of Catholic social doctrine. But, while awaiting the eventual corporative reorganization of the working class, Ketteler applied himself tirelessly to the encouragement and promotion of progressive social legislation, not hesitating to call on State intervention to defend the workers against the abuses of Liberalism.

Ketteler died in 1877, but the ideas he launched did not die with him. While the Center Party, made up of German Catholics, was allying itself with the socialists in the Parliament to pass social legislation (introduced after 1878 and especially after 1881, giving Germany a notable head-start on other countries in this matter[12]), the theologians began to take interest in questions of social morality, for example Fr. Cathrein, in a series of articles published in *Stimmen aus Maria Laach* from 1879 to 1882, or Fr. Lehmkuhl, in his *Theologia moralis* (1883).

The ideas put forth by Ketteler and his collaborators did not take long to spread beyond Germany. The baron Karl von Vogelsang,[13] a German noble (converted to Catholicism by Ketteler) who had retired to Austria in 1864, founded in 1879 the *Oesterreichische Monatschrift, fur Gesellschaftswissenschaft and Volkswissenschaft,* in which he brought to light, following his teacher Ketteler, the social function of property and undertook a violent criticism of the capitalist system, based solely on the pursuit of profit. He insisted on the necessity of organizing the professions, not, as the Socialists wanted, along State-run lines, but after the manner of medieval corporations.

Vogelsang managed to bring a group of young Austrian Catholics to his way of thinking, such as Schindler, who would succeed him as head of the Austrian social school, Lueger, future mayor of Vienna, where he would do remarkable social work, and the prince Charles von Löwenstein, who organized meetings of Social Christians on his property from 1883 to 1888, from which would come, among other ideas, the "theses of Haid."[14] The labor contract is of a completely different nature from the property contract because of the moral aspect of human activity; salary must be determined taking into account the essential needs of the worker and his family; large industries must be organized corporatively and, among other things, corporative insurance funds instituted.

These theses, which were unheard of at the time outside of revolutionary circles (and which were met moreover with strong reticence on the part of the Austrian episcopate, extremely conservative and governmental on the whole), were spread abroad thanks to an international journal, the *Correspondance de Genève*, founded and run by a member of Vogelsang's group, the count von Blome,[15] a convert also of German origin.

The Catholic groups preoccupied with the workers problem in Germany, Austria, France, Belgium, and Italy, were not complete strangers to each other. They knew each other through their respective publications and somewhat occasional contacts took place, notably in Rome, where a noble Austrian of Vogelsang's group, Count Kuefstein,[16] who spent winters there, had in 1882 set up a circle for social studies with the help of a Canadian priest, Father Villeneuve[17] and especially of a young Roman prelate, extremely dynamic, Msgr. Domenico Jacobini.[18] This Union for the Social Studies, which met at prince Borghese's home under the direction of Msgr. Mermillod,[19] Bishop of Geneva who, expelled from Switzerland by a radical government, lived in exile in Rome, had fixed himself as statutory goal "to study all questions of social economics in the light of Catholic doctrine and especially those concerning the workers, to discover the true principles, how the current economy can be measured against them and how to make them prevail at the core of all societies."[20] Found there among others were the Jesuit M. Liberatore[21] of *La Civiltà cattolica*, long concerned by the social problem, Msgr. Talamo,[22] one of the pioneers of neothomism in the field of legal philosophy, the German Dominican Denifle,[23] Count Blome, La Tour du Pin on occasion, and several extremely anti-Liberal Italian aristocrats. Contrary to what has sometimes been said, this group had absolutely no official status and received little if any support from the Curia,[24] but the Pope was kept informed of its doings.

* * *

Leo XIII had in fact been long interested in the workers question. Still young, as a nuncio in Belgium, he had become familiar with the questions raised by industrialization and the spread of capitalism. He had read and meditated on the works of Ketteler, whom he would one day call "my great predecessor." Already as bishop of Perugia, he had published in 1877 an episcopal mandate in which he denounced the "law of bronze" by virtue of which the contractor of physical labor ignored the man in the worker, and in it wishfully called for legislation "which puts a stop to this inhuman traffic."[25]

But beyond the problems of the working class, it is the entire "social question" which long retained his attention from the perspective of restoring the "Christian social order" destroyed by the French Revolution, child of the "Lumières" of the 18th century. For, contrary to what has often been claimed, Leo XIII was in no way an advocate of "modernity" and, in the first sentence of his 1891 encyclical, will yet stigmatize "the thirst for novelty which has taken hold of society."[26] Leo XIII meant to continue the combat begun by Pius IX against "modern society" as conceived of by the Liberals of his time, that is to say, on the one hand, a secularized and 'laicized' society, which believed that the Church should confine itself to helping individuals find eternal salvation without claiming to have a say in the organization of the society of this world, and, on the other hand, a society which had destroyed the intermediary bodies politic, leaving faceto-face only the State, organ of a small, wealthy minority, and the mass of exploited workers.

This combat for the restoration of a unified Christian social order, which alone could return happiness and peace to a society split into opposing camps, will be led by Leo XIII on two fronts: against Liberalism, which delivers isolated individuals into exploitation by the rich arbiters of economic and political power, a Liberalism whose dangers he will not cease to denounce if his legitimate aspirations are not regulated by the Church, interpreter of divine law; but equally against Socialism, in his eyes a cure worse than the disease, which, in his encyclical program of 28 December 1878 on the errors of modernity, he had stigmatized in these terms, which today seems like caricature to us:

> We are speaking of the sect of men who called themselves variously, and by almost barbarous names, socialists, communists, and nihilists. Spread across the earth, bound to each other by a pact of injustice, they no longer keep to the shadows of occult meetings, but appear without fear in the full light of day, laboring to bring to term their already ancient design, to ruin the foundations of all of civilized society.[27]

Condemning in one stroke Bakounine and the anarchists, very active in Italy at the time, who, in the name of their ideal of liberty, preach rebellion against all authority, in heaven and on earth, and the disciples of Proudhon ("property is theft"), of Karl Marx (private ownership of the means of production is at the root of all class struggles) and of Lassalle, or of Jules Guesde, he reproaches them for questioning the principle of authority and the right of ownership, "sanctioned by natural law," and for shaking the traditional foundation of society. This theme will at various times be taken up in his later writings, even where one would least expect to find them, for example in the encyclical *Aeterni Patris*, advocating a return to Thomist philosophy, in which one finds this declaration:

> Surely, the family and civilized society would enjoy a more perfect peace and a greater security if, in the universities and in the schools, were taught a doctrine more sane and more in conformity with the teachings of the Church, a doctrine such as that found in the works of St. Thomas Aquinas. What St. Thomas teaches us about the true nature of liberty, which nowadays is degenerating into license, about the divine origin of all authority, about the obedience due to one's superiors, about the mutual charity which must reign among men, what he tells us about these and other analogous subjects has power that is enormous, invincible, for overturning all these principles of the new law, full of danger for civil order and public safety.[28]

Leo XIII's reaction to the real and imagined excesses of socialism does not however prevent him from better realizing, as the years pass, that the social problems created by the increasing industrialization of the Western world are becoming more and more critical, and that the Church, in the name of morality, must intervene to propose a solution. He sees one in an adaptation of collaborative relationship between employers and workers that had existed before the French Revolution, at least in theory and as it was presented in the nostalgic, romantic historiography of the Middle Ages. Already in the encyclical *Quod apostilici*, alongside a reminder about the Socialists' intentions concerning the Church's teachings on private property, one sees appear, next to the intentional atomization of the workers' world by the Liberals, an encouragement to "societies of workers and craftsmen which, instituted under the patronage of religion, are able to render all their members content with their fate and resigned to working."[29] The point-of-view is still essentially religious and even clerical. Five years later, in the encyclical *Humanum genus* of April 20, 1884, against the Freemasons, Leo XIII encourages the return to "these workers' guilds destined to protect the interests of labor and the mores of the workers under the tutelage of religion."[30] In the following years, he comes back to this same theme in allocutions addressed now to the Christian employers, now to the pilgrimages of French workers in Rome, organized by Léon Harmel, demanding that there be restored "at least insofar as their substance, in their multiple and charitable virtues and in whatever form the new conditions of the times will permit, these arts and trades guilds which, in the past, informed by Christian thought and inspired by the maternal solicitude of the Church, providing for the material and religious needs of the workers, facilitated their labor, took care of their savings, and supported, in the desired measure, their legitimate demands."[31] It is seen that, more and more, it is not only the religious role of these guilds which is underscored, but the aid which they can bring to workers, organized for the purpose of backing, against the employers, their "legitimate demands." At the same time, the Pope begins to call attention to another theme: the aid that the public powers can and even must bring to the workers so that justice can reign in economic and social life. Thus, on the 18th of October 1887, after having evoked actions taken by the Church in the Middle Ages so that its concerns for the poor and working classes might penetrate into "the ordinances and laws of the publics powers," he declares:

> Doubtless, the intervention and action of these public powers are not of an indispensable necessity, when, in the conditions which rule the work and exercise of industry, there is encountered nothing that offends the morality, the justice, the human dignity, the domestic life of the worker. But, when one or the other of these blessings finds itself threatened or menaced, the public powers, by intervening appropriately and in just measure, will be doing work of social salvation, for it belongs to them to protect and to safeguard the true interests of the least of their citizens.[32]

And two years later, in October 1889, he names among his wishes measures in favor of the workers, especially the regulation of the labor of women and children, all the while inviting employers to no longer merely practice generous charity in favor of the poor but to observe "the rules of equitable justice" and to renounce the pursuit "of rapid and disproportionate profits."[33]

If Leo XIII was expressing himself more and more clearly on the Church's position *vis-a-vis* the workers problem, it is because he was, from the middle of the 1880s on, more and more often solicited to speak.

* * *

When in 1883, Msgr. Mermillod had managed to return to his diocese, he had ceded leadership of the Roman Social Committee to Msgr. Jacobini, but La Tour du Pin suggested that he organize an International Committee in Fribourg, where representatives from the Committee of Rome, the Council of Studies in Paris, and the German-speaking group of Catholics presided over by Löewenstein could meet and compare their views. Mermillod immediately accepted the proposal and, beginning in 1884, each year members of the three organizations met, constituting what was named the *Union of Fribourg*. The bishop, who presided over it, was greatly assisted by a Swiss layman, Gaspard Descurtins, who had translated the works of Ketteler into French and assiduously frequented Vogelsang, whose friend he was.

The result of these meetings was to reveal the conformity of tendencies among the different groups and to encourage them by permitting them to no longer work in a dispersed fashion. Little by little a complete social plan was elaborated, hostile to economic liberalism and even to a certain extent to the capitalist system itself, affirming the necessity of a reorganization of society on a corporative basis imposed by the state, demanding the intervention of the public powers to counterbalance the power of capital, and in particular to impose the payment of a just salary, hoping finally for an international understanding among governments for the legal protection of labor.[34]

Through the intermediary of Msgr. Mermillod, especially, Leo III was kept regularly informed of the works of the "Union of Fribourg." Elsewhere, he accumulated documentation, and we know that when, in the course of an audience, Catholics from diverse countries broached the social problem; he did not fail to ask that they submit to him a written report on the question. Gradually, the idea took shape of exposing the Holy Sees point-of-view on the matter, no longer just on the occasion of a discourse given before a small group of adherents, but in a document destined for the universal Church. We know that already in 1885, one day when Msgr. Jacobini was introducing to him René de La Tour du Pin, observing that he and those who thought like him were called socialists in certain Catholic circles, the Pope exclaimed: "Socialism! It's Christianity. Our adversaries do not suspect the fundamental principles of the Christian social order... Very well! The Pope will make it known to them. Wait for my next encyclical."[35]

If, however, it was necessary to wait six years more before the publication of *Rerum novrum,* it is that Leo XIII realized the complex character of the question. On one hand, he was well aware of the diversity of the social and economic conditions of various countries, and also of the fact that the workers question was only one aspect of the "social question," that is to say of the restoration of the society shaken to its foundation by the French Revolution and its aftermath; he judged it therefore necessary to clearly mark out the terrain with a series of encyclicals on the true Christian concept of society (to which *Rerum novarum* will refer furthermore in several instances): *Immortale Dei,* on the Christian make-up of States (November 1, 1885); *Libertas,* on the exact notion of freedom and liberties (June 20, 1888); *Sapientiae christianae,* on the principal civic duties of Christians (January 10, 1890). Moreover, this was the first time that the ecclesiastic Authority was going to take a position regarding the workers question, and Leo XIII knew very well that opinion was far from unanimous among Catholics as to the concrete solutions to be adopted to improve the situation of the workers, so he was careful to avoid giving the impression that the Holy See was inopportunely taking sides in academic discussions favoring any one solution among them.

However, various events came to reinforce him in the idea that intervention was becoming an urgent matter: the pilgrimages of *La France du Travail* (working France) to Rome, organized since 1885 by Léon Harmel with a view to bringing the working masses closer to the Pope and to putting the latter in direct contact with the world of the factory;[36] the mandate of the American Cardinal Gibbons, Archbishop of Baltimore, in 1887-88, with a view to avoiding condemnation by the Holy Office of the Knights of Labor, the first American workers organization, whose trappings of a secret society were reproached by certain bishops, which made them suspicious of a compromise with anarchism;[37] the support given in 1889 by Cardinal Manning, Archbishop of Westminster, to the London dock strike, which had repercussions throughout Europe;[38] emperor Wilhelm II's decision in 1890 to convene an international workers conference in Berlin,[39] and finally, in that same year 1890, a new flare-up, on the occasion of the Liège Social Congress, of the controversy opposing Catholics in favor of the State's intervention in social problems and those who were in principle opposed to all intervention of this sort and attached to the Liberal economy.

The Bishop of Liège, Msgr. Doutreloux,[40] aided by the professor of morals from his major seminary, Canon Pottier,[41] had organized international congresses in his episcopal city in 1886, 1887, and 1890, where social questions were widely discussed; German and Austrian participation was considerable and several of the organizers were in close contact with the "Union of Fribourg." Still in a timid fashion at the first two congresses, but much more clearly at the third, was affirmed the necessity of State intervention in social and economic life, and the legitimacy of unions charged with defending the workers' just demands vis-a-vis employers.[42] A segment of Catholic opinion rebelled against what seemed to it to be excessive concessions to socialism. There were among the opposition people who were very open-minded from a social point of view, but suspicious regarding all State intervention (this was the case notably of Léon Harmel); most however tended to be conservative and paternalistic. They gathered around the Bishop of Angers, Msgr. Freppel, who organized in response to the Congress of Liège another congress during the year 1890.[43] To the "School of Liège," the "School of Angers" responded in kind, and the controversy was threatening to escalate when, the following year, the Pope at last published the encyclical *Rerum novarum,* which came down on several important points in favor of the School of Liège.

* * *

The encyclical *Rerum novarum* is thus the result of multiple initiatives, which developed outside Rome, and we remark once more the importance of laymen in the concrete life of the Catholic Church. It remains nonetheless Leo XIII's work as well. On the manner in which his text was elaborated, we are fairly well informed because, relatively rare occurrence, the different preparatory drafts have been found.[44] It is in the beginning of the summer of 1890, doubtless spurred by William II's decision to convene an international conference on the problems of labor in Berlin, that the Pope, who never wrote his own encyclicals,[45] charged the Jesuit Liberatore with drawing up a draft. Not satisfied with it, he demanded another from the Dominican Cardinal Zigliara,[46] who submitted his text in September, a text considerably more developed (66 pages instead of 33). The Pope judged that this new draft remained too abstract and did not relate sufficiently to the concrete problems of the times. Liberatore was thus called on in November to rework the draft once more.[47] This third version, on which the Jesuit Cardinal Mazzella collaborated as well, was then translated from Italian into Latin by Msgr. Volpini, one of the Vatican's most distinguished Latinists. This was not an easy task, being a matter of expressing modern problems in an ancient tongue, and thus of either forging neologisms or finding adequate circumlocutions, "which respect the gravity of the Curia's style without however obfuscating the clarity of thought" (B. Riposati). This Latin version was completed on January 31, 1891, but according to the recollections of a contemporary, Leo XIII, after having carefully read and reread it, is to have declared: "Yes, here we have the entire subject, but the tone is wrong. It must be thrown out and redone yet again." It is Msgr. Boccali, one of the Pope's secretaries, who was charged with the task. Certain passages, to judge by the manuscripts found, were reworked another three or four times. This was notably the case for the initial sentence (*Rerum novarum...*), which only appeared in its definitive form in the last version, dated May 10, 1981.

In comparing these different versions, reread meticulously in each instance by the Pope himself, one observes that "the affirmation of a guild system gradually disappears and is replaced by professional associations."[48] The first draft by the Fr. Liberatore recommended in effect the restoration of a guild system, considered to be the only one consistent with the Christian social order. Zigliara rejected this system, which was a response to the views of the La Tour du Pin School and of the Austrian School, views sanctioned for the most part by the "Union of Fribourg." He limits himself to advocating the expansion of professional associations, to which, wary of the abuses of 'statism', he refuses to attribute a character of public domain, insisting on their free, private, and voluntary nature. The preferences of Zigliara and of those who revised his draft moved toward mixed associations, where employers and workers collaborate. But a few days before the publication of the encyclical, Leo XIII had an incidental clause added, specifying that the professional associations that he hoped to see growing more and more could be "either composed of workers only, or mixed, bringing workers and employers together at one time."[49] It is with good reason that Fr. Jarlot observes that this "very short insertion, seemingly insignificant, changed the direction of the encyclical."[50]

Moreover, if the initial option in favor of the State's intervention in economic and social life was maintained, upon meeting with the excessive liberalism of the School of Angers, the numerous nuances and hints introduced progressively into the text show well enough the hesitation with which the Holy See embarked on this path. To understand the reticence of Leo XIII one must realize that, while trying to act in the name of scholastic tradition, based on the common good, against an individualistic conception of society and property, he was careful not to show any of the totalitarian signs often found in the doctrinal socialism of his time. Moreover, as has already been said, he was very careful to respect freedom of discussion insofar as concrete solutions were concerned, and to limit himself to recalling the great principles of the tradition without imposing on the entire Church what amounted to an academic thesis. Finally, if the very clear recognition of the State's right to regulate economic and social life through legislative measures (recognition justified by long developments[51]) marks a decisive turning point in the history of social Catholicism, the Pope nevertheless advances only very prudently in this direction. He in no way imagines that the intervention of the public authorities could aim at changing the basic structures of the existing system . Their role is clearly more limited, for "they must not go forward nor undertake anything beyond that which is necessary to reprimand the abuses and avert the dangers." Obviously, Leo XIII did not wish to follow the much more radical path suggested by the "Union of Fribourg," whose members would have wished a condemnation of the capitalist system as such. As noted by Fr. Bédouelle during a recent colloquium of the French School of Rome, the encyclical *Rerum novarum* met the aspirations of the "Union of Fribourg" more than its inspirations, and historians have exaggerated the influence that it supposedly exercised on this first formulation of the Church's social doctrine.

* * *

Exalted in certain Catholic circles as the "workers' charter," the encyclical *Rerum novarum* was considered by others to be an essentially anti-socialist document, all in all one whose inspiration was rather reactionary, and one whose influence was in any case small in the workers emancipation movement.

It is certain that Leo XIII's interest in the workers question was in part inspired by the hope of finding for the Church, in the popular masses on their way to obtaining universal suffrage, a counterbalance to the anti-clerical politics so often practiced by the bourgeois secular state ['legal country'].[52] It is no less certain that the encyclical *Rerum novarum* was written from the perspective of restoring Christianity: social problems will not be solved until society is Christian once more. From this, "a series of moralizing sermons" (Candeloro) addressed as much to the poor as to the rich, and the less than angelic insistence on the necessity of fraternity between social classes to regulate the workers question. From this too, the fact that "the text is prisoner of a certain moral reformism, which fails to see that poverty in society is as much an objective social disorder as it is a moral problem"[53] and that, thereafter, the true roots of this evil, the structures of the concrete capitalist system such as it was at the end of the 19th century,[54] are only denounced in a superficial manner. Even a summary critical examination of the modern means of production is lacking, and the encyclical limits itself to developing abstract philosophical considerations at the point where, today, one would expect to find precise sociologic and economic analyses.[55] Particularly noteworthy is the absence of reflection on the notion of capital: the encyclical only speaks of employers, viewed as a social class, but it does not deal with capitalism from an economic perspective. As for its considerations of private property, these seem above all aimed at the possession of the family dwelling and of the small field beside it, in other words, that they are situated in the perspective of a relatively primitive agrarian economy without regard to the particular conditions which hold for industrial ownership in a complex capitalist economy. Add to this, along these same lines, that the treatment of socialism is highly superficial. It is identified with totalitarian communism or with anarchism, whereas by 1890, *Sozialdemokratie,* especially in Germany but not only in Germany, had already clearly distanced itself from these utopian currents; the encyclical, in its "metaphysical" defense of private property, seems particularly unaware of the problem that was at the heart of socialist thinking at the time—that of ownership of the means of production.

The encyclical *Rerum novarum* thus had without question its limitations and its weaknesses. However, it is necessary to recognize that it had its positive aspects as well, which should not be minimized.

In the first place, while most social Catholics of the preceding decades had been nostalgic for the traditional, preponderantly rural society, reacting against bourgeois society from a pre-capitalist perspective and advocating the return to a more-or-less modernized version of the traditional guild system (which was a dead-end at the level of the great modern industries), Leo XIII had the great merit of disengaging himself from these romantic utopias and taking his place alongside the realists, on [philosophical] ground analogous to that of reformist socialism, seeking the uplifting of the working class within the framework of existing institutions: he condemns neither wage-earning nor lending on interest, foundations of the capitalist system, but he affirms insistently that their functioning must respond to the demands of justice and that, to insure that justice is respected, an intervention by the State may prove to be legitimate and even unavoidable. He encourages moreover, to assure the protection of the workers faced with the power which capitalists and employers are tempted to abuse, the formation of professional associations, which can eventually take the modern form of labor unions.

It must be further observed that if Leo XIII's involvement came late—the founding of the first International had occurred more than a quarter century earlier—it was not something unimportant that for the first time the rights of workers and the injustice of the entire liberal system were solemnly proclaimed by the highest spiritual authority. Catholics were quite forced to admit, despite numerous reservations, that, faced with the conditions of "undeserved poverty" whose victims were the great mass of workers, a change was needed, and the most open-minded began to follow the path of Christian democracy. But the importance of Leo XIII's stance went far beyond Catholic circles. Assuredly, well before *Rerum novarum,* the labor movement was up and running and the credit for the initiative goes essentially to the socialists. But for the first time this labor movement received the solemn sanction of one of the principal forces of order in the world, and such a sanction was bound to help remove the revolutionary label which it had till then worn in the eyes of the great majority of the middle class. From the psychological point of view—and it is a point-of-view which has its historical importance—this was far from being trivial.

One can conclude that although the encyclical *Rerum novarum* reveals a still relatively timid attitude, and today appears at various points as manifestly obsolete, it at least opened certain doors and pointed the Catholic Church in the right direction. In spite of its imperfections, this first solemn pontifical document having for its object the problems of industrial society marked, for the later thought and actions of Catholics, a decisive step.

Notes

[1] See for example a certain number of articles by P. Droulers collected as a volume under the title *Cattolicesimo sociale nei secoli XIX e XX*, Rome, 1982, especially *L'épiscopat devant la question oouvrière en France sous la Monarchie de Juillet*, in *Revue historique*, t. CCIX, 1963, pp. 335-362, as well as the paragraph on "Les premieres réalisations sociales des catholiques allemands," in R. Aubert, *Le pontificat de Pie IX*, Paris, 1952, pp. 488-89.

[2] Cf. P. Droulers, *Question sociale, Église, État, dans "La Civiltà cattolica" à ses debuts*, in *Chiesa e Stato nell'Ottocento. Miscellanea in onore di P. Pirri*, Padoue, 1962, pp. 123-47.

[3] Proposition 58, which denounces the exclusion of morality from the relations between capital and labor.

[4] See among others the nuanced article by J. Lecler, *Les catholiques libéreaux et la question sociale en 1848*, in *Études*, February 1948, pp. 145-65.

[5] This aspect, long lost from sight, has often been stressed by recent historiography. One will find discussions suggestive of this view in the work of É. Poulat, *Église contre bourgeoisie*, Tournai-Paris, 1977, in particular chapter 5: "Un conflit triangulaire."

[6] See A. Gambasin's fundamental study, *Il movimento sociale nell'Opera dei Congressi (1874-1904)*, Rome, 1958. Since then, numerous monographs have studied the diverse regional manifestations of the movement. See also the recent synthesis by S. Agocs, *The troubled origins of the Italian Labour Movement, 1878-1914*, Detroit, 1988, as well as the *Dizionario storico del Movimento cattolico in Italia*, under the direction of Fr. Traniello and G. Campanini, Turin, 1981-1984, especially t. I, vol. 1 and 2: *I fatti e le idee*.

[7] Long neglected by official historiography, Giuseppe Toniolo (1845-1918), professor of the University of Pisa, is for the past few years the subject of renewed interest. See especially: P. Pecorari, *Giuseppe Toniolo et il socialismo*, Bologna, 1981; S. Burgalassi, *Alle origini della Sociologia: G. Toniolo e la scuola pisana (1878-1918)*, Pisa, 1984; D. Sorrentino, *G. Toniolo. Una biografia*, Milan, 1988; A. Spicciani, *G. Toniolo tra economia e storia*, Naples, 1990.

[8] On Albert de Mun (1841-1914), see R. Talmy, *Albert de Mun. Introduction et choix de textes*, Paris, 1964; Ch. Molette, *Albert de Mun, 1872-1890. Exigences doctrinales et préoccupations sociales chez un laïc catholique d'après des documents inédits*, Paris, 1970; Ph. Levillain, *Albert de Mun. Catholicisme français et catholicisme romain du Syllabus au ralliement*, Paris-Rome, 1983.

[9] On René de la Tour du Pin (1834-1924), see R. Talmy's thesis, which refers to numerous unpublished documents: *Aux sources du catholicisme social. L'École de La Tour du Pin,* Tournai-Paris, 1983.

[10] See A. Louant's account of him in the *Biographie Nationale* (of Belgium), t. XXX, col. 665-71, as well as R. Kothen, *La pensée et l'action sociale des catholiques,* Louvain, 1945, pp. 139-150.

[11] Besides his definitive biography by F. Vigener, *Ketteler. Ein deutches Bischofsleben aus dem XIX. Jahrhundert,* Munich, 1924, see especially: L. Lenhart, *Bischof Ketteler. Staatspolitiker, Sozialpolitiker, Kirchenpolitiker,* t. I, Mainz, 1966; R.J. Ederer, *The social teachings of W.E. von Ketteler,* Washington, 1981; E. Iserloh, *W.E. von Ketteler, sein Kampf ür Freiheit and soziale Gerechtigkeit,* Stuttgart, 1987.

[12] The Catholics of Germany adopted all the more easily these anti-capitalist positions in that the most dynamic elements of the Catholic community came, more so than in Italy or in France, from socially modest backgrounds (farmers, craftsmen, laborers), and in that, additionally, the general hostility toward the bourgeoisie increased during the *Kulturkampf,* of which the Catholic Church was a victim in the years 1870-80. See especially: B.H.A. Hermans, *Das Problem der Sozialpolitik und Sozialreform aus den deutschen Katholikentagen von 1848 bis 1891. Ein Beitrag zur Geschichte der katholisch-sozialen Bewegung,* Bonn 1972; E. Ritter, *Die katholisch-soziale Bewegung Deutschlands im 19. Jahrhundert und der Volksverein,* Cologne, 1954; E. Hanisch, *Konservatives und revolutionäres Denken. Deutsche Sozial-Katholiken and Sozialisten im 19. Jahrhundert,* Vienna-Salzburg, 1975; *Geschichte der christlich-demokratischen und christlich-sozialen Bewegungen in Deutschland,* t. I, Cologne, 1986.

[13] On Karl von Vogelsang (1818-90) and his school, see J.Ch. Allmayerbeck, *Vogelsang. Vom Feudalismus zur Volksbewegung,* Vienna, 1952.

[14] Cf. A.M. Knoll, *Der soziale Gedanke im modernen Katholizismus. Von der Romantik bis "Rerum novarum,"* Vienna-Leipzig, 1932, pp. 96-98 and pp. 132-143, as well as R. Kothen, *op. cit.,* pp. 203-12.

[15] On Gustav von Blome (1829-1906), see A. von Briczo, *Graf G. Blome, ein oesterreichischer Sozialreformer,* in *Jahrbuch der Vereinigung katholischer Edelleute in Oesterreich,* Vienne, 1930, and *Neue Deutsche Biographie,* t. II, p. 315.

[16] On Franz von Kuefstein (1841-1918), son of the president of the Austrian House of Lords, a former miltary man influenced by the ideas of Msgr. Ketteler, see *Oesterreichisches biographisches Lexikon, 1815-1950,* t. IV, Vienna-Colongne, 1969, p. 321. He was the author of several works on political economics, notably *Die Familie und die Volkswirtschaft* (1877) and *Die Entwicklung zur Weltwirtschaft* (1879).

[17] On Fr. Alphonse Villeneuve (1843-98)—whom G. Jarlot confused with the future cardinal archbishop of Québec, Rodrigue Villeneuve—see É. Poulat, *Catholicisme, démocratie et socialisme,* Tournai-Paris, 1977, pp. 143-44.

[18] On him, see M. Casella, *Il Cardinale Domenico Maria Jacobini (1837-1900),* in *Rassegna storica del Risorgimento,* t. LVIII, 1971, pp. 557-617, especially pp. 590-93.

[19] On the future cardinal Gaspard Mermillod (1824-1892), see Ch. Comte, *Le cardinal Mermillod d'après sa correspondance,* Paris, 1924, and J. Gadille, in *Dictionnaire de Spiritualité,* t. X, col. 1053-55.

[20] Cited by H. Rollet, *L'action sociale des catholiques en France (1871-1901)*, Paris, 1947, p. 109. On this Roman circle, see especially: S. Tramontin, *Un secolo di storia della Chiesa*, t. II, Rome, 1980, pp. 75-76.

[21] On Matteo Liberatore (1810-1892), one of the guiding forces of *La Civiltà cattolica* for forty years and one of the crafters of the Thomist revival, see T. Mirabella, *Il pensieero politico di P. M. Liberatore ed il suo contributo ai rapporti tra Chiesa e Stato*, Milan, 1956; on his influence in the realm of social ideas, see in particular pp. 283-346.

[22] On Salvatore Talamo (1844-1932), professor of philosophy at the seminary of Naples, called to Rome by Leo XIII in 1879 as professor of philosophy of law at the Apollinaris, see A. Piolanti, *La Filosofia cristiana in Mons. S. Talamo, inspiratore della "Aeterni Patris"* (Studi tomistici, 29), Vatican City, 1986, in particular pp. 21-22: "Il sociologo cristiano," as well as F. Duchini, in *Dizionario storico del Movimento cattolico in Italia*, under the direction of F. Traniello and G. Campanini, t. II, *I Protagonisti*, Casale Monferrato, 1982, pp. 633-635, which affirms that "the desire to interpret the complete reality of a society in transformation seen by the light of Christian philosophy is particularly present in the numerous articles that Talamo published from 1874 to 1893 in the review *Scienza e Fede*."

[23] The Austrian Dominican Heinrich Denifle (1844-1905), specialist in scholasticism and in medieval mysticism and curator of the Vatican Archives, was also socius to the general of the Dominicans and in close contact with the group from the Austrian church of the Anima in Rome. See on him A. Walz, in *Dictionnaire d' Histoire et de Géographie ecclésiastiques*, t. XIV, col. 221-245, and A. Redigonda, *Il P.E. Denifle, O.P. Cenni biografici e alcune lettere*, Florence, 1953.

[24] Kuefstein affirms that when he tried to form a committee for the study of social questions in Rome, he got no response from the Vatican (cf. Zanata [= A. De Gasperi] *l tempi e gli uomini che prepararono la "Rerum novarum,"* Milan, 1928 [1941], p. 140 sq.). And G. Goyau reports the following: "I saw Father Villeneuve. He told me that in 1882, when he founded the Union of Social Studies in Rome with Count Kuefstein, they went to make known their intentions to Cardinal Pecci, brother of the Pope. The Cardinal began to laugh and told them: 'I well understand what you are trying to do, but it will take a lot of courage. Do you think the other cardinals worry about the social question?' And indeed several cardinals shrugged their shoulders" (letter of 19 April 1893, cited in J.Ph. Heuzey-Goyau, *Dieu premier servi, G. Goyau*, Paris, 1947, p. 115.)

[25] Cf. M. Spahn, *Leo X111*, Munich, 1905, pp. 185-194, and J.-M. Mayeur, *Catholicisme social et démocratie chrétienne*, Paris, 1986, pp. 47-48.

[26] "Rerum novarum semel excitata cupidine, quae din quidem commovet civitates."

[27] *A.S.S.*, t. XI, 1878-79, p. 369.

[28] On this "conservative" aspect of the Thomist restoration, see especially the work, arguable but in spite of all provocative, by P. Thibault, *Savoir et pouvoir. Philosophie thomiste et politique cléricale au XIXe siècle*, Québec, 1972 (and the commentary by É. Poulat, in *Archives de sciences soeiales des religions*, t. XXXVII, 1974, pp. 5-21).

[29] *A.S.S.*, t. XI, 1878-79, p. 376.

[30] *A.S.S.*, t. XVI, 1883-84, p. 431. And he pursues: "We ardently hope to see them reestablished, under the auspices or the patronage of the bishops, these guilds appropriated for the needs of the present. This is no small joy for Us to have seen

associations of this type formed in several places, as well as societies of employers; the aim of both being to come to the aid of the honest class of proletariats, to assure their families and their children the benefits of a nurturing patronage, to furnish them with the means of keeping, along with good morals, familiarity with religion and the love of piety."

[31] *Leonis Papae Xlll, Allocutiones...*, t. III, *1887-89*, Bruges, 1893, pp. 280-285.

[32] *Ibid*, pp. 13-15.

[33] *Ibid.*, p. 283.

[34] See, C. Massard, *L'œuvre sociale de Mgr Mermillod: l'Union de Fribourg d'après les documents inédits*, Louvain, 1914, as well as G. Jarlot, *Doctrine pontificale et histoire. L'enseignement social de Léon Xlll, Pie X et Benoit XV, vu dons son ambiance historique*, Rome, 1964, pp. 195-203. For the last point, see J. Joblin, *L'appel de l'Union de Fribourg à Léon XIII en faveur d'une législation internationale du travail*, in *Archivum historiae pontificiae*, t. XXVIII, 1990, pp. 357-72.

[35] Cf. G. Hoog, *Histoire du catholicisme social en France (1871-1931)*, Paris, 1946, pp. 24-25, and Ph. Levillain, *Albert de Mun*, pp. 801-803.

[36] On Léon Harmel (1829-1915), who was not a theoretician but a doer and a man of action, see G. Guitton, *Léon Harmel*, Paris, 1927. On the "Pilgrimages of Working France," see also G. Hoog, *Histoire du catholicisme social en France (1871-1931)*, Paris, 1946, pp. 37-39.

[37] On this intervention, see the work by H.J. Browne, *The Catholic Church and the Knights of Labour*, Washington, 1949. This work, written from original sources, while still emphasizing the role played under the circumstances by the archbishop of Baltimore, "demythified" somewhat the latter's image as a pioneer of the Christian social movement. Indeed, although Gibbons lucidly discerned how much a condemnation of the *Knights of Labor* would have discredited the Church in the eyes of labor, he never positively supported their actions and, unlike Manning, he cannot be considered, contrary to a widespread cliche, a champion of workers' causes.

[38] See E.S. Purcell, *Life of cardinal Manning*, London, 1896, t. II, pp. 638-671. Manning's role in social work is also brought to light by V.A. McClelland, *Cardinal Manning. His public life and influence (1865-1892)*, London, 1962.

[39] See M. Baumont, *L'essor industriel et l'impérialisme colonial, 1878-1904 (Peuples et civilisations*, XVIII, Paris), 1937, pp. 452-453; J. Joblin, *L'Église et la guerre*, Paris, 1988, p. 224 and 259; as well as *La lettera dell'Imperatore Guglielmo ll e la riposta del Papa*, in *La Civiltà cattolica*, Ser. XIV, vol. VI, 1890, pp. 178-82 (the Holy See, which had at the time no official international status, was not invited to send a representative to the Berlin Conference, but Wilhelm II informed Leo XIII of his initiative).

[40] On Victor-Joseph Doutreloux (1837-1901), see P. Gérin, in *Dictionnaire d'histoire et de géographie ecclésiastiques*, t. XIV, col. 748-51.

[41] On Antoine Pottier (1849-1923), see J.-L. Jadoulle, *La pensée de l'abbé Pottier. Contribution à l'histoire de la Démocratie chrétienne en Belgique*, Louvain-la-Neuve, 1991.

[42] Cf. P. Gerin, *Les origines de la démocratie chrétienne à Liége*, Bruxelles-Paris, 1958, pp. 87-101.

[43] Cf. R. Kothen, *op. cit.*, pp. 292-302, and G. Guitton, *Léon Harmel*, t. I, p. 134 sq. and t. II, p. 50 sq.

[44] See the capital work by G. Antonazzi, *L'enciclica "Rerum novarum," testo autentico e redazioni preparatorie dai documenti originali,* Rome, 1957 (its conclusions are summed up by B. Riposati in *Vita e pensiero,* t. XL, 1957, pp. 626-635, French translation in *La Documentation catholique,* t. LV, 1958, col. 53-62). It is Msgr. Tardini who had searched for and found the precious dossier in question (cf. C.F. Casula, *Domenico Tardini,* Rome, 1988, pp. 255-56).

[45] On his method of preparing encyclicals, see B. Riposati, *art.cit.* (Fr. translation in *La Documentation catholique,* t. LV, 1958, col. 56), which refers notably to a work by Msgr. V. Tarozzi *(Un segretaro di Papa Leone XIII,* Bologna, 1919, p. 98): "He almost never wrote anything: he would give ideas, organize the work, and indicate how it should develop and in what direction, even dictate the most delicate points and leave to his secretaries the editing of the actual text; this text, before taking definitive form, written and re-written, corrected and re-corrected several times, would pass again and again under his gaze, which never seemed satisfied, and here he would lend order to ideas, there underline errors of style and spelling, now he would insert small spaces and indentations to make transitions clearer, now he would note one or another point to make stand out in a distinct fashion."

[46] On Tommaso Maria Zigliara (1833-1893), one of the principal promoters of the Thomist revival in Rome, prefect of the Congregation of the Studies from 1889, see *Dictionnaire de théologie catholique,* t. XV, col. 3692-94, and G. Marco in *Memorie domenicane,* new series, t. VI, 1975, pp. 167-339.

[47] On this new contribution from Liberatore, whose role was ultimately decisive, see S. Lombardi, *"La Civiltà cattolica" e la stesura della "Rerum novarum." Nuovi documenti sul contributo del P. M. Liberatore,* in *La Civiltà cattolica,* 1982, vol. I, pp. 471-76.

[48] Cf. G. Jarlot, *Les avant-projets de "Rerum novarum" et les anciennes corporations,* in *Nouvelle Revue Théologique,* t. LXXXI, 1959, pp. 60-77.

[49] It is between April 21 and May 10 that, to the sentence "Vulgo coiri ejus generis societates gratum est" was added the famous incidental clause: "sive totas ex opificibus conflatas, sive ex utroque ordine mixtas" (lines 1613-15). ["It is gratifying to know that there are actually in existence not a few associations of this nature, consisting either of workmen alone, or, of workmen and employers together."]

[50] *Doctrine pontificale et histoire, op. cit.* (note 34), p. 214. Could this last-minute addition be the result of Cardinal Gibbons' influence, as suggested by G. Jarlot, *ibid.,* p. 214, and by B. Lai, *Finanze e finanzieri vaticani fra 1'800 e il 900,* Milan, 1979, pp. 140-41, n. 1? Perhaps we need to recognize the influence of Msgr. Satoli, former apostolic delegate to the United States (cfr. Daniel-Rops, *Un combat pour Dieu,* Paris, 1963, p. 229 and n. 33).

[51] In particular, it is in the name of defending the dignity of the human being that the State has the right and the duty to intervene. To be noted moreover that, in Leo XIII's view, the State, charged with safeguarding the common good, must be subordinate to the Church in all matters concerning man's highest purpose, including the material conditions of his life (on this last point, see especially: J. L. Jadoulle, *La pensée de l'abbé Pottier,* pp. 46-48).

[52] The Italian communist historian G. Candeloro calls this "anti-bourgeois demagogy" *(La doctrine sociale chrétienne et l'encyclique "Rerum novarum," in Recherches internationales à la lumiére du marxisme,* n. 6, March-April 1958, p. 112). It must be remembered that, at the end of the 19th century, in many regions the decris-

tianization of workers was far less advanced than certain recent socio-historians have asserted, having too hastily generalized a few situations belonging to certain regions of France.

[53] J. Famerée, *De "Rerum novarum" à "Octogesima Adveniens,"* in *Nouvelle Revue Théologique,* t. CIV, 1982, p. 89.

[54] That is to say, in the framework of pure and simple economic liberalism, before it was increasingly amended by a century of social-democracy.

[55] See for example L. Duquesne de la Vinelle, *Le Marché et la Justice. A partir d'une lecture critique des encycliques,* Gembloux, 1987, chap. I. He concludes, p. 15: "These observations in no way cast doubt on the social philosophy of the encyclical. But they do suggest the existence of a gap between its philosophic thought and its concrete recommendations. The latter would doubtless have been different and less ambiguous if they had been supported by a less inexact understanding and a less rudimentary analyses of the problems of economic organization." As for sociological analyses, they are not completely absent from *Rerum novarum* (cf. P. de Laubier, in *L'Église et la question sociale aujourd'hui,* under the direction of O. Hoeffe, Fribourg, 1984, pp. 84-87), but they remain rather superficial.

The Great Themes
of the Social Teachings of the Popes
from Leo XIII to Paul VI
1992

There has been an incontestable continuity in the social teachings of
the Popes for the last century, continuity which they took to heart
to underline in the very titles of their great social encyclicals, which
look back explicitly to the seminal document that was *Rerum novarum: Quadragesimo anno, Octogesima adveniens, Centesimus annus*:
they obviously mean to situate themselves in the tradition of Leo
XIII's encyclical. Still, the various pontifical documents treating the
social question are not limited to repeating what Leo XIII had said.
An evolution can be observed, explainable by three factors. First,
the particular personalities of the various Popes, each of whom ap-
proached the question from his own point of view. Next, the fact
that the more that Catholic theologians and sociologists explored the
exigencies of social justice in the light of Holy Scripture and social
philosophy, the more they discovered the complexity of the problem:
new reflections led to asking new questions and the popes tried to
contribute elements of the response. And finally, and foremost, the
fact that in one hundred years the givens of the social problem have
changed profoundly, because social and economic reality itself has
been profoundly transformed, which has necessitated a nuancing and
occasionally a modification of initially stated positions (for, if man
remains in pure abstraction, one always takes a position in relation
to something and indeed, most often, in opposition to something).
The capitalism of small and mid-sized businesses of the second half
of the 19th century, in which employers generally had the possibility
of maintaining "human" relations with the worker, evolved over the

course of the first half of the 20th century into something that Pius XI called "hypercapitalism," a capitalism centered on a few oligopolies and multinational corporations, in which relations between the executives at the top and the tens of thousands of salaried employees dispersed across several continents become impossible, and in which financial games increasingly take priority in the decision-making of executive boards. Socialism, for its part, likewise evolved a great deal between the foundation of the First International and the end of the 20th century: from its revolutionary beginnings, of which the Paris Commune of 1879-71 was the symbol for Leo XIII's contemporaries, it gradually changed into "social-democratic" reformism, denounced with disgust by the communists, and then even became, more and more, a workers' humanism, separated from all anti-religious ideology, which explains why an increasing number of Christians look sympathetically on the idea of reconciliation and even collaboration.

* * *

The Encyclical *Rerum novarum*: Culmination of a Slow Maturation

The first "social" encyclical, which was published in May 1891 by Leo XII, was, to use an expression of Jean-Marie Mayeur recently taken up by René Rémond at the international colloquium on the encyclical organized by the French School of Rome, a "foundation text": it in fact constituted a point of departure for later reflection by Catholic theologians and sociologists, and at the same time for the more-and-more decisive action of the Christian Democrats, anxious to react against the "undeserved poverty" of the working class. Still, as is often the case with pontifical documents, this encyclical was also situated in a continuum: not only did it inscribe itself as a new element in the overall project to restore Christian society that Leo XIII had elaborated bit by bit from the beginning of his pontificate,[1] but it moreover consecrated a series of initiatives, both doctrinal and practical, taken more or less everywhere, over the course of the two preceding decades, by the ecclesiastical community—bishops, priests, and clergy, but also laity—animated by the desire to translate the evangelical message into the daily life of the society of their times.

The leadership of both ecclesiastics and laity had taken a long time to become aware of the problems posed to Christian reflection by the Industrial Revolution, which progressively substituted for traditional rural society an increasingly urban world, built around factories and capitalist institutions, and in which the living conditions of the working masses had changed profoundly. Contrary to what has long been thought, the precursors of modern social Catholicism, which found its first official expression in the encyclical *Rerum novarum,* were not the Liberal Catholics, those champions of democracy faced with an ecclesiastic hierarchy which was for the most part allergic to the "principles of 1789," but were rather to be found among men who at first glance seem to be "reactionaires." They in fact were from several points of view—and who doubly detested—because they were anti-clerical and because they would have substituted the power of money for traditional social authority—the Liberal bourgeois oligarchy that then dominated the business world.

One finds Catholics concerned with social problems in the years 1870-80 in Italy gathered around Professor Toniolo, and in France around Albert de Mun and René de La Tour du Pin, but it is especially in the Germanic countries, even though industrialization came later there, that the most realistic Catholic social movement is located, one favoring limitations on economic liberty through social legislation. One man played an especially important role in this process: Msgr. Ketteler, Bishop of Mainz,[2] who appears as the first theoretician of corporatively-based organic social organicism, which will constitute for more than half a century the foundation of Catholic social doctrine. But, while awaiting the eventual corporative reorganization of the working class, Ketteler applied himself tirelessly to the encouragement and promotion of progressive social legislation, not hesitating to call on State intervention to defend the workers against the abuses of Liberalism. Inspired by his suggestions, the *Zentrumspartei,* which included a good many German Catholics in the Parliament, allied with the Socialists to pass a series of social laws that gave Germany a notable head-start on other countries in this arena.

The ideas put forth by Ketteler did not take long to spread beyond Germany. In Austria, between 1883 and 1888, a group of young Catholics elaborated what is called the "theses of Haid," in which it was among others affirmed that the labor contract is of a completely different nature from the property contract, because of the moral aspect of human activity, and that salary must be determined taking into account the essential needs of the worker and his family. At the same time, an Austrian noble of the same group, Count Kuefstein, who spent winters in Rome, there started with the help of a young and very dynamic prelate of the curia, Msgr. D. Jacobini, a circle of social studies presided over by a Swiss bishop expelled from Geneva by an anti-clerical government, Msgr. Mermillod. This group had no official status, but the Pope, who had long been interested in the question,[3] was kept regularly informed of its doings. When, in 1883, Msgr. Mermillod was able to return to his diocese, La Tour du Pin suggested that he organize an International Committee where representatives from the Committee of Rome, the Council of Studies in Paris, and the Haid group could meet and compare their views. The result of these annual meetings was to demonstrate the general conformity of tendencies among the different groups (who remained nevertheless a tiny minority among their fellow Catholics).

Through the intermediary of Msgr. Mermillod, relations with Rome were frequent and, from year to year, Leo XIII became more and more decided on taking an official position. Various and further events came to reinforce him in the idea that intervention was becoming an urgent matter: the pilgrimages of *La France du Travail* ("working France") to Rome, organized since 1885 by the model Catholic patron Léon Harmel with a view to bringing the Pope into direct contact with the world of the factory; the mandate of the American Cardinal Gibbons, Archbishop of Baltimore, in 1887-88, with a view to avoiding condemnation by the Holy Office of the Knights of Labor, the first American workers organization, which was suspected of anarchism by certain bishops; the support given in 1889 by Cardinal Manning, Archbishop of Westminster, to the London dock strike, which had repercussions throughout Europe; Emperor Wilhelm II's initiative in 1890 to convene an international workers conference in Berlin; and finally, in 1890, on the occasion of the third Congress of Social Works called to meet in Liège by Msgr. Doutreloux, a new flare-up of the controversy that, in the eyes of paternalistic liberal Catholics led by Msgr. Freppel, Bishop of Angers, for whom the solution to the workers question was strictly a matter of charity, opposed the idea of the necessity of State intervention in economic and social life and the idea of the legitimacy of unions charged with defending the workers' just demands vis-a-vis the employers.

As to the way in which the text of the encyclical was elaborated between July 1890 and May 1891, we are fairly well informed because the various preparatory drafts have been found in the Vatican archives.[4] From the first draft written by the Jesuit Liberatore, to the new version done by the Dominican Zigliara, afterwards reworked by Fr. Liberatore with the collaboration of Cardinal Mazella, and finally to the definitive text minutely reviewed by the Pope himself, we can see how the idea of a guild system gradually gives way to one of professional associations. It can likewise be observed that, if the initial option in favor of State intervention in economic and social life was maintained against the excessive Liberalism of the School of Angers, the numerous nuances and hints introduced progressively into the text show well enough the prudence and hesitation with which the Holy See embarked on this path, careful not to give any sign of the totalitarian tendencies often found in the socialism of the era.

The encyclical opened with an introduction deploring "the thirst for novelty which has taken hold of society" ("Rerum novarum excitata cupidine") and announcing the intention of refuting erroneous opinions concerning the condition of the workers by opposing them with the Catholic doctrine on the subject. The Pope began with a severe criticism of the effects of economic liberalism, preached and practiced "by men greedy for profit, men with an insatiable cupidity," but he rejected the socialist solution even more energetically, because its basic principle, the substitution of collective property for private property, is "absolutely to be repudiated" as being contrary to natural law: "let it therefore be well established that the first principle to be put forth by all who sincerely desire the good of the people, is the inviolability of private property."

While still recognizing that the current situation has "divided the body public into two classes and dug an abyss between them," the Pope reproves "the capitalist error, which consists of believing that the two classes are enemies of each other, as if nature had armed the rich and the poor so that they might combat mutually in an obstinate duel." He likewise reacted against egalitarian utopias:

> It is impossible that, in civilized society, everyone should rise to the same level. Doubtless, this is what the Socialists were after; but against nature, all efforts are in vain. It is nature, in effect, which has distributed among men differences as varied as they are profound: differences of intelligence, of talent, of ability, of health, of strength; necessary differences, from which unequal conditions are spontaneously born.

And the Pope reminds us that "pain and suffering are the lot of humanity," that this earth remains "a place of exile," and that "it is only when we will have quit this life that we shall begin to live." But, this said, "let no one think that the Church is so absorbed with the care of souls, that it neglects that which pertains to terrestrial life." Much to the contrary, "in particular for the working class, the Church makes every effort to extract them from their poverty and procure for them a better fate." It means to react against the abuses of the present system, and the majority of the encyclical is dedicated to sketching several fundamental positions based on the Thomist distinction between *dominium* and *usus*: it is important to distinguish between the rightful ownership of riches and their legitimate use.

If, contrary to socialism's aims as understood by the Pope, economic society must rest on the right of private property and free will, capitalism nevertheless cannot be given free reign: economics must be subordinated to ethics. This is true for example insofar as the labor contract is concerned, the exigencies of justice give it precedence over application of the famous basic principle of economic liberalism, "laissez faire, laissez passer" ("don't interfere, let it pass"):

> Let the employer and the worker therefore make as many and as varied agreements as they please, let them notably agree on the amount of salaries, above and beyond their free will there is a higher and an older law of natural justice, to wit, that salary must not be insufficient to the sober and honest subsistence of the worker. If, constrained by necessity or spurred by fear of a greater evil, he accepts difficult working conditions which, besides, it was not lawful

for him to refuse, because they are imposed on him by the employer
or the one who makes the offer of employment, this is suffering a
violence against which justice protests.

Now, to uphold respect for the exigencies of justice - not only in the
matter of fair salary, but equally to protect the Sunday rest, to limit the
work day taking into account the relative difficulty of various jobs, to
limit or, when necessary, forbid the labor of women and children - a
certain involvement of the State, guardian of the common good, is
necessary. Historical development justifies this intervention. Assuredly,
the State cannot absorb the individual or the family, but it is its duty to
protect the rights of all citizens and in particular the weakest of them,
who have only it to shelter them from injustices. Legislative action
seeking to protect workers' rights is all the more justified in that the
labor of the proletariat, peasants and workers, "has such fecundity and
such efficaciousness that one can state, without fear of error, that it is
the unique source from which springs the prosperity of nations."

This very clear recognition of the State's right to intervene through
legislative measures regulating economic and social life marks a decisive
turning point in the history of Social Catholicism. The Pope, however
only proceeds in this direction very cautiously. He in no way imagines
that the interventions of the public powers could aim at modifying
the basic structures of the existing system. Their role is clearly more
limited, because "they must neither advance nor undertake anything
beyond what is necessary to repress abuses and prevent dangers."
Obviously, Leo XIII did not try to take the much more radical path
suggested by the Union of Fribourg, whose members would have
wished for a condemnation of the capitalist system *per se*. As stated
by Fr. Bédouelle during a recent colloquium of the French School of
Rome, the encyclical *Rerum novarum* met the aspirations of the Union
of Fribourg more than its inspirations, and historians have exaggerated
the influence that it supposedly exercised on this first formulation of
the Church's social doctrine.

It is especially with a view to skirting the always-threatening
peril of the totalitarian state that the Pope insists on the utility of the
intermediary bodies-public, which had been suppressed by the Revolution of 1789. It is not a matter, as the Union of Fribourg would have
wished, of re-establishing the guild system, but instead of developing

professional associations, to which, still wary in regards to 'statism,' he refuses to attribute a character of public domain, insisting on their free, private, and voluntary nature. In the schema elaborated by Zigliara and reviewed by Liberatore, it was specified that these professional associations should be "mixed," that is to say they should encompass employers and workers. But a few days before the publication of the encyclical, Leo XIII had an incidental clause added, specifying that the professional associations that he hoped to see steadily growing could be "either composed of workers only, or mixed, bringing workers and employers together at one time." It is with good reason Fr. Jarlot observes that this "fiery short insertion, seemingly insignificant, changed the direction of the encyclical"[5] by according pontifical approval to modern labor unions. Certainly, the encyclical affirmed that these professional associations, which normally would be confessional, must "aim above all at the moral and religious education" of the workers, but the encyclical added that these associations must not be limited to this plan and it also invokes their functions in the matter of aid and assistance, as well as mediation in the case of conflicts between employers and workers.

Exalted in certain Catholic circles as the "workers' charter," the encyclical *Rerum novarum* was considered by others to be an essentially anti-socialist document, all in all one whose inspiration was rather reactionary, and one whose influence in the workers emancipation movement was in any case minimal.

It is certain that Leo XIII's interest in the workers question was in part inspired by the hope of finding for the Church, in the popular masses on their way to obtaining universal suffrage, a counterbalance to the anti-clerical politics so often practiced by the bourgeois secular state ['legal country']. It is no less certain that the encyclical *Rerum novarum* was written from the perspective of restoring Christianity: social problems will not be solved until society is Christian once more. From this, "a series of moralizing sermons" addressed as much to the poor as to the rich,[6] and the less than angelic insistence on the necessity of fraternity between social classes to regulate the workers question.

From this too, the fact that "the text is prisoner of a certain moral reformism, which fails to see that poverty in society is as much an objective social disorder as it is a moral problem"[7] and that, thereafter, the true roots of this evil, the structures of the concrete capitalist system such as it was at the end of the 19ᵗʰ century, are only denounced in a superficial manner. Even a summary critical examination of the modern means of production is lacking, and the encyclical limits itself to developing abstract philosophical considerations at the point where, today, one would expect to find precise sociologic and economic analyses. Particularly noteworthy is the absence of reflection on the notion of capital: the encyclical only speaks of capitalists, viewed as a social class, but it does not deal with capitalism from an economic perspective. As for its considerations of private property, these seem above all aimed at the possession of the family dwelling and of the small field beside it, in other words, that they are situated in the perspective of a relatively primitive agrarian economy without regard to the particular conditions which hold for industrial ownership in a complex capitalist economy. Add to this, along these same lines, that the treatment of socialism is highly superficial. It is identified with totalitarian communism or with anarchism, whereas by 1890 *Sozialdemokratie,* especially in Germany but not only in Germany, had already clearly distanced itself from these utopian currents; the encyclical, in its "metaphysical" defense of private property, seems particularly unaware of the problem which was at the heart of socialist thinking at the time, that of ownership of the means of production.

The encyclical *Rerum novarum* thus had without question its limitations and its weaknesses. But it is necessary to recognize that it had its positive aspects as well, which should not be minimized.

In the first place, while most social Catholics of the preceding decades had been nostalgic for the traditional, preponderantly rural society, reacting against bourgeois society from a pre-capitalist perspective and advocating the return to a more-or-less modernized version of the traditional guild system (which was a dead-end at the level of the great modern industries), Leo XIII had the great merit of disengaging himself from these romantic utopias and taking his place alongside the realists, on [philosophical] ground analogous to that of reformist socialism, seeking the uplifting of the working class within the framework of existing institutions: he condemns neither wage-earning nor lending on interest, foundations of the capitalist system, but he affirms insistently that their functioning must respond to the demands of justice and that, to insure that justice is respected, an intervention by the State may prove to be legitimate and even unavoidable. He encourages moreover, to assure the protection of the workers faced with the power which capitalists and employers are tempted to abuse, the formation of professional associations, which can eventually take the modern form of labor unions.

It must be further observed that, if Leo XIII's involvement came late—the founding of the first International had occurred more than a quarter century earlier—it was not something unimportant that for the first time the rights of workers and the injustice of the entire liberal system were solemnly proclaimed by the highest spiritual authority. Catholics were quite forced to admit, despite numerous reservations, that, faced with the conditions of "undeserved poverty" whose victims were the great mass of workers, a change was needed, and the most open-minded began to follow the path of Christian democracy. However, the importance of Leo XIII's stance went far beyond Catholic circles. Assuredly, well before *Rerum novarum,* the labor movement was up and running, and the credit for the initiative goes essentially to the socialists. But for the first time this labor movement received the solemn sanction of one of the principal forces of order in the world, and such a sanction was bound to help remove the revolutionary label that it had till then worn in the eyes of the great majority of the middle class. From the psychological point of view—and it is a point-of-view that has its historical importance—this was far from being trivial.

One can conclude that although the encyclical *Rerum novarum* reveals a still relatively timid attitude, and today appears at various points as manifestly obsolete, it at least opened certain doors and pointed the Catholic Church in the right direction. In spite of its imperfections, this first solemn pontifical document having for its object the problems of industrial society marked, for the later thought and actions of Catholics, a decisive step.

* * *

The Difficult Beginnings of Christian Democracy under Leo XIII and Pius X

In the decade which followed the publication of *Rerum novarum,* an increasing number of Catholics, especially among the youngest, began to follow the path of Christian Democracy,[8] which integrated a part of the Catholic liberal heritage into the Catholic social program, in increasing measure with the realization that the utilization of modern liberties in the framework of political democracy was in fact the necessary condition of a march toward social democracy (the demand for universal suffrage in Belgium; pleading in favor of the reintegration of Catholics into the national political life of France and Italy, where that reintegration was contested in the first place by those nostalgic for the monarchy and in the second because of the Rome question).

But this evolution toward "Christian Democracy" did not go forward without problems.

First, because many of those who admitted that henceforward institutional modifications were necessary to ameliorate efficiently the situation of the working masses, meant for these transformations to be implemented according to the old adage: "everything for the people, nothing by the people."

Leo XIII, who was aware at the time of the necessity for going beyond conservatives' limited point-of-view and very careful to maintain the unity of Catholic forces, attempted to channel the effervescence of the Christian Democrats with the encyclical *Graves de communi* of January 18, 1901. While admitting the legitimacy of its expression—contested in certain Catholic circles, notably by the *Civiltà cattolica*—the Pope, inspired by the ethico-social point of view of Professor Toniolo, the great Italian Catholic authority on the subject, gave Christian Democracy a very restrictive definition: "in the present circumstances, it can only be employed by removing all political meaning from it, and in attaching to it no other significance than that of a charitable Christian action among the people." Which clearly kept its distance from the formula extolled by the Christian Democrats: "everything for the people and by the people." This pulling in of the reins did not however close the door on the pursuit of a moderate reform action, and this was notably the case in Belgium. With the support of, among others, Cardinal Mercier (who had not hesitated to publicly recognize that "when it works for a more equitable redistribution of public wealth, socialism is right"), an entire series of concrete projects could be undertaken and, on the eve of the Great War, Belgian Christian democracy possessed all the traits that would characterize it during the half-century which followed: it had become an essential factor in the Catholic Party and, in the form of unions, of friendly societies ["mutualités"], of co-operatives, constantly expanding, it had increasingly become a presence in the professional, economic, cultural, and religious life of the country.

However, elsewhere, things were not so easy. In France, and still more in Italy, the democratic priests (who were the vanguard of a movement in which laymen were not very numerous) often had a tendency to free themselves, in the arena of political and social choices, from the control of a hierarchy that was still very timid and, honestly, often conservative. Now, this pretension, which could have been seen as the precursor to demands for a "democratization" of the internal government of the Church, was for the most part unacceptable to the bishops and in particular to Pius X, who declared to the Belgian ambassador: "In Belgium, you have good democrats, because they obey their bishops." It is a "clerical" reflex of this sort that explains largely the condemnation of *Sillon* by Pius X in 1910. [9]

But there was yet another more profound problem. In the expression "Christian Democracy," which sought to mark its distance from radical and individualist "false democracy," what exactly was the meaning of the reference Christian? Was it a matter of assembling a confessional party, definitively determined to re-establish a Christian State on a popular basis, or was it one of contentment with a simple Christian inspiration in accepting part of the liberal heritage, namely the secular State, in the heart of which believers and non-believers collaborated for the sake of greater social justice? On this point, the ideas of Pius X were unequivocal: there was no question of renouncing the ideal of a completely Catholic social order, whose restoration had been the goal of pontifical politics since the French Revolution.

One can understand that under these conditions, the pontificate of Pius X seemed like the crossing of the desert for many of the Christian Democratic leadership. But the historian must also declare along with Fr. Jarlot: "if, in the aftermath of the First World War, labor, agricultural, and professional Catholic organizations were able to federate on a national and international scale, it is because they were first planted under the reign of Pius X: in Germany, Holland, Belgium, France,

Italy, and elsewhere. The seeds sown by Leo XIII germinated under Pius X and would flourish under Pius XI."[10]

It is obviously not possible here to follow the vicissitudes of the movement in the various countries, as it takes on very different shapes according to local cicumstances[11]: sometimes overtly supported by the hierarchy, as in Australia, where the Cardinal Moran, archbishop of Sydney, does not hesitate to present himself as an adept of "Christian Socialism" and to incite his flock to vote for Labor; sometimes fostered by enterprising vicars from working-class parishes, such as Fr. Alfons Ariëns in the Netherlands, who, influenced by the German social movement, founds as early as 1889 the first Catholic organization made up exclusively of workers and, two years later, the first Catholic union of factory workers; sometimes on the contrary over the objection of suspicion of a clergy too little sensitive to the problem, as result of its too-close relations with the ruling classes, as in Spain, or again the object of objections by the theoreticians of the new guild system, as in Austria, where the courageous founder of the first Christian unions (beginning in 1892) had great difficulty in making the demands of the workers movement understood at the core of the People's Christian Social Party, which was in fact focused on the petite bourgeoisie.

In particular, the Christian trade-unions were the object of a very lively controversy during the last years of Pius X's pontificate, in the context of the fundamentalist reaction against modernism. In effect, the adversaries of Christian Democracy, beginning with the encyclical *Pascendi,* denounced it as one of the heads of the modernist hydra, "social modernism" and "political modernism" appearing to them as a consequence of religious modernism. Those who touted "fundamental Catholicism" and believed that "the social question is above all a moral question and hence a religious question, which will only be resolved by strictly Roman Catholic doctrine," would after 1909 attack with increasing vehemence these Social Catholics who, for reasons of expediency, split from the then-accepted model of Christian civilization by organizing the workers defense on a professional basis, and who, while still keeping a confessional etiquette for the unions, placed the accent on their economic and social roles, without putting their moral and religious goals in the foreground. The conflict developed simultaneously throughout Western Europe, but its epicenter was located in Germany. [12]

Since the beginning of the century, an ideological rupture opposed what was called the Berlin faction, which had remained faithful to the traditional formula of Catholic workers' associations, and the Cologne faction, rapidly growing, whose formula was inter-confessionalism and de-clericalization. Pius X, whose sympathies for the first faction were evident, but who had to account for the strength of the second, and for the fact that it had behind it the great majority of the episcopate, tried to arrest the ever more venomous controversy by publishing, in September 1912, an encyclical on the unions, in which he approved the Berlin formula without reservation but admitted that one could tolerate the other formula in order to avoid a greater evil. This pontifical intervention, far from appeasing intellects, only succeeded in stirring up things, and the controversies redoubled in intensity, not only in Germany, where each party cried victory, but likewise in France, where the fundamentalists took advantage to renew their attacks against Christian Democracy, then in Rome, where in February 1914, the *Civiltà cattolica* published an obviously inspired article; it appeared as a trial balloon prefiguring a new and more severe pontifical document meant to put Christian syndicalism on guard against an evolution which was increasingly removing it from the social ideology which, although certain historical apologists have tried to deny it after the fact, seemed to Pius X to be the only one truly in conformity with Catholic orthodoxy. All those who realized that the Pope, in this regard, was prisoner of an outdated "model" (in the sociological sense of the term) and who were preoccupied with not further retarding the Church's adaptation to the evolution of modern society, attempted to parry the blow which threatened. The debut of international organization among Christian unions that had been preparing for several years made their task easier. The Cardinals Maffi and Mercier, the general of the Jesuits, Toniolo and Harmel, among others, intervened discretely, and Pius X preferred to postpone. The Christian Democrats, in this "last great battle of the pontificate,"[13] had finally gained the advantage over their fundamentalist adversaries.

* * *

Between the Two Wars: Benedict XV and Pius XI

The two decades from the First to the Second World War marked a period of great vitality for Christian Democracy in general and for Catholic reflection on the social problem in particular. A very lively reflection, stimulated notably by the Russian Revolution of 1917 and its aftermath, by the progress of the Socialist movement in all the countries of Western Europe, then by the anti-capitalist but also anti-democratic reaction of the fascist regimes. But the fields of research and intellectual positions upheld were extremely varied. A superficial glance suffices to recognize this great diversity in the teachings of a don Sturzo[14] (who emphasizes the importance of the intermediary bodies politic); of a Jacques Maritain (whose influence in Latin America is well-known); of a Jacques Leclercq in tome IV of his *Lessons of Natural Law;* of the group of Catholic Workers in the United States, led among others by Dorothy Day[15] (reacting vigorously against the materialist principles which it denounces at the base of the socio-economic capitalist system); of the Austrian School of Johannes Ude and Anton Orel,[16] whose radical condemnation of the capitalist system, as intrinsically flawed, will be in its turn condemned by the Austrian episcopate in a collective letter of Spring 1932; of the circle of German Jesuits under Konigswinter, in which the effort of elaborating a conception of society as far removed from liberalism as from socialism, based on scholastic natural law, inaugurated at the end of the 19th century by the Frs. Cathrein and Heinrich Pesch, is pursued between the wars by Oswald von Nell-Breuning and Gustav Gundlach.[17]

It is precisely this ever more vivid awareness of the multitude of directions taken by social studies research in the Catholic Church, and of the problem there was in plumbing these new questions pell-mell, which was at the origin of the International Union of Social Studies of Malines. The idea was put forward by two veterans from before the war, the Belgian Georges Helleputte and the Frenchman Eugene Duthoit, president of *Semaines sociales* [Social Weeks], who proposed the idea to Cardinal Mercier, haloed with international glory after the First War. Upon reflection, the latter accepted and entrusted the secretariat general to one of his former students, Maurice Defourny, professor of political economics at the University of Louvain. The Union had three objectives: to study social problems from the perspective of Catholic morality; to transmit concrete directives and resolutions approved in common after deliberations to the public at large and specifically to men of charity (a Social Code was published in 1927); and eventually, to create a bureau of social consultations which would play a role analogous on the international level to that played by the Jesuits' *Action populaire* in France.[18]

In this gradual maturation of Catholic social doctrine, the encyclical *Quadragesimo anno* marks an important step and constitutes in some measure a new point of departure. Not only because of its content, to which we shall return in a moment, but also because of two aspects of the historical context in which it was published. On one hand, the growth of Catholic social movements, a phenomenon characteristic of the period, which would furnish particularly fertile ground for the spread of the Church's social doctrine for some years: the text of the encyclical would be debated in innumerable circles of study, where the future Catholic elite was being formed. On the other hand, beginning in the 1930s, a new world is taking shape, dominated simultaneously by the great economic crisis and by the rise of totalitarian regimes of the right and the left, which casts serious doubt on the liberal democratic conception of society.

Pius XI became interested in the social problem and in particular in the workers question from the beginning of his pontificate.[19] It should be sufficient to recall his reiterated encouragement to the "Semaines sociales" of France and to the campaigns of the J.O.C. [Young Christian Workers], as well as the famous 1929 letter addressed to the bishop of Lille, Msgr. Lienart, who had supported the demands of the Christian trade-unions against the reactionary industrialists of Northern France.[20] The 40th anniversary of the encyclical *Rerum novarum* in May 1931, seemed to the Pope to be an occasion to take stock and to put up a certain number of new signposts. This document, the longest of Pius XI's pontificate, was prepared by Fr. Oswald von Nell-Breuning, greatly aided by his colleagues of the Konigswinter circle and in particular by Fr. Gundlach. But this first version was judged to be too theoretical and too abstruse and also too marked by a social philosophy, belonging to the German Jesuit, which could not be imposed such as it was on the Church at large. The general of the Jesuits, Fr. Ledochowski, to whom the Pope had assigned preparation of the encyclical, called upon, on the one hand, Fr. Desbuquois from *Action populaire* of Paris, who along with a colleague elaborated another, more concrete segment, and on the other hand, upon a Belgian Jesuit and friend of Fr. Gundlach, Fr. Albert Muller, a remarkably clear intellect. It was he who became "the veritable orchestrator of the whole, combining the elements furnished from here and there and bringing to them the nuances required by the Vatican."[21]

The encyclical *Quadragesimo anno* presents several distinctive traits in relation to *Rerum novarum*. First, by its pains to specify the theological criteria on which the Catholic Church's social message is based. Leo XIII positioned himself essentially within the perspective of natural law. Pius XI, while still attaching great importance to natural law, equally emphasizes the Christian originality of the social model proposed by the Church, a third way between Liberalism and Socialism-Communism. The very title of the encyclical is a sign of this new emphasis: "on the restoration of the social order in full conformity with the precepts of the Gospel"; throughout the encyclical are numerous references to the Fathers of the Church, notably to Origen (who had reflected a great deal on the question of property as a function of creation); the document's finale insists on social *charity*, the complement of social justice. Moreover, there is a detectable change of perspective between the two encyclicals, the first looking at person in relation to the State, whereas in the second, it is a matter of the Church's relationship to civil society.

But above all, this anniversary document is not a simple commentary on *Rerum novarum*. To be sure, it insists on the continuity of the Church's social teachings, especially concerning morality's precedence over economics, and on the church's right to intervene in these matters and to make judgement on society's economic and social organization. But various specifications are added, illuminated by forty years of reflection within the Church (and especially by the numerous episcopal documents on the subject). This is the case for example for the familial salary, a topic on which Leo XIII had voluntarily remained vague, whereas now its necessity is clearly affirmed (the solution of familial allocations had been found in the interim). This is also the case for the way in which the right of ownership is seen: *Rerum novarum,* conceived from the perspective of a rural society undergoing industrialization, was centered — the Socialists have reproached it thus often enough — on the defense of private property (the family home, the fields for cultivation, the factory for production) as matrix of the social order; *Quadragesimo anno,* written in the fullness of industrialized society, in which giant corporations increasingly make their own law in economic and social life, insists much more on the limitations which the common good imposes on the use of property rights, and does so by distancing itself from a conception inherited from Roman law, in which the absolute character of ownership was grounded.

But beyond these particular points, there is something in *Quadragesimo anno* that is newer still. To a renewed criticism of socialism,[22] it adds a warning against the excesses of the sort of capitalism that was evolving. It is in effect between the two wars that a capitalism of small, often family-run businesses, subject to the familiar market forces of the 19th century, is increasingly replaced, beginning in the United States, by a capitalism of large financial groups which aspire to domination of the market. Faced with this new situation, Pius XI means to do more than Leo XIII in the way of profoundly reorganizing the economic and social system as a whole, by separating the Church's position from that of economic liberalism, not only insofar as the relation between employers and workers (especially relative to fair wages) is concerned, but in a much larger perspective, encompassing all aspects of business. For the first time, a solemn pontifical document envisaged the redistribution of the gross national product in terms of the common good, and the necessity of a certain workers' involvement in the operations of business enterprises.

The concrete solution considered ideal by the encyclical, greatly influenced as it was by the German Jesuits,[23] is the guild system. Certainly not, although some have affirmed it in more or less good faith, a State-controlled guild system such as had been achieved by fascism in Italy,[24] but a collection of bodies politic, intermediary between the individual and the State, organizing its members "not according to the position that they occupy in the labor market (employers on one side, workers on the other), but according to the various branches of social activity to which they belong," in other words by profession. This insistence on an ideal guild system is today the decrepit aspect of *Quadragesimo anno*,[25] an aspect on which the Christian Democrats of the day were likewise more or less silent - the commentaries on the encyclical published in Belgium or in the Netherlands are typical in this regard—but an aspect which would be voluntarily orchestrated for some ten years in numerous Catholic circles.[26]

Yet, another point is worthy of attention. Pius XI calls attention to the ties that must exist between social action and Catholic Action, thus its full development. Catholic Action, he says, must be at the service of social action, especially in preparing its members to enter into Christian secular institutions, intent on reconstituting an ersatz Christianity. This is another aspect which seems outmoded today, but which at least had a positive side: these exhortations prodded many Christians of the next generation "to get out of the sacristy" and to become ardently involved in temporal action.[27]

* * *

Pius XII and the Restoration of the Christian Social Order

Pius XII did not present his social teachings in doctrinal syntheses comparable to the encyclicals *Rerum novarum* and *Quadragesimo anno*. Apart from a few wartime messages that give related statements, the majority of his social teaching is found in much more concise documents, treating particular problems suggested by current events (especially groups received in audience). One example among others: the speech which he addressed to members of the International Council of Social Studies in June 1950, in which he pronounced against co-management *(Mitbestimmung)* of business enterprises by workers and employers, an idea dear to the German Christian unionists.[28]

The particular form which Pius XII gave to his social teachings shows that his plan was to apply the permanent general principles formulated by his predecessors to various concrete situations, which he called "the social doctrine of the Church"[29]: not *a* doctrine or a current of thought encouraged by the Holy See, but indeed *the* official doctrine of the Church, that is to say a coherent whole which had been gradually elaborated over the course of the preceding half-century and which was being proposed by the supreme authority of the Church.

It is here obviously not a question of passing in review these very numerous texts, nor even of trying to sketch a synthesis thereof. I will limit myself to pointing out a few general traits, which distinguish the interventions of Pius XII from those of his predecessors. First, mention has often correctly been made of the high technical level often found in the interventions of Pius XII, who believed strongly in consulting experts before expressing himself. But one is struck foremost by displaced perspective in which the problem of social injustice is viewed: the contrast between the rich and the proletariat within industrial societies is increasingly supplanted in the Pope's concerns by the contrast which exists between rich countries and developing countries. This new contrast even becomes an habitual theme in the speeches and documents of the last years of the pontificate. Pius XII states that, in Western societies, a great majority will henceforward enjoy growing security and a more-or-less well-founded hope of new improvements to come, whereas, simultaneously, in the Third World, the virtually absolute poverty of the great mass of the population is increasing, following the destruction of traditional structures by the impact of technological civilization and foreign capitalist exploitation.

An important remark must be added to the preceding considerations. To have an exact idea of Pius XII's position on the questions which concern us here, it is not enough to consult the texts of his speeches or his messages, his concrete attitudes must also be considered, his practical options when faced with the problems posed by the reorganization of society following the great confrontation between democratic and totalitarian ideologies.

Pius XII had deluded himself in the hope — maintained by the American delegate to the Vatican, Myron Taylor — that he would be invited to participate in the peace negotiations and involved, within the framework of the U.N., in the reconstruction of the post-war world.[30] But he was soon forced to admit before the political leadership the few means of direct action at the Holy Sees disposal and, reaping the consequences of this isolation, he had to limit his involvement to the moral level, addressing himself directly to the people, so as to take every occasion to remind a de-centered world of the vision of Christian society, seeking in particular to mobilize the Christian masses, thanks to intensive use of the media, so that they would become actively engaged in the pursuit of that ideal. Without giving up on, when it seemed possible, consolidating the Church's freedom of action through government accords, he tried above all to exercise a moral authority which, making appeal largely to natural law, sought, through the faithful of the Catholic Church, to make the Pope the leader of world public opinion. "It is with Pius XII that a new interpretation of the role of the papacy reached its full scope, the one we see continuing before our eyes, and which leads contemporary popes to hold a much more substantial discourse on the problems of their times than that of their predecesors. ..."[31]

In an earlier time, Pius XII, conforming to the tradition of previous Popes, stressed foremost the profound differences between the Christian understanding of society and the liberal-and-lay-inspired ideology of the Anglo-Saxon world, observing in particular that "although the Church condemns the current Marxist regimes, it cannot ignore nor refuse to see that the worker, in his efforts to improve his condition, comes up against a social system which, far from conforming to nature, is opposed to the order established by God and to the end that He has assigned to the fruits of the earth" (Sept. 7, 1947). But as he came to see totalitarian communism as an ever greater threat, he increasingly stressed the positive values of Western democratic ideology and, although not wanting to engage in an anti-Soviet "crusade" alongside the United States—which caused a part of American public to accuse him of playing a neutralist game - he decided, unlike a K. Barth for example, to bring the not negligible support represented by his moral authority to the Western camp. The disavowal of the "Christian progressives," the decree by the Holy Office of July 1ˢᵗ 1949, excommunicating Catholics who give their support to the Communist Party, like the unequivocal involvement of Italian Catholic Action under the leadership of Gedda in the 1948 elections, can be seen from this perspective. Even attempts at peaceful co-existence with the communist parties, undertaken by some of the clergy in countries located beyond the iron curtain, were badly received at the Vatican, where conversely a great tolerance was shown toward Franco's Spain, Salazar's Portugal, and the South American dictators. However, this anticommunist option did not prevent Pius XII, increasingly preoccupied by the situation in the Third World, from continuing to denounce the economic disorder of the capitalist world and the so-called "social order" which is "neither profoundly Christian nor really human" (Dec. 31, 1952). Although one cannot deny the influence of Cardinal Spellman, which was great in the Vatican for many years, nor the Pope's intense desire to see American Catholics contribute generously to furnish the Holy See with the materials necessary for his vast apostolic and caritative projects (especially founding the bank of the *Opere di Religione*), it would be nevertheless inaccurate to speak of a pure and simple alignment with American policy.

The project to restore "Christian civilization" nurtured by the Pope just as much as his concern to strengthen the West's resistance to Soviet pressure without being swallowed by the American bloc, led him to encourage with voice and pen, and also with the support of pontifical diplomacy, the Christian Democratic parties in power in Italy, Germany, France, and the Benelux, with an eye to constituting "the Europe of the Six," to the point that at one time, some spoke - with much exaggeration - of a "Vatican Europe."[32]

Let us conclude with a final observation.[33] Pius XII's social project, greatly influenced by the Jesuit Gundlach, situated in the perspective of the *restitutio in integrum* of a social order infected by sin, emphasizes the leadership role in the organization of social life to which the Church's hierarchy must return. It is true, Pius XII does not deny the important role of lay people, but he sees them principally as executors of the ecclesiastical hierarchy's plan, without much autonomy in the choice of solutions. On this point, an important change of direction would be initiated by John XXIII and followed up on by Paul VI in the framework of the Vatican II Council.

* * *

Under the Sign of Vatican II: John XXIII and Paul VI

In order to understand better the changes of perspective in the social teachings of the recent Popes, it is important to take into account the profound mutation the world has undergone since the end of the Second World War. In the first place is the global spread -not only in the Mediterranean and Eastern Europe, but also in the Third World, with its exploding "megalopolises"—of industrial society and urban civilization, with its corollary, the disappearance of traditional agrarian cultures ["peasant civilizations"]. This evolution has had as its consequence the development of a "consumer society," that is to say a society of opulence which, thanks to social legislation, many workers have profited from: salaried workers now seem less and less to be "the damned of the earth." Still, poverty has not disappeared for all that, but it wears a new face; immigrants, the new slaves of modern times, at the service of consumer society; what is called the "Fourth World," exploited not only by foreign capitalists but just as much by the new local "elite." Moreover, although the accumulating misery of he Third World originally favored the spread of communism in these regions, which had greatly worried Pius XII, increasing awareness of the true nature of the "Soviet paradise" resulted in the steady decline of Marxist ideology, in which many after the war, including a considerable number of "progressive Christians," thought they saw the ideal model for industrial societies. Another important phenomenon of the last few decades: accelerated decolonization has had as a consequence, along with the lessening of Western influence, of drawing attention to the plurality of cultures and therefore to the error of those who claim to hold the only solution,—"made in U.S.A." or in Moscow or in the Vatican- for the socioeconomic problems of today's world. Furthermore, the increasing role—for political as well as demographic reasons—played by the countries of Africa and especially Asia in international affaires has resulted in the further growth of the deChristianized character of the world, or in any case its deconfessionalization: from now on, not only are the "old" Christian countries less-and-less Christian, but in addition they hold an increasingly limited place in world affairs, and we are forced to realize that it is increasingly illusory to try to have Christian recipes for the solutions to socioeconomic problems adopted everywhere in the world.

It is in this new historical context that we have begun to ask the question: is there a reason to speak of a "social doctrine of the Church," in the sense that there could be an ideal Catholic "model" of societal organization, deduced *a priori* from a few philosophical or theological principles, an ideal organizational system which would present itself as a third way between the capitalist system and Marxist socialism? In other terms: is it legitimate that the official authority of the Church should present a collection of propositions and directives which govern the entire Church, everywhere and always, whose content constitutes a more-or-less organic doctrine formulated within very specific social and religious categories? The question began to be heard in the 1960s, but has been expressed and developed in particularly piercing fashion by Father Chenu in a small book first published in Italian in 1977[34] and translated soon thereafter into French under the more engaging title: La *"doctrine sociale" de l'Église comme idéologie.*[35] According to Chenu, it is necessary to reject the presentation of an abstract, monolithic doctrine, which is only one ideology among others, "making sacred in reality a particular hierarchical structure of the social order," and substitute for "an abstract social doctrine, accepted on authority, enunciated through out-dated categories, a social methodology, illuminated and inspired by the Gospel, in the conscious participation in the construction of the world and the movement of history, both becoming theological places" (p. 51). In sum, instead of juxtaposing a formulated *a priori* Catholic model with the American and Soviet models, Christians, enlightened by the Gospels, should join with their unbeliever brothers in the world Socialist movement in the pursuit of just solutions, in each country adapted to the real-life situations of social evolution.

Fr. Chenu's work was enthusiastically received in certain Catholic circles, but it was greatly argued about in others, and especially in Rome, and it must be recognized that it too often lacks nuances and that it contains a certain number of excessive affirmations, sometimes even inexact ones. It is nevertheless true that it stated in cutting fashion an uneasiness felt more or less embarrassingly toward the end of Pius XII's pontificate: the Church's social doctrine such as it had been laid out in pontifical documents, and especially in the manuals which attempted to codify it, seemed increasingly like an abstract and impractical ideology, but was in fact closely linked to Western concepts such as they had been gradually incarnated in the projects of Christian Democratic governments, admirable projects it is true but often timid ones, and governments assuredly and clearly opposed to totalitarianism on the right and the left but, in a majority of cases, ultimately dominated by conservative reflexes (the most typical case being that of the German C. D. U.). In particular, the Church's social teachings in the first half of the 20th century were reproached for having given insufficient attention to the reality of the Politician, which is increasingly the true battleground between the exploiters and the exploited.

It is in the context of these questions and these doubts that the great "social" documents of the Church were written over the last thirty years.

First to come, for the 70th anniversary of *Rerum novarum,* John XXIII's encyclical *Mater et Magistra.* Therein is indeed found an echo of the earlier social teachings of the Popes in social matters, and notably a long defense of private property written from an anticommunist perspective. But also found are certain clarifications of the traditional doctrine taking into account new elements introduced into the makeup of society since the end of the Second World War. And to begin with, that remarkable statement: "Socialization is one of the characteristic aspects of our era." The phenomenon of socialization, to which the encyclical devotes long passages, is presented as being "both cause and effect of governmental involvement" in socioeconomic life and as implying the establishment of new legal institutions. Now, this evolution, provided that it is accomplished with respect for the human being, is seen by the Pope with a favorable eye, whereas Pius XII had shown clear reservations concerning use of the term "socialization," too evocative of the official socialism rejected by the Church.[36] Another point in which *Mater et Magistra* separates itself from Pius XII: reprising a theme already outlined by Pius XI but swept under the rug by his successor, John XXIII's encyclical deals at length with the problem of workers' participation in business decisions and considers co-management desirable.

Moreover, surpassing *Quadragesimo anno,* the new encyclical not only reaffirmed the right to form labor unions, but it hoped to see unions take their place among the public powers-that-be, on condition that they retain their autonomy. It likewise expands on Pius XI's evaluation of the problems posed by the spread of corporations, this time squarely facing the increasingly frequent problem of a business enterprise's ownership being divorced from its management.

The entire second part of the encyclical concentrates on the problem of the underdeveloped regions, a problem which had already been looked at by Pius XII. This last aspect is reprised and expanded on in the encyclical *Pacem in terris (1963),* which is not a social encyclical in the usual sense of the term, but in which social questions maintain an important place. In pursuit of social order and social justice, John XXIII assumes an international and even a global perspective, and the link between peace and economic development, as a necessary condition of social improvements, is clearly marked. It becomes increasingly clear that "Social Catholicism" is not limited to finding a solution to the problems of workers in industrial society, but that it must, in a larger perspective, seek to resolve the problem of the world's developing countries and, to resolve it, and a global authority which will stimulate, guide, and watch over social progress must be seen to assert itself. We thus pass from the socioeconomic to the political level.

Another passage of *Pacem in terris* received attention in its day. In the pastoral directives with which the document concludes, John XXIII makes a distinction of capital importance:

> It must be borne in mind, furthermore, that neither can false philosophical teachings regarding the nature, origin, and destiny of the universe and of man be identified with historical movements that have economic, social, cultural, or politcal ends, not even when these movements have originated from those teachings and have drawn and still draw inspiration therefrom.
>
> This is so because the teachings, once they are drawn up and defined, remain always the same, while the movements, working in constantly evolving historical situations, cannot but be influenced by these latter and cannot avoid, therefore, being subject to changes, even of a profound nature. Besides, who can deny that those movements, insofar as they conform to the dictates of right reason and are interpreters of the lawful aspirations of the human person, contain elements that are positive and deserving of approval?
>
> It can happen, then, that meetings for the attainment of some practical end, which formerly were deemed inopportune or unproductive, might now or in the future be considered opportune and useful.
>
> But to decide whether this moment has arrived, and also to lay down the ways and degrees in which work in common might be possible for the achievement of economic, social, cultural, and

political ends which are honorable and useful, are problems which can be solved only with the virtue of prudence, which is the guiding light of the virtues that regulate the moral life, both individual and social.

Therefore, as far as Catholics are concerned, this decision rests primarily with those who live and work in the specific sectors of human society in which those problems arise, always, however, in accordance with the principles of the natural law, with the social doctrine of the Church, and with the directives of ecclesiastical authority. For it must not be forgotten that the Church has the right and the duty not only to safeguard the principles of ethics and religion, but also to intervene authoritatively with her children in the temporal sphere when there is a question of judging the application of those principles to concrete cases."

Fr. Chenu, citing this passage, omitted the last sentences, which show that, whatever he may think about it, John XXIII continued to speak, like his predecessors, of a "social doctrine of the Church," but it remains nonetheless true that he officially opened the door at last to a collaboration, under certain conditions, of Catholics with the socialist movement.

Between the two encyclicals of John XXIII and the social documents of Paul VI, which we have yet to discuss, is situated the Vatican II Council and in particular the constitution *Gaudium et Spes,* in which an entire chapter (chapter III) is dedicated to "socioeconomic life." This time, mention of a "social doctrine of the Church" was avoided by design and the presentation of an ideal system was not attempted. It is strictly a question of the great and permanent principles of morality, from which all research concerning concrete solutions *hic et nunc* must draw inspiration. These principles logically revolve around two axes: labor and property. Let us briefly review them.[37]

Concerning labor:
a) Primacy of labor over every other aspect of economic life, from the fact that it engages the dignity of the individual, whereas capital is only a tool.

b) Salaries must permit the worker and his family access to a life which is worthy on a material, social, cultural, and spiritual level.

c) Labor must be humane and allow sufficient time for rest and leisure.

d) It is necessary to encourage the active participation of workers in the management of the enterprise.[38]

e) The workers' right of association is a fundamental right of the individual.

f) In case of conflict, the right to strike must be recognized as necessary, although it should only be exercised as a last recourse.

Concerning property:

a) Usufruct in common of all the goods and bounties of the earth, which implies especially that the rich "are bound to aid the poor, and not only by means of their surplus."

b) Investments must be made as a function of the common good, with a view to better distribution of wealth, and taking into account the pressing needs of developing regions.

c) Private property is legitimate insofar as it is an expression of the individual and an extension of human liberty, but it takes extremely diverse forms and the State has the right "to prevent the abuse of property which is contrary to the common good, because property is draped in a social character."

d) Nationalization is legitimate, provided there is fair compensation; likewise, in developing countries where there exist *latifundia* of abusive size or inefficient management which impose indigent revenues and living conditions on the workers, expropriation is legitimate, in accordance with the exigencies of the common good.

Following the Council, Paul VI published two important documents on social issues.

First, the encyclical *Populorum Progressio*,[39] in March 1967. The preparation of this document, in whose refinement Msgr. Poupard played an important role, went on for four years, beginning in 1964, and the Pope called on numerous experts, in particular Fr. Lebret, the editor of *Économie et humanisme*. It can be seen that, contrary to what had usually been the case in pontifical documents, this one cites numerous contemporary authors: Maritain, Fr. Chenu, Fr. De Lubac, the Brazilian bishop Msgr. Larrain, etc. It is developed in two parts: the principles which must rule the development of man; and the actions which must be undertaken in order to obtain a "fraternal ["solidaire"] development of humanity." As it is impossible to linger on this nevertheless very important document, I limit myself here to pointing out its essential affirmation: "the social question has become global." More concretely: from now on, it is no longer so much a matter of the relations between workers and employers or the holders of capital, but of relations between the rich nations and the poor nations. Many elements of this encyclical are already found in chapter III of the Vatican II constitution *Gaudium et Spes,* but relatively few people have read the council documents, whereas the encyclical *Populorum Progressio* found its target and it is typical that, as for *Rerum novarum,* the need will be felt, twenty years later, to celebrate its anniversary, which indeed underscored its innovative character.

Paul VI's second important document is not an encyclical in the formal sense, but a letter addressed to the Canadian Cardinal Roy in 1971 on the occasion of the encyclical *Rerum novarum's* 80th anniversary, which begins with the words: *Octogesima adveniens.* In it are two very important new things.

In the first place, Paul VI insists on the political stakes, namely that the solution to social problems is not only a question of sociology or of theology, but of the political will necessary to make the economic renewal operational and to bring about restructuring (which had already been emphasized by the first Christian Democrats of Leo XIII's time, but which had always been left in the shadows by pontifical documents). It is with good reason that Fr. Famerée wrote on this subject: "Paul VI's letter could be titled 'the Christian's political responsibility'."[40] Even more, Paul VI, applying the distinction between doctrines and the movements which spring from them, already enunciated by John XXIII in *Pacem in terris,* believes that this Christian political action may eventually be brought to the heart of the socialist parties. Finally recognizing "a certain fragmentation of Marxism, which until now seemed to be a monolithic ideology,"[41] and observing that socialism had greatly evolved in a century, Paul VI prudently acknowledges the consequences of this metamorphosis and no longer rejects *en masse* the entire Socialist movement in its many forms:

> Today, some Christians are attracted to Socialist currents and their diverse incarnations. They seek to identify therein a certain number of aspirations, which they carry in themselves in the name of their faith. They feel thrust into this historic current and want to do their part in the work. Now, depending on the continent and the culture, this historic current takes different forms under the same name, even if it has been and remains, in many cases, inspired by ideologies incompatible with faith. A careful discernment is called for. Too often, Christians attracted to Socialism have a tendency to idealize it in terms that are moreover very generous: a desire for justice, solidarity, and equality. They refuse to recognize the constraints of historical Socialist movements, which remain conditioned by their ideology of origin. Among Socialism's various levels of expression -- a generous cause and a search for a more just society, historical movements organized politically for political ends, an ideology which claims to give us a total and autonomous vision of mankind - it remains to establish distinctions which will guide the concrete choices. However, these distinctions must not strive to consider these levels as completely separate and independent. The concrete ties which, depending on circumstances, exist between them, must be lucidly identified [marked out], and this perspicacity will permit Christians to see what degree of participation is possible along that path, keeping the values of freedom, responsibility, and openness to spirituality, which guarantee the complete flowering of mankind.

However, there is a still more important innovation in the letter *Octogesima adveniens*. Paul VI, keeping his distance from what Fr. Chenu called "the unrealistic psychology and sociology"[42] of many previous pontifical documents, states that the diversity of concrete situations around the world is such that the Holy See no longer feels qualified to "speak unilaterally," to "propose a solution having universal value." And he added this just as remarkable clarification:

Such is not our ambition nor even our mission: it remains for the Christian communities to analyze objectively the situations in their own countries, to illuminate them in the light of the Gospel's inalterable words, to delve the principles of reflection, of the norms of judgement, and of the directives for action in the social teachings of the Church, such as it has been elaborated in the course of history and especially in this industrial era, since the historic date of Leo XIII's message on the condition of the workers, whose anniversary we have the honor and joy of celebrating today. It is left to the Christian communities to discern, with the help of the Holy Spirit, in communion with the responsible Bishops, having dialogue with other Christian brothers and all men of good will, the options and the involvement which must be exercised in order to effect the social, political, and economic changes which are proving to be urgently necessary in many cases.

Contrary to the long-dominant perspective, Paul VI deems that the Church should not aim to authenticate an inherited structure or a pre-fabricated model of society, but that it must limit itself to enlightening men, and in particular laymen, in their search for the best-adapted solutions to the diverse concrete situations in which they live.

* * *

Leo XIII became Pope in 1878. Paul VI died in 1978. Over the course of these 100 years, the social teachings of the Popes appear as a particularly suggestive example of that which is the "Living Tradition," which does not stop at repetition, but appears as a progressive deepening and enrichment, all the while careful to remain "in the line": *Nova et Vetera.*

Notes

[1] Contrary to what has often been claimed, Leo XIII was in no way an advocate of "modernity" and, in the first sentence of his 1891 encyclical, will yet stigmatize "the thirst for novelty which has taken hold of society." Leo XIII meant to continue the combat begun by Pius IX against "modern society" as conceived of by the Liberals of his time, that is to say, on the one hand, a secularized and `lay-icized' society, which believed that the Church should confine itself to helping individuals find eternal salvation without claiming to have a say in the organization of the society of this world. This combat for the restoration of a unified Christian social order, which, according to Leo XIII, could alone return happiness and peace to a society split into opposing camps, will be led by him on two fronts: against Liberalism, which delivers isolated individuals into exploitation by the rich arbiters of economic and political power, a Liberalism whose dangers he will not cease to denounce if his legitimate aspirations are not regulated by the Church, interpreter of divine law; but equally against Socialism, in his eyes a cure worse than the disease, which, in his encyclical program of 28 December 1878, on the errors of modernity, he had already severely stigmatized, for - confusing the Anarchists, who preach rebellion against all authority in heaven and on earth, the Marxists, who denounce the private ownership of the means of production as the origin of class struggle, and the Socio-Democrats—he reproaches the "Socialists" for shaking the traditional foundation of society by questioning the principle of authority and the right of ownership, "sanctioned by natural law."
In the eyes of Leo XIII, the workers' question was only one aspect of the "social question," that is to say of the restoration of the society shaken to its foundation by the French Revolution and its aftermath and, before taking a position on the workers question, he had judged it necessary to mark out clearly the terrain with a series of encyclicals on the true Christian concept of society (to which *Rerum novarum* will refer furthermore in several instances): *Immortale Dei,* on the Christian make-up of States (November 1, 1885); *Libertas,* on the exact notion of freedom and liberties (June 20, 1888); *Sapientiae christianae,* on the principal civic duties of Christians (January 10, 1890).

[2] Besides his definitive biography by F. Vigener, *Ketteler. Ein deutches Bischofleben aus dem XIX. Jahrhundert,* Munich, 1924, see especially: L. Lenhart, *Bischof Ketteler. Staatspolitiker, Sozialpolitiker, Kirchenpolitiker,* t. I, Mainz, 1966; R.J. Ederer, *The Social Teachings of W.E. von Ketteler,* Washington, 1981; E. Iserloh, *W.E. von Ketteler, Sein Kampf für Freiheit und soziale Gerechtigkeit,* Stuttgart, 1987.

[3] Earlier, as a nuncio in Belgium, he had become familiar with the questions raised by industrialization and the spread of capitalism. He had read and meditated on the works of Ketteler, whom he would one day call "my great predecessor." And as bishop of Perugia, he had published in 1877, an episcopal mandate in which he denounced the "law of bronze" by virtue of which the contractor of physical labor ignored the Man in the worker, and in it wishfully called for legislation "which puts a stop to this inhuman traffic."

[4] See the capital work by G. Antonazzi, *L'enciclica "Rerum novarum," Testo autentico e redazioni preparatorie dai documenti originali,* Rome, 1957 (its conclusions are summed up by B. Riposati in *Vita e pensiero,* t. XL, 1957, pp. 626-635, French translation in *La Documentation catholique,* t. LV, 1958, col. 53-62), and equally

L'Enciclica "Rerum novarum" e il suo tempo, edited by G. Antonazzi and G. De Rosa, Rome, 1991.

[5] *Doctrine pontificale et histoire.* *L 'enseignement social de Léon XIII, Pie X et Benoit XV, vu dans son ambiance historique*, Rome, 1964, p. 214. - Could this last-minute addition be the result of Cardinal Gibbons' influence, as suggested by G. Jarlot, *ibid.*, p. 214, and by B. De Lai, *Finanze e Finanzieri vaticani fra 1'800 e il '900*, Milan, 1979, pp. 140-141, n. 1? Perhaps we need to recognize the influence of Msgr. Satoli, former apostolic delegate to the United States (cfr. Daniel-Rops, *Un combat pour Dieu*, Paris, 1963, p. 229 and n. 33).

[6] G. Candeloro, *La doctrine sociale chrétienne et l'encyclique "Rerum novarum,"* in *Recherches internationales à la lumiére du marxisme*, n° 6, March-April, 1958, pp. 120-125, in particular p. 121.

[7] J. Famerée, *De "Rerum novarum" à "Octogesima adveniens,"* in *Nouvelle Revue théologique*, t. CIV, 1982, p. 89.

[8] The term seems to have originated in Belgium after the founding of the "Belgian Democratic League" by Helleputte in 1891.

[9] Cf. J. Carom *Le Sillon et la Démocratie chrétienne, 1894-1910*, Paris, 1967.

[10] *Op. cit.*, pp. 13-14.

[11] See for example *150 ans de mouvement ouvrier chrétien en Europe de l'Ouest*, under the direction of S. H. Scholl, Brussels, 1966.

[12] Cf. E. Deuerlein, *Der Gewerkschaftstreit*, in *Theologische Quartalschrift*, t. CXXXIX, 1959, pp. 40-81.

[13] This is the title of an article by É. Poulat, in *Rivista di storia della Chiesa in Italia*, t. XXV, 1971, pp. 83-107.

[14] The number of works in Italian on the thought and action of Luigi Sturzo has multiplied in the last decades. See among others G. Morra, *Luigi Sturzo. Il pensiero sociologico*, Rome, 1979, and the Acts of the International Congress of Palermo: *Luigi Sturzo nella storia d Italia*, Rome, 1973, 2 vol.

[15] N. L. Robert, *Dorothy Day and the Catholic Worker*, Albany, 1984.

[16] See for example, by the first, *Eigentum, Kapitalismus, Christentum* (1930), and by the second, *Oeconomia perennis* (1930).

[17] See J. Schwarte, *Gustav Gundlach, S. J. (1892-1963), Massgeblicher Repräsentant der katholischen Soziallehre während der Pontifikat Pius XI and Pius XII*, Paderborn, 1975.

[18] Founded in 1903 by Fr. H. Leroy and run magisterially from 1905 to 1946 by Fr. G. Desbuquois, its aim was "aid action" by putting Catholics in contact with all movements which wanted to work in the social arena and by documenting them thanks to a remarkably equipped library and especially by its publications, its speakers, and its councilors. See P. Droulers, *Politique soeiale et christianisme. Le P. Desbuquois et l'Action Populaire. Débuts. Syndicalisme et intégristes (1903-1919)*, Paris, 1969, and *Le P. Desbuquois et l'Action Populaire, 1919-1946*, Paris, 1981.

[19] Cf. G. Jarlot, *Pie XI. Doctrine et action (1922-1939)*, Rome, 1973, in particular chapter X, pp. 247 sq.

[20] On this letter of the *Congrégation du Concile* (dated June 5, 1928, and made public August 9, 1929), which "marks a new step in the Church's attitude toward Christian unionism" (P. Droulers), see R. Talmy, *Le syndicalisme chrétien en France (1871-1931). Difficultés et controverses*, Paris, 1965, pp. 205-230.

[21] P. Droulers, *Le P. Desbuquois et l'Action Populaire, 1919-1946,* Paris, 1981, pp. 152-156. It points out that there were 8 successive versions and that notably "the page against the guild system of the Fascist State is by the Pope's own hand" (p. 155, note 139).

[22] A critique still not nuanced enough, which does not sufficiently distinguish Labor unionism of the Anglo-Saxon type from Marxism in the radical form it had assumed since 1917.

[23] *Quadragesimo anno* has been described by some, with the exaggeration typical of all expressions of the sort, as "ein grandioses Plagiat an Gundlach."

[24] They were not fooled in Italy: "the anger of Mussolini and of his press proved well enough that in spite of diplomatic circumlocution, (the warning against it) had been understood" (P. Droulers, *Le P. Desbuquois et l'Action Populaire, 1919-1946,* p. 155, note 139).

[25] It is typical for example that the *Code social* published by the International Union of Malines, which was given a pro-guild retouch in 1934, abandons this point-of-view in the reedition of 1948.

[26] This was notably the case for the *Semaines sociales* (Social Weeks) of France. And when the Vichy government promulgated the Labor Charter, which was conceived, in conformity with the then-dominant ideology, in the image of the guild model ["in a corporative perspective"], the Assembly of French Cardinals and Archbishops declared (December 23, 1941) that it "followed too well the Church's social doctrine to not rally the votes of all Catholics."

[27] In this exposé *"per summa capita"* on the social teachings of the modern Popes, I do not mention the encyclical *Divini Redemptoris* of 1937 against "atheistic Communism," for the same reason as that of Fr. E. Charbonneau in his work on the sources of the encyclical *Populorum progressio* (published as appendix to the collective volume *L'Église dans le monde de ce temps. Études et commentaires autour de la constitution pastorale "Gaudium et Spes" de Vatican II avec une étude sur l'encyclique "Populorum progressio"* edited by G. Barauna and H. Crouzel, Paris-Bruges, 1967-68): "One can wonder why we do not here analyze the encyclical *Divini Redemptoris,* which deals *ex professo* with the Communist problem and condemns Marxism as 'intrinsically evil.' Our omission is based on that of Paul VI himself, who, when he mentions the 'great social encyclicals,' omits mention of *Divini Redemptoris.* This official omission (is) extremely significant" (p. 782, note 5).

[28] The anger provoked in these circles by Pius XII's speech was profound, and the *Osservatore Romano* dedicated not fewer than three articles to limiting the damage.

[29] It is with him that we first find the explicit expression, but Pius XI, in *Quadragesimo anno,* was already speaking of a *"doctrina de re sociali et economica."*

[30] Cf. I. Garzia, *La diplomazia vaticana e il problema dell' asseto postbellico,* in *Pio XII,* A. Riccardi, Bari, 1984, pp. 218-227.

[31] J.-M. Mayeur, in the journal *Relations internationales,* no. 28, winter 1981, p. 414.

[32] See P. Cheneaux, *Une Europe vaticane? Entre le Plan Marshall et les Traités de Rome,* Louvain-la-Neuve, 1990.

[33] One suggested to us by the work of A. Acerbi, *La Chiesa nel tempo. Sguardi sui problemi di relazioni tra Chiesa e società civile negli ultimi cento anni,* Milan, 1979, pp. 130-178 ("Il 'progretto storico' di Pio XII").

[34] *La dottrina sociale della Chiesa. Origine e sviluppo (1891-1971),* Brescia, 1977.

[35] Paris, Éditions du Cerf, 1979, 96 pp.

[36] It is moreover important to observe that the encyclical recalls the earlier condemnations of Communism and Socialism. Looking back to *Quadragesimo anno,* the Pope notes that Pius XI believed that "it can in no way be allowed that Catholics give their allegiance to moderate socialism: whether because it is a way of understanding life centered on the temporal, in which physical well-being is considered society's supreme objective; or because it seeks a social organization of the common life, only at the level of production, to the great detriment of human liberty; or that every true principle of social authority is lacking in it."

[37] Following Fr. Charbonneau, *op. cit.* (to note 27), pp. 791-793.

[38] *Quadragesimo anno* (§ 65) and *Mater et Magistra* (§ 77) were limited to saying that co-management was "to be hoped for" or "desirable."

[39] See especially *Il magistero di Paolo VI nell' encyclica "Populorum Progressio." Giornata di Studio* (Pubblicazioni dell' Istituto Paolo VI, 10) Brescia, 1989.

[40] In *Nouvelle Revue théologique,* t. CIV, 1982, p. 90.

[41] It had already been several decades since sociologists and political scientists, including a certain number of Catholics, had observed it.

[42] *Op. cit.,* p. 89.

Some Reflections on the Historical Perspectives of Catholic Social Teaching 2002

To understand Catholic Social Doctrine, it is indispensable to grasp the historical context in which it was formulated. Catholic Social Doctrine developed from an effort to apply Christian moral principles to rapidly changing social and economic relationships. As a result, Catholic Social Doctrine, though rooted in basic principles, is a work in progress. A continual effort is required to assess new social conditions and relations in light of these principles. (Just as there is often stubborn resistance against changes in social life, there is more frequently a stubborn reluctance on the part of the institutional church, which is bureaucratic, to rethink the application of doctrine to new social circumstances.)

Human experience is historical. An individual's knowledge grows with experience. A person defines himself or herself in terms of a life story. Perceptions and interpretations are broadened as a person encounters new phenomena; with growing experience and reflection upon those experiences thought becomes more sophisticated. Just like individual life, social life is historical. It evolves as new circumstances are encountered. Social forms change, life impacted by these changes is altered, and humans are forced to rethink how they should behave when confronted with new circumstances.

We are indeed obligated to Canon Roger Aubert for his historical perspectives on Catholic Social Doctrine. What we now need to do is make our reflections on the doctrine itself and on his reading of it, and to make some comments on the philosophy of the doctrine. We need to examine where it came from, what ideologies were at work, what schools of thought were involved, what consequences in people's lives it brought about, if any, and from an ethical point of view, what position must one take in the face of it.

To do this, I propose seven steps. First, we should read and reread Canon Aubert's articles. They give the history of the doctrine in a nuanced, accurate, and honest way. Second, we should spell out in a philosophical way what the key doctrines are. Third, we should summarize some important studies completed at the beginning of this millennium. Fourth, we should familiarize ourselves with the best source on Catholic Social Doctrine found in German, that is, Cardinal Höffner's classic text on Christian Social Teaching.[1] In addition, we should look into the recent study by European theologians and philosophers on the Social Doctrine of the Church.[2] And, we should look at length into the recent book by Fr. Charles Curran, who not only wrote a preface to this book, but has recently given us the best one-volume exposition and analysis of Catholic social teaching in our times.[3] Fifth, we should consult the popular presentations of the doctrine, which we find in pamphlet form today.[4] Sixth, we would be amiss if we did not look into the summary form that the American Catholic bishops produced. And finally, we should consult the wise and learned Fr. Jean-Yves Calvez to see what he calls the "silences" of Catholic Social Doctrine.

However, before we begin, let us make three general observations. First, Catholic social thought should not be restricted only to what is called Catholic social teaching ("CST"), which comes only from the popes and conferences of bishops. It should include Catholic nonofficial social thinking ("CNOST"). There are many other thinkers, usually neglected, such as von Ketteler, Sturzo, and John A. Ryan. They all frequently acted in the past as precursors, stimulators, and developers of the official teaching. So, let us use in a generic way the notion of Catholic Social Teaching ("CathST") as having two specific forms, namely ("CST") from the pope and hierarchy and "CNOST" from theologians, philosophers, and social scientists.

Second, as I have written elsewhere, we should correct what seems to be a common historical inaccuracy.[5] Catholic Social teaching began long before the last century. Professor Michael J. Schuck has shown that the social teaching of the papal encyclicals began in 1740 under the pontificate of Benedict XIV (1740-58).[6] What Professor Schuck calls the pre-Leonine period (1740-1877) will show that by a "textually inclusive and topically broad-gauged approach," a previously unacknowledged body of papal social teaching emerges, primarily aimed against the Enlightenment and, of course, the French Revolution and its aftermath.

Nine popes from 1740 to 1877 made negative judgments regarding the erosion of communal unity in traditionally Roman Catholic countries and regions. This erosion is significant in religious, political, family, economic, and cultural life. The popes believe that all of this erosion is due to false ideas, which were rampant in the 18th and 19th centuries, all a product of the Enlightenment.

Also, the popes offer what Schuck calls a "territorial" communitarian ethic. This ethic is based on the papal understanding of the self and society. That self is embedded in the tradition of a territorial community. This embeddedness provides a person's sense of identity and purpose and defines one's function and obligation. The popes also understand this social ethic as "theological." The source is God's will mediated through Scripture, patristics, and Church tradition, which is primarily handed down from the top to the bottom. The metaphor is of a shepherd and a flock.

Professor Schuck also corrects an historical misunderstanding by establishing a coherence between the pre-Leonine period and all subsequent periods (Leonine 1878-88, post-Leonine 1959-89). To avoid distorting the understanding of encyclical teaching, Professor Schuck proposes a new method, now appearing in encyclical commentaries, which calls for an inclusive, holistic reading of a given pope's encyclical corpus.

Second, his method will show that the encyclicals demonstrate serious interest in social relations involving not only economic affairs, but also political, religious, family, and cultural affairs. He also claims that the pope's encyclicals contain several critical judgments of Enlightenment, premises that become constituent of encyclical social teaching. These criticisms are not simply "historical artifacts." And because the method employed by Professor Schuck shows the methods employed in arriving at the social teachings by the popes are eclectic, substantive contradictions occur in encyclical social thought. No single source nor method molds encyclical thought as a whole. Thus, to base them all on natural law thinking or on Thomistic, neo-Scholastic theology is, in Professor Schuck's opinion, inaccurate.

Yet, because the encyclicals from 1740 until today share several common recommendations on God, the world, humanity, and issues of religion, politics, family, economics, and culture, these recommendations are communitarian in nature and, combined with the persistent negative judgments made by the popes, form and constitute a coherence of encyclical social teaching.

The interesting results of the methodological approach made by Professor Schuck opens papal teaching to European political thought and Third World liberation theology. With the decentering of natural law theory and the passing of neo-Thomism as the sole philosophical approach, the way is open between papal thought and Protestant social ethics in North America and Europe. There is also a development of new links between the critiques of Western liberalism, child of the Enlightenment, and papal social teaching so interpreted. We are in Professor Schuck's debt.

Third, as a sobering note, we should remind ourselves of two conclusions that came to us from studies done near or on the centennial of Leo XIII's encyclical *Rerum novarum* of 1891.

Richard L. Camp, in his book *The Papal Ideology of Social Reform*, gives a very minimalistic evaluation of the impact of Catholic social teaching ("CST") on the world.[7] Papal social pronouncements may have contributed to the change in attitude found in Catholic labor circles granting Catholicism relevance in the modern industrial society.

There is even a stranger sobering note sounded by a seminar conducted by the Von Hügel Institute of Cambridge, England, and the Centre for Catholic Social Thought of the Faculty of Theology of the Catholic University of Leuven in Belgium. This seminar, conducted in April of 1999, prefaced all their remarks with this paragraph:

> Neither in the current bubbling debate on political theory nor in the heated exchange of ideas on national and international politics does Catholic social thought make an effective entry on the public stage in our day. Externally, it is all too often ignored even the "people of good will" appealed to in the papal encyclical *Centesimus annus*. Inside the Catholic Church, it is more frequently neglected than

vigorously adopted or put into action. Even among interested parties, it labours under a certain crisis of identity. On a wider canvas it finds itself in a vortex of challenges posed by liberal individualism and crude capitalism, by widespread social injustice and division in contemporary society, and by dominant currents of thought which, while sympathetic in some ways to Christian values, do not seem to want or need the sacred, the spiritual or the ecclesial.[8]

So, after reading and rereading Canon Aubert's articles, we can spell out seven distinct areas or major themes in Catholic social teaching ("CathST"). In a June 1998 statement of the American Bishops, we find these themes listed thus:

Modern Catholic Social Teaching has been articulated through a tradition of papal, conciliar, and episcopal documents, which explore and express the social demands of our faith. In these brief reflections, we wish to highlight several of the key themes which are at the heart of our Catholic social tradition.

1. Life and Dignity of the Human Person
In a world warped by materialism and declining respect for human life, the Catholic Church proclaims that human life is sacred and that the dignity of the person is the foundation of a moral vision for society. Our belief in the sanctity of human life and the inherent dignity of the human person is the foundation of all the principles of our social teaching. In our society, human life is under direct attack from abortion and assisted suicide. The value of human life is also being threatened by the increasing use of the death penalty. The dignity of life is undermined when the creation of human life is reduced to the manufacture of a product, as in human cloning or proposals for genetic engineering to create "perfect" human beings. We believe that every person is precious, that people are more important than things and that the measure of every institution is whether it threatens or enhances the life and dignity of the human person.

2. Call to Family, Community Participation
In a global culture driven by excessive individualism, our tradition proclaims that the person is not only sacred but also social. How we organize our society — in economics and politics, in law and policy

— directly affects human dignity and the capacity of individuals to grow in community. The family is the central social institution which must be supported and strengthened, not undermined. While our society often exalts individualism, the Catholic tradition teaches that human beings grow and achieve fulfillment in community. We believe people have a right and duty to participate in society, seeking together the common good and well being of all, especially the poor and vulnerable. Our Church teaches that the role of the government and other institutions is to protect human life and human dignity and promote the common good.

3. Rights and Responsibilities

In a world where some speak mostly of "rights" and others mostly of "responsibilities," the Catholic tradition teaches that human dignity can be protected and healthy community can be achieved only if human rights are protected and responsibilities are met. Therefore, every person has a fundamental right to life and a right to those things required for human decency. Corresponding to these rights are duties and responsibilities — to one another, to our families, and to the larger society. While public debate in our nation is often divided between those who focus on personal responsibility and those who focus on social responsibilities, our tradition insists that both are necessary.

4. Option for the Poor and Vulnerable

In a world characterized by growing prosperity for some and pervasive poverty for others, Catholic teaching proclaims that a basic moral test of any society is how its most vulnerable members are faring. In a society marred by deepening divisions between rich and poor, our tradition recalls the story of the Last Judgment (*Mt. 25*) and instructs us to put the needs of the poor and vulnerable first.

5. The Dignity and Rights of Workers

In a marketplace where too often the quarterly bottom line takes precedence over the rights of workers, we believe that the economy must serve people, not the other way around. Work is more than a way to make a living; it is a form of continuing participation in God's creation. If the dignity of work is to be protected, then the basic rights of workers must be respected — the right to productive work, to decent and fair wages, to organize and join unions, to private property and to economic initiative. Respecting these rights promotes an economy which protects human life, defends human rights, and advances the well-being of all.

6. Solidarity

Our culture is tempted to turn inward, becoming indifferent and sometimes isolationist in the face of international responsibilities. Catholic Social Teaching proclaims that we are our brothers' and sisters' keepers, wherever they live. We are one human family, whatever our national, racial, ethnic, economic, and ideological differences. Learning to practice the virtue of solidarity means learning that "loving our neighbor" has global dimensions in an interdependent world. This virtue is described by Pope John Paul II as "a firm and persevering determination to commit oneself to the common good; that is to say to the good of all and of each individual, because we are all really responsible for all" (*Sollicitudo Rei Socialis, No. 38*).

7. Care for God's Creation

On a planet conflicted over environmental issues, the Catholic tradition insists that we show our respect for the Creator by our stewardship of creation. Care for the earth is not just an Earth Day slogan, it is a requirement of our faith. We are called to protect people and the planet, living our faith in relationship with all of God's creation. This environmental challenge has fundamental moral and ethical dimensions which cannot be ignored.

This teaching is a complex and nuanced tradition with many other important elements. Principles like "subsidiarity" and the "common good" outline the advantages and limitations of markets, the responsibilities and limitations of government, the constructive role of government in our own society, and the essential roles of voluntary associations.

There will be legitimate differences and debate over how these challenging moral principles are applied in concrete situations. Differing prudential judgements on specifics, however, will not deter us from pursuing the common good and defending the dignity of the human person.[9]

There have been a number of studies done to celebrate the centennial of Pope Leo's *Rerum novarum*. As David J. O'Brien and Thomas A. Shannon point out, the social doctrine of the Church reached a climax in America with the very radical publication called the *Bishops Program of Social Reconstruction* in 1919. It was Msgr. John A. Ryan who led that charge.

During the Depression, the bishops gave support to unions and called upon government involvement in the workplace and in the marketplace to restore fiscal solvency to a depressed economy. Although the encyclicals were nostalgic for the *Ancien regime*, triumphalist in their ecclesializing, and antidemocratic and conservative, they were put into a democratic mode by John XXIII, Paul VI, and the Second Vatican Council. The modern encyclicals communicate a vision of the Church as servant to humanity, a renewed concern for the human person and human rights, an increasing emphasis on popular participation, and a more open and humble acknowledgment of the historically conditioned character of human life and consciousness. The social teachings of the modern Church also reflect the ideas and perspectives of the emerging Christian communities of the Third World. Still somewhat European-centered, the documents are nonetheless far more universal in origin, spirit, scope, and impact than ever before.

The history of the Social Doctrine of the Church, of course, began with the Church. But it was not until the Middle Ages that a synthesis was found in the work of St. Thomas Aquinas. This synthesis enabled Christianity to embrace both the radical demands of the primitive Gospel and the pressing demands of a religious establishment. The use of natural law was involved to solve this tension. As O'Brien and Shannon state:

> Eternal law existed in the mind of God from all eternity. Natural law was the apprehension of eternal law by human reason, in theory capable of knowing God's will and acting on it, but in practice flawed by sin. The state was both a punishment and a remedy for sin; it provided for the common good, most notably by the repression of evil. The church, of divine origin, possesses revealed truth and directs people and institutions to their final, supernatural end.
>
> The church is therefore superior to the state; it interprets the demands of natural law and imposes sanctions on both institutions and individuals. Some, called by God to a special vocation, practice the heroic virtues demanded by the Gospel, while church and state cooperate to enforce more moderate, realistic moral demands on society at large.

The person thus stands at the center of two intersecting lines, the natural and supernatural, united through the eternal and natural law and through the church and the state. On this basis Aquinas envisioned an organically unified universe in which there were transcendent norms to assist in understanding and evaluating human experience. There was in this universe a proper ordering of all things and harmony within and among the several orders. Individuals occupied particular roles or functions within a hierarchical society. They were bound to one another and to social institutions by duties inherent in their state of life. What held society together and gave it ethical discipline and coherence was a theory of social obligation that sprang from the very nature of society and was related to a hierarchical universe presided over by God. Social obligations thus took priority over individual desires and wants.[10]

This medieval world was shattered by modernity. Modernity heralds the triumph of subjectivity and the loss of objective realism. Again our author points out:

Perhaps most important, one of the major consequences of the breakup of the medieval unity of civilization was the perception that individuals stood in an adversary relationship to the larger society, a perception which, together with the opportunity for choice presented by contending religious factions, fostered a deeper sense of individual autonomy and personal worth. As a result of this new perception of the individual's place in society, a new theory of the proper relationship between the individual and society was needed.[11]

Emphasizing the subjective enhanced the value of the individual by making the person, not society, the locus of natural law. Not one's state in life, but obligations agreed upon by individuals became normative. Thus, conflicts arose. In such a world where truth is equated with positive certitude, where mechanism explains the world, and where religion is disparaged by making it a private thing, anyone who would insist on order and harmony backed up by a divinely constituted authority capable of announcing and enforcing the demands of nature and nature's God would come face to face with tensions upon tensions. The Catholic Church's rejection of modernity and its fellow, the Enlightenment, provides the basic background for the Social Doctrine of the Church for the last one hundred years. Our authors point out that in reading the texts of the Social Doctrine of the Church, one must make an effort to distinguish with the Church its need to be both prophetic and responsible in order to be significant in the contemporary world. To overcome what appears to be insurmountable problems, we must be both idealistic and real. If we do not believe that justice is possible, then fatalism will make things worse. Contrariwise, we cannot be dreamers. We have to face hard and ambiguous choices; otherwise, forces beyond our control will enhance the inhuman world.

A hard-nosed reading of the texts shows that the prophet and the politician are both necessary to bear true witness to the truth of the Church. Our authors are very right in describing these tensions between prophet and politician. They correctly maintain that:

> The tension between the Gospel and social analysis thus remains at the heart of Catholic social teaching. Even the simplest reflection on the beatitudes forces two conclusions: 1) that Christians are called to an ethic of perfection by the revelation in Christ of a God Who is love; and 2) that the Church and its members must respond to that vocation in the midst of a history in which real, complex human beings live. It is not a simple matter to be both a good Christian and a good citizen, any more than it is simply to be the Church and to share responsibility for the problems of a pluralistic society. The documents collected in this volume reflect this ever present-tension and pervasive ambiguity. So it is simply wrong to abstract any one statement or issue from the context of the overall teaching, for it is precisely that larger framework of integrity and responsibility which is the unique contribution of Catholic social teaching. If this is true, then certain conclusions follow:
>
> 1) The contemporary documents need to be examined in light of the continuing historical effort to relate Christian faith to the problems of modern society, that is, to Catholic theology broadly understood.
>
> 2) The documents need to be examined as well in the context of the overall life of the contemporary church; these teachings are one, but only one, important expression of Catholic faith and life.

They can be understood and evaluated only in relation to other expressions of Catholicism, from the spiritual lives of individuals through the worship and fellowship of congregations to the ongoing development of Catholic theology.

3) The documents are best read and evaluated from the viewpoint of the laity. More than other formal documents of the church, these are located at the intersection of the church and the world, the sacred and the secular. Of their very nature they deal with the problems of living the Christian life in the midst of ordinary human relationships. Individuals who devote their lives to the organizations of the Church, of course, have something to contribute to the implementation of these teachings. But as the Second Vatican Council affirmed, social, political, and economic problems are the special concern of the laity. They are uniquely qualified to describe what in fact is going on and to evaluate what should be done. In the past there has been too little effort to consult the laity in the development of these teachings, too little effort to ask lay people what they think before telling them what to do. Given the situation of the church in the modern world, and given the experience of all local churches since the Second Vatican Council, it is clear that this will no longer be acceptable, if it ever was. It is the laity who must reshape the course of history. It is they who must act and, if they are to act, they will have to be more fully enlisted in the process that determines what that action should be. Of course there are elements of faith which for Catholics evoke the unique charisma of the hierarchy; but it is not hard to determine in these documents where such matters of doctrine end and more complex matters of applied theology, including morality, begin. At that point the laity have the right, and indeed the obligation, to speak up and to act.[12]

Finally, a sincere faith and familiarity with what the popes and bishops say must always be combined with an alertness to what is going on around us and a willingness to inform ourselves about public life. We must be familiar not only with the theological formulation of the documents, but also with the concrete solutions to which they could or do refer.

One of the reactions to modernity and to the Enlightenment is to challenge their method of knowing. At the moment, the average person in the street is obedient to three imperatives: the technological, the economic, and the company policy. This bureaucratic, technocratic, managerial, and instrumentalist rationality has to be broken open. What is being suggested by the Social Doctrine of the Church is that one uses the Scriptures. The Scriptures are exhortative, not normative. Use them to provoke you to think bigger than the utilitarian ethic of modernity, with its residue of a minority.

The Scriptures are rich in defending the sacredness of the human person. How are we to protect the sacredness of the human person in every age? The Old Testament is complemented by the New Testament. Every human is joined to the humanity of Christ when He became flesh. He must be recognized in all His neighbors, especially the poor, the widows, and the children. Catholic social teaching uses Biblical language, which transcends time and place, and is surely not restricted to the instrumentalist causality of modernity.

During the last one hundred years, we have gone through at least four stages. First was the industrial stage (1891-1941), wherein the Church defended human rights by defending the rights of working people. They also insisted on the government's right to intervene in economic affairs. Then came the globalization stage (early 1940s to the present), the establishment of the United Nations, prevention of genocide, limitation of nuclear weapons, and protection of the rights of workers in the Third World. Pope John XXIII's great encyclical, *Peace on Earth,* addressed the rights of workers as well as political and civil rights in connection with economic rights. From 1971 on came the post-industrial-secular stage, which moved the world from rural and manual labor to urban technological centers. The Church must now deal with this.

Finally, we have the social teaching of Pope John Paul II. He speaks of human dignity and human rights. Throughout it all, there is a consistent moral trend in that Catholics believe that God is the Creator of life and humans have no right to end another person's life. While Catholics cannot do all the good in the world, they can avoid doing harm.

In the summer of 1991, a conference at Cambridge in England entitled "Four Revolutions: An Unfinished Agenda" was held. The revolutions referred to were the industrial, the liberal capitalist, the socialist, and the one which has not yet taken place, the Christian social revolution.

Five different groups assembled to discuss five different topics: 1) social philosophy, 2) the historical context of *Rerum novarum*, 3) social services and ethics/theology, 4) political thought and the theory of the State, and 5) economics in a modern advanced economy. The conference corrected two mistakes. One, there was no substantive encyclical teaching before *Rerum novarum*, as we mentioned above.[13] Two, there is only one model of Catholic social teaching, namely, that of *Rerum novarum*. Yet, there is common agreement that Pope Leo XIII's *Rerum novarum* inaugurated a special period of encyclical social teaching, which acquired a remarkable and monolithic continuity from 1891 until the death of Pius XII in 1958.

This conference found that natural law continues to be an important element in the Catholic tradition. Europe was pointed out as being of historical importance to the whole nature of Catholic social teaching. Canon Aubert's articles underline this and emphasize the relationship as mediator between political theories and economics to Catholic social thinking.[14]

Another book celebrating the centennial of *Rerum novarum* was published by the Center for Ethics at the University of Notre Dame.[15] This book contains twenty essays that reflect on the development and evolution of Catholic social teaching and analyzes its positive application for the contemporary world. From the earliest origins, the Catholic Church has tried to influence society, and society has, to varying degrees, shaped the Church. Recently, with the demise of the Marxist alternative to capitalism, Catholic social teaching has assumed the role of the major international force challenging free enterprise to be more humane. What does the Church have to say about the world's current situation and the possibility of a new world order, and how has this message evolved over the past one hundred years?

In light of heightened awareness that Catholic social thought has an increasingly major role to play in the international forum, these clear-sighted analyses of the past, present, and future of Catholic social thought and its continuing influence on personal and communal life in our times will appeal to scholars and laypersons alike.

The idea of a new world order was given prominence by former U.S. President George Bush during the Gulf War and the last years of his administration. President Bill Clinton clearly demonstrated his resolve to carry forward that theme in his Inaugural Address on January 20, 1993:

> To renew America, we must meet challenges abroad as well as at home. There is no longer a clear division between what is foreign and what is domestic. The world economy, the world environment, the world AIDS crisis, the world arms race — they affect us all.
>
> Today, as an old order passes, the new world is more free but less stable. Communism's collapse has called forth old animosities and new dangers. Clearly, America must continue to lead the world we did so much to make.
>
> While America rebuilds at home, we will not shrink from the challenges nor fail to seize the opportunities of this new world. Together with our friends and allies we will work to shape change lest it engulf us.[16]

As Canon Aubert (who is everybody's teacher and precursor in these matters) has reminded us, one has to go to the Rhineland to look for the origins of Catholic social thought. Today, we have the writings of Joseph Cardinal Höffner of Cologne. He has left us a marvelous book entitled *Christian Social Teaching*.[17]

Christian Social Teaching is composed of two parts: Foundations and the Structure of Social Order. The first part, Foundations, has three sections. Section one has two chapters on the social nature of humanity, community, society, and the loss of individuality. Section two spells out the principles of the social order in three chapters: the solidarity principle, the common good principle, and the subsidiarity principle. The third section has two chapters, law as a norm of social life and the virtue of justice. The second part of the book is on the structure of the social order. It has five sections, the first on marriage and the second on the family. The second section is on work and profession. This is divided into the concept and definition of work, the meaning of work and profession, the meaning of work and leisure, the professional conditions in industrial society, and Christian ethics.

The third section concerns the economy. In this section, the Cardinal spells out the material object of the economy, the order of the economy, the order according to socialism, and, in great detail, the order of priests' ownership as the foundation of the economic order in Christian social teaching. Here he lists five components: 1) the community of goods in paradise, in the monastery, and in the world; 2) the reasons for the system of priests' ownership; 3) the natural law character of priests' ownership; 4) the individual and social formation of ownership; and 5) the crisis of the economic formation of priests' ownership in modern society. The third chapter of this section is concerned with the distribution of the social product. Here, the Cardinal speaks about rent, interest, income, profits, and social security.

The final section concerns the State and Government. What is its origin, its authority, its rights and duties? What is resistance? What are the roles of Church and State? He concludes his book with chapters on the role of the united or community of nations. What is the legacy of colonialism and what is our obligation of development? This is a marvelous book, especially for beginners, outlining the social doctrine of the Church. Especially interesting is the story of the author.

Joseph Höffner was born in 1906 into a rural family of eight children in a small village in Germany. In 1929, he obtained a Ph.D. at the Gregorian Papal University in Rome; after being ordained in 1932, he was awarded a theology doctorate in 1934 with a dissertation on *Social Justice and Social Love*. With his study, *Peasant and Church in Medieval Germany*, he also obtained a German theology doctorate from the University of Freiburg in 1938. At the same university, he studied economics under Walter Eucken and wrote a dissertation on *Business Ethics and Monopolies in the 15th and 16th Centuries*.

In 1945, Höffner became professor of pastoral theology and Christian social teaching at the Trier Seminary; in 1951, he was appointed professor of Christian social sciences at the University of Münster, where in 1960 he founded the *Yearbook of Christian Social Sciences*.

Apart from his teaching and research work, he was involved in Germany's post-war political and social reconstruction as a member of advisory committees to the federal ministries for family and youth, housing, labour, and social affairs as head of the social affairs department of the Central Committee of the German Catholics and as advisor to the Federation of Catholic Entrepreneurs. Höffner's *Christian Social Teaching* appeared in the year he was appointed Bishop of Münster, 1962. In 1969, he became Archbishop of Cologne and Cardinal, in 1976 Chair of the German Bishops Conference. Through his numerous publications and his visits to many parts of the Third World, Höffner acquired increasing esteem as an ambassador of the Church's social teaching. He died in 1987.

Perhaps the most interesting of the centennial studies is published by the Catholic University of Leuven. There, in 1999, eighteen mostly European Catholic intellectuals called upon other experts in the field of Catholic social teaching. Their initiative was directed by "more than encyclicals" and there they studied the causes, notions, and implications of the neglect of nonofficial Catholic social thought.

Taking a distance from official Catholic thought of the popes and bishops, they studied long-standing but relatively neglected translations of Catholic nonofficial thought (CNOST). They felt it was essential to do this to have an effective Catholic intellectual presence in contemporary public debate. In defense of this singular perspective, the authors felt:

> …it must be said that it is not adopted in any un-ecumenical spirit but in the interests of a deepening of a tradition which does possess some critical mass both historically and conceptually, and which, it is hoped, may thus be made available to others in a richer form. More general approaches often end up with a sharing of abstract, under-explored generalities.[18]

Besides that, these

> …essays converge in criticizing or distancing themselves from a number of past excesses and mistakes in CathST, both official and nonofficial: notably a frequent rigidity or pseudo-precision, over-confident or triumphalist claims to provide "solutions," a rule-book rather than a guidebook approach. They do not accept a widespread limitation of CathST to the *magisterium* of the Church or the official social declarations of the Popes and Councils (while according to these, of course, the appropriate close attention and respect).

The assumption is that the drive and inspiration which comes from the Church's official social teaching, essential and vital as it is, particularly in proclaiming over-arching values and guidelines, needs to be complemented and carried forward by thinking which is able to adapt to varying geographical and cultural contexts, to take greater risks (including political risks), to offer alternative approaches to policy or prescriptions for social, political, and economic improvement, and hence, often, to be prepared to be controversial among Catholics as well as in the world outside.[19]

All of these essays show strong commitment to Catholic belief and Christian values and they seek engagement with the social, political, and economic circumstances that influence social justice.

The authors bring to the discussion what may be called "middle-level social thinking;" that is, thinking in the large and complex areas that lie between broad values and principles, and, on the other hand, concrete action and decisions. This kind of thinking will use:

a) models of society, politics, or the economy; b) theories of history and of social, political, and economic relationships; c) empirical observation and analysis; and d) thinking about policy and "improvement." All of these will be found here in various mixtures, along with pervasive, underlying influences from philosophy, social ethics, and theology. Many of the essays use leading contemporary thinkers on the borders of Christian social thought or, more likely, "outside the camp" altogether, as interlocutors.[20]

Jean-Yves Calvez, S.J., a veteran leading authority in the Social Doctrine of the Church, raises in his commentary the persistent unease in challenges not met. We will see at the end of this essay how he spells this out in his latest book, *Les Silences de La Doctrine Sociale Catholique.*

Stof Hellemans wonders what will happen with the passing of "ultramontane mass Catholicism" when modernity finally gives way and the Second Vatican Council works out its still incomplete "post-modern" mutation. After all, the search for an adequate conception of transcendence appears far from finished. How does the necessary allow genuine contingency? How does the contingent affect the nature of necessity? These questions are far from answered; but humankind will not rest till they are.[21]

Can neo-Thomism be of any help here? What emphasis should be placed on the hermeneutics of sacred Scripture? How should CNOST be consulted for not only theory, but praxis and policy? Above all, does Catholic social teaching have anything distinctive to say? If so, where does the difference come from? Is there something distinctive about Catholic social thought? Do we know something other people do not?

The natural law theory has to be rethought, updated, and made relevant. Does not Catholic social thought include not only rational, philosophical arguments, but also, and decisively, both reflection and praxis as a continuous relationship of hermeneutic interpretation and inspiration with Gospel narrative, poetry, and metaphor, which challenges us to a constant deepening renewal?

It is questioned whether Catholic social thought is not pretentious or divisive; and what is suggested is that Catholic social thought made an honest effort for justice and for cooperation with secular thought, which taking a cue from "discourse ethics" draws on a universally accessible set of rules for fair and rational discussion.

Again and again the question is raised why Catholic social thought is so often esoteric or misunderstood internally and externally. The imperatives that secular society obey were under constant scrutiny and the question is asked why cannot or why has not Catholic thought addressed or related to them? Let us quote their summary:

> Certain guiding threads run through these and other essays: namely, 1. Christian anthropology (the freedom and dignity of the human person, the social and communitarian aspects of human nature) as implying cooperation with some parts of contemporary secular thinking, confrontation with others; 2. the "peak notion of solidarity" in various forms, as "community" or "relationality," or in lesser ways as "civic spirit," "interdependence," "culture of giving," "reciprocity," "communion of goods," key aspects of "social capital"; 3. "subsidiarity" in terms of "civil society," "power-sharing" or "intermediate associations"; 4. "justice" and "option for the poor." But although these may be good guiding principles, they still need a lot of working through and connecting, by way of middle-level

thinking, to ideas for policy. The contributions in this book do no more than point to some possible ways forward.[22]

In their final set of essays, five levels of action are touched on: health and social care, Third World development, reform of international finance, cooperative enterprise, and the inclusion of the poorest section of society. Donal Dorr finds Church practices and attitudes still critically and tragically deficient. He advocates more radical methods of "being with" and "listening to" the socially deprived and marginalized.

We should pause here and listen closely to what he says. Option for the poor is at the extreme end of the Catholic social teaching spectrum. If we focus only on what seems potentially realistic at any given time, we are failing to give the Church its prophetic role and voice. A major purpose of the Church is to stand for, and give witness to, a different and better future that is bound to seem unrealistic in present day times.[23] The prophetic dimension of the Christian vision would be betrayed. The option for the poor is an integral part of Catholic social teaching.

What Dorr means by the option for the poor is explained when he says:

> When I speak of option for the poor in a biblical sense I have in mind a spirituality inspired by the belief that God chooses the weak to confound the strong, chooses the foolish to show up the wisdom of the wise (*1 Cor 1:27-8*). Again and again in the Bible we see the weak ones, the unlikely ones, being chosen by God in order to show that what matters if not human power but trust in and reliance on divine initiative and power. … It is rather a matter of taking the side of those who are the most marginalised and weakest people in society. There is no serious likelihood that the widows, the orphans, the "strangers" (that is, the refugees), the prostitutes or the tax-collectors will ever become major political powers in society. To opt for the poor is not to make a carefully calculated political gamble but to throw oneself on the mercy of God. It is to renounce any likelihood of political success in the conventional sense, but rather to redefine radically the very notion of success. It is a deci-

sion to find joy and fulfillment in ways that are incomprehensible in conventional terms.[24]

He outlines for us two important aspects of the "Option for the Poor." First, a "solidarity" aspect, which is about lifestyle. It is a deliberate choice to enter in some degree into the world of those who have been left on the margins of society, and a sharing in their experiences of being left behind, bypassed, mistrusted, or left helpless. Solidarity allows one to become one with the other, or, even better, one of the other.

Solidarity is a virtue; that is, it is a habitual attitude and style of being and relating that causes one to be sensitive to the needs and feelings of others in the group and to devote oneself generously to the common good.

Second, the "Option for the Poor" has to do with analysis and political or quasi-political action. There are stages in this aspect. First, careful discernment and analysis of the situation. Second, ensuring that one is not unconsciously colluding in the process of marginalization. Third, joint action to challenge the marginalization. Fourth, searching for realistic alternatives to the present state of marginalization.

On the one hand, it is very difficult to say that the option for the poor is not a truly Christian thing; on the other hand, there is resistance to it when taken in its full meaning. It is too radical for the authorities. They are inclined to avoid it or to tone it down without realizing, as Dorr says, "they are distorting a crucial aspect of the faith they profess."[25] He spells out this problem in strong language when he says:

> The problem gets much more serious when the institutional life of the Church comes into the question, as it usually does. As part of its evangelizing mission the Church sees itself as called to insert Christian values and, perhaps, some elements of "a Christian ethos" into the community in different countries, and even into international relations. In recent centuries, Church leaders have operated on the assumption that one of the most effective ways to do this is to own or control some of the major "instruments of culture" such as schools, hospitals, newspapers, and other media. So, the institutional Church frequently becomes quite a powerful

agent in society, part of "the establishment." Consequently, Church leaders often have a certain vested interest in preserving the main structures of the society in which they live, even while they seek to bring about certain changes for the better. Church leaders and many theologians belong to a rather privileged class of people in society; and they can scarcely avoid being influenced in their opinions and values by those with whom they mix.

The new emphasis on option for the poor calls into question this whole model of Church influence and the corresponding status of the institutional Church and church leaders and theologians in society.[26]

He concludes with the observation:

It is quite evident that the outcome of all this has been a rather obvious disparity between the official teaching and the practical action of the Roman authorities. I have said that there are references to a preferential option for the poor in some of the Pope's addresses in Latin America. But they are hedged around with provisos and warnings. And, whatever may be thought about the addresses of the Pope, it is quite clear that there is little or no practical support from the Vatican for any really radical option, using that term in the rather technical sense I have outlined here. Concern for the poor, yes; "option" for the poor, not yet, and perhaps not at all.[27]

This study from Cambridge and Leuven has some common traits. In all the essays there is a clear refection of an apparently hegemonic form of present day capitalism, characterized as individualistic, market-imperialist, consumerized, and grossly unequal. But, there is no nostalgia for some "golden days" in our past. No longing for the *Ancien regime.*

When they speak of "community" or "solidarity," "responsibility," as well as rights, "devaluation," "civil society," and "social inclusion," all of these ideas our authors insist must take on flesh and blood. They must result in a more effective, concrete recognition of human rights. They present neither a unitary paradigm nor a comprehensive prospectus because, as yet, many policy issues are not addressed.

Finally, what all the authors call for is the need to re-explore the values and principles themselves, and particularly their continuous stimulation from religious beliefs and practices. What has to be done, as John Milbank suggests, is that we draw out the consequences of the recognition of the priority of the other-worldly as the precondition of justice. As he says, "politics of time seeks, first of all, to ritualize life as a passage, in order to capture in the passage certain traces of the eternal. In this sense it is fundamentally liturgical."[28]

It is in Charles Curran's latest work that we find the first comprehensive analysis and criticism of the development of modern Catholic social teaching (CathST) from the perspective of theology, ethics, and Church history.[29] As he points out in the preface to this book, today an historical and critical hermeneutic has been brought to the study of Catholic social teaching. Thus, his newest book is a perfect complement to Canon Aubert's articles.

Building on Aubert and on his other works, Curran contends that the fundamental basis for Catholic social teaching comes from an anthropological perspective that recognizes both the inherent dignity and the social nature of the human person. Thus, there is charted a middle cause between the two extremes of individualism and collectivism. As Aubert before him, Curran's systematic analysis reveals the significant historical developments that have accrued over the course of more than a century. Thus, there is pointed out discontinuities between the documents. When one examines, as does Curran, the fundamental changes that have occurred in the theological, ethical, and ecclesial methodologies, significant discontinuities do exist. The danger of ideology is possible if one does not recognize the discontinuities, if not outright mistakes.

Curran treats these matters under the title of "Tensions and Problems Connected with Authoritative Teaching."[30] Besides the above problem of discontinuities, there are five others. First, a very real tension from the fact that Catholic social teaching claims to be both authoritative Church teaching and a matter of natural law. How do we put the two of them together?

Second, the tension between an authoritative Church and a skip away from a triumphalistic Church with all the answers. Nowadays, we are in dialogue with all others working for a better world.

Third, does not the teaching Church also learn? Fourth, there is a tension in the citing of sources. Would citation from other than Scripture, the fathers, Aquinas, and previous popes, would they not also be welcomed without diminishing the truth of the documents? And finally, who wrote these documents that the popes have signed? All of these texts have to be interpreted.

To do that, at least six steps are needed: a) we must understand the complexity of the text; b) we must understand the author(s). Who wrote these texts for the pope's signature? What was their education? From what schools of thought did they come? What ideologies are operative? What defensive interests are manifest or hidden? Real tensions are obvious when one seeks out the ghost author. c) We must then understand the "schools" to which the author(s) belong. d) We must understand the social context of both text and author. Do not get the texts out of context, which means to e) understand the "world of the text;" and, f) we must understand the *wirkungsgeschichte* of the texts.

In his introduction, Curran points out that his perspective on the Social Doctrine of the Church comes from the discipline of Catholic ethics, which:

> …as a second-order discourse, endeavors to study the social teachings in a thematic, systematic, and scientific way. Systematic and scientific study of these documents gives great importance to methodological aspects. Although these documents themselves do not explicitly develop their methodology at length, methodological approaches play a very significant role in all of them. The discipline of social ethics also is concerned with the major themes and positions taken, but it tries to put all the aspects together in a logical, thematic, and systematic manner.[31]

Curran's book centers on anthropology as the basis for Catholic social teaching; it is the key to understanding the teaching.

The anthropology found in Catholic social teaching has four aspects. First, there is an emphasis on human fulfillment. Second, there is a danger of optimism. Human happiness will not come in this world; it will come only in the next. Third, Catholic social teaching insists on both faith and good works. Fourth, as Curran clearly states:

...morality is intrinsic, not extrinsic. Extrinsic morality regards the moral norm as something imposed on the human being from outside. Intrinsic morality regards morality as coming from within the human person and contributing to her or his fulfillment and happiness. Despite some lapses in practice, the best Catholic theory has always insisted on intrinsic morality. Something is commanded because it is good, not the other way around. Thus, human fulfillment and happiness constitute the summary of our duties.[32]

Catholic social teaching rests on two fundamental anthropological principles: the dignity or sacredness of the human person and the social nature of the person.

In Catholic thought, human dignity is God-given. All humans have the same fundamental dignity because all are created and redeemed by God. All human beings are equal inasmuch as they have the right to be respected as they are and not reduced by another to what the other might think they are. All human beings are different inasmuch as they are all in different stages of development and, therefore, are in need of others' help. These ideas of equality and difference are well expressed in the philosophy of Emmanuel Levinas.[33]

The present pope bases the dignity of humans on an anthropology that is directly theological in nature. Suppose one does not believe in Christian theology? How could you discuss with him or her human dignity? Are the rights of humans founded only on theology or on theology and human reason? What would the reason be? We remember what John XXIII said in *Pacem in terris*:

> (9) Any human society, if it is to be well-ordered and productive, must lay down as a foundation this principle, namely, that every human being is a person; that is, his nature is endowed with intelligence and free will. Indeed, precisely because he is a person he has rights and obligations flowing directly and simultaneously from his very nature. And as these rights and obligations are universal and inviolable, so they cannot in any way be surrendered.
>
> (10) If we look upon the dignity of the human person in the light of divinely revealed truth, we cannot help but esteem it far more highly; for men are redeemed by the blood of Jesus Christ, they

are by grace the children and friends of God and heirs of eternal glory.[34]

As we shall see later on, does not a restriction of the Social Doctrine of the Church to theology alone limit it from what we thought it might be? Is theology sufficient to appeal to all persons of good will?

The Social Doctrine of the Church never adopted an individualistic conception of humanity. They meant what they said when they put DesCartes on the Index. Humans are not extrinsic to their environment. The bourgeois conception of humanity is flawed. DesCartes' *cogito* is not an equation. There is no consciousness which is not conscious of something other than oneself. The ethical implication of this is what is worked out in existentialism and phenomenology. As Curran says, "the social aspect of human existence is not something added on to the person but an essential part of the human reality."[35]

Catholic tradition is Aristotelian-Thomistic. This means a form of realism, not idealism. The subject is informed by the object, not vice-versa. This relationship in human matters means that humans are social and political by nature. Insisting on the human's social nature is against modernity and the Enlightenment and surely against DesCartes. To bring this out, one needs a neo-Thomism, which uses the new to renew the old. Leo XIII wanted to do it the other way. It was Cardinal Mercier and the Louvain School that turned the procedure around.[36] This will result in a use of contemporary thought, existentialism and phenomenology, to correct the errors of modern anthropology. Very simply, the way DesCartes discussed consciousness, the way he said we are, is not the way we are.

Thus, in contemporary thought, realism arises once again in the philosophical world and, thus, in anthropology. Pope John Paul II is a phenomenologist of distinction. His making solidarity a central theme in his social teaching is indicative of this mentality:

> When interdependence becomes recognized in this way, the correlative response, as a moral and social attitude, as a "virtue," is solidarity. This then is not a feeling of vague compassion or shallow distress at the misfortunes of so many people, both near and far. On the contrary. It is a firm and persevering determination to commit

oneself to the common good; that is to say, to the good of all and of each individual because we are all really responsible for all.[37]

The strongest part of Curran's book is found in pages 133-135, for here he spells out the context in which he draws out the implications of Catholic social teaching for the United States. He engages himself in dialogue within the context of this society. He says:

> This insistence on the fact that all human beings are sisters and brothers who are called to live and to work together in solidarity flies in the face of the rampant individualism in the United States that regards the individual as the be-all and end-all. The self-made person remains a strong mythic and iconic figure even in contemporary American culture. The self-made person is able to do whatever he or she wants if he or she works hard enough. Many commentators have pointed out the danger of individualism in American society. The anthropology developed in Catholic social teaching opposes an individualism that emphasizes the person as a self-made individual. None of us is self-made. We are obviously dependent on God but also on many other human beings — family, friends, teachers, various associations, and the political community.[38]

We must not forget that we are at the end of an age. Our poets, artists, and playwrights have gone before us. Our philosophers are just now correcting the past errors. When all of your geniuses are critics, you know something is wrong. We are on the verge of a new breakthrough. We are moving from raw individualism towards a new communitarianism. This is what the Catholic Social Doctrine has called for. As Curran points out, the social and communitarian nature of human existence shows itself in many ways. And despite the American myth of the self-made person, experience reminds us, if we do not lack profound thinking, that we are social by nature and find fulfillment and true development only in and through social relationships and social structures.

Catholic social teaching recognizes both the dignity of the human person and the human's social nature. Very simply, I need a we to be.

Ethics begins when I begin. It is coterminus with my existence. I have first of all to preserve myself in being. I have to build myself up so that I can recognize and help the other person. Otherness is equated with needfulness. When I consult the sacred Scriptures as to how it is I ought to be, the good Samaritan is pointed out as one who is as he ought to be with his neighbor. Do not fail to notice that he is about his business; that he has a jackass with saddlebags loaded for emergencies; that he has money to pay the innkeeper. So he has taken care of himself, but, and this is the moral of the story, ethics is an interruption in life. All were on the road from Jerusalem down to Jericho — that is the road of life where self-interest obtains. Only the good Samaritan interrupts that life; he denies himself to be of help to the other who by being other is needful. Jesus gives, in one sentence, the ethics lesson of all time, "Go and do likewise" (*Luke 1:37*). To do it you must be another self than the self-promoting individual. It is what Levinas calls the responsible self.[39] Curran, in one sentence, passes sentence on the United States with this insightful remark:

> In all of these areas, Catholic social teaching finds the greatest opposition in the United States from the perspective of an individualistic ethic that does not give enough importance to the social nature of the human person.[40]

The Church, for Curran in his interpretation of the Social Doctrine, is an agent for progress. Being Catholic is all about trying to change the world, about becoming a "transformation agent." And the danger is always that as American Catholics, we will instead give in to the individualistic culture and *status quo*. Individualistic is here understood as understanding oneself to be extrinsic to and not responsible for your environment. The other person is seen as an obstacle or as a possibility for one's own development. On the road from Jerusalem to Jericho, which is the road of life, we do not feel any obligation for the person in the ditch, who is other, who has been used and beaten up by others. We understand ourselves as self-defined, as extrinsic. We are in Sartrian terms *bougeoisie*. The other is hell and an obstacle.

We, lacking fundamental questioning, fail to see how our definition of ourselves is too narrow, too abstract, childish, selfish, and greedy.

How is it that we ought to be with the other? It surely is radically different than how we are.

When Christ humbled Himself and came among us, He at least showed us how one ought to be with the other. True spirituality, for the Christian, has to be based on the imitation of Christ. How to re-say who we are, how to re-say it in a more adequate way is one of the problems found in the Social Doctrine of the Church. Over the last one hundred years, attempts were made by resurrecting a Thomist-Aristotelian paradigm for redefining our anthropology. Not all these attempts were successful.

The problem with neo-Thomism is where does one start? What Thomistic principles would one use? The attempt became diverse and in many cases pluralistic. Thus, again, I think Cardinal Mercier was correct in demanding that one start where people are and then see how Aristotle and Thomas might shed some light on the subject. Metaphysics is a demand for realism, but at the moment we are still centered on the philosophy of the subject as a source of meaning traditionally reserved to a transcendent source of power.[41] Phenomenology has been successful in helping us redefine our nature of the self. While isolation may be, in our nostalgia of the past, desirable, yet today, total involvement is the reality. How then should we be with the other? That person beaten up and lying in the ditch along the road of life has begun to catch our attention. That is one small reason why we have a pope. The pope is not only against abortion, he is also, and very much so, against ignoring that beaten up person in the ditch.

I suspect the ordinary person walking the streets in America begins to suspect that something is wrong. September 11, 2001, was more than a wake-up call. For years now, labor unions have addressed themselves to the undeserving poor of the industrial world yet still only about twenty percent of American workers have successfully brought about safety in the workplace.

And, there is something which now looms more important than ever to an aging population — successful retirement programs. We also know that reason alone leaves us with a utilitarian ethics, with a residue of abandoned people. The greatest good for the greatest number does not include everyone. With the introduction of Sacred

Scripture into the Social Doctrine of the Church, it demands that no
one be left out. Again, what is in store is an attempt to break open
the limited hermeneutic horizon of our time, marked by an iron
cage of bureaucratic, technocratic, managerial, and instrumentalist
rationality.[42]

It is here that Curran, following Paul VI, correctly calls for a learning
process on the part of a teaching process:

> ...[T]he social teaching of the Church should be considered as
> the result of a dialogue between the magisterium of the pope, the
> bishops (including their general and regional synods and the texts
> made in the context of bishops conferences), the specialists in social
> ethics and social sciences and the people of God.

Paul VI in *Octogesima Adveniens* (nr 4) expressed a methodological
option to this "learning process" when he said:

> In the face of such widely varying situations it is difficult for
> us to utter a unified message and to put forward a solution
> which has universal validity. Such is not our ambition, nor
> is it our mission. It is up to the Christian communities to
> analyze with objectivity the situation which is proper to
> their own country, to shed on it the light of the Gospel's
> unalterable words and to draw principles of the church
> (...) It is up to these Christian communities, with the help
> of the Holy Spirit, in communion with the bishops who
> hold responsibility and in dialogue with other Christian
> brethren and all men of good will, to discern the options
> and commitments which are called for in order to bring
> about the social, political and economic changes seen in
> many cases to be urgently needed.[43]

Curran encapsulates the key documents in his book. He says these
documents develop the basic anthropology — the human person as
sacred and social — which transcends times and cultures. American
bishops and bishops everywhere can use this anthropology to criticize the one-sided individualism so prevalent in our own society and
worldwide.

Curran is mostly concerned in his book with the methodology found
in papal documents. How natural law has been interpreted bothers

him and rightly so. From Leo's pontificate on a hierarchial schema of scholastic thought, in which the Church as a supernatural entity stands morally above the natural human sphere, it dominated official Catholic pronouncements until the Vatican Council of the mid 1960s. It surely was there that a more democratic, dialogical model focused on the subject and a more collegial appreciation of the Church's role within national and world affairs was unveiled. However, the old methods and the new methods still exist in strong tension, as Curran makes clear. Thus, he is not so concerned as to what the Church teaches as to the competing methodological frameworks that shape the style, interpretation, and direction of the teaching.

As Curran points out, three generic models exist for moral theology:

> The deontological model understands morality primarily in terms of duty or law and conformity to duty or law. The teleological model considers morality in terms of ends or goals. One decides the normative ends or goals and judges means in relationship to obtaining these ends. The third model, relationality-responsibility, sees the human person in multiple relationships with God, neighbor, world, and self and acting responsibly within these relationships.
>
> These models are generic and broad, and many different varieties of ontology and teleology exist. One important difference for our purposes in teleological approaches concerns intrinsic or extrinsic teleology. Extrinsic teleology, which is identified with consequentialism and utilitarianism, regards the end as extrinsic to the human person and her or his act. These ends are consequences that follow from the act. Intrinsic teleology regards the ends as constitutive inclinations of the human person, who obtains fulfillment by achieving the ends to which the person is inclined.[44]

The third model based on the shift to historical consciousness and on the emphasis on the person as subject causes us difficulty when speaking of an unchanging eternal law with specific guidelines. Especially, we should note that the conversion of the subject helps us become more aware of the interdependence among all individuals and all nations. I am responsible for all and everyone and I more than anyone else. Solidarity constitutes the virtue that deals with this interdependence and responsibility. Spelling out the role of this relational-responsibility model of ethics now becomes the task of Catholic social thinking.[45]

Curran's book is essential reading for anyone interested in the Church's social teaching. His emphasis on anthropology, his description of how ethics works, his study of the tensions at work in the social teaching, and his evolution of its role is crucial to understanding the teaching. For Curran, the human is the sign of the Divine presence and activity in our midst. How is Christ in the world? How is the Divine present? How is the natural law to be interpreted? How do we use Scripture? What is a "good will"? Why is there not a consistent, coherent, and integrated theological approach? Who is the audience? People of the Faith? People of good will? What is the implication of the historicity of consciousness? Are we caught in ideologies? What if the significance of finding out the claims to be universal, neutral, value-free were limited, blind, prejudicial? What is the implication that all commentators agree that the Social Doctrine is authoritative, non-infallible teaching? How binding then are the encyclicals and pastoral letters? What response is owned them? Should they be specific or general? All these questions are raised in Curran's book and we would do well to meditate on all of them.

Among the number of smaller books on Catholic social teaching, one stands out as an excellent introduction and guide. It is a small book of over two hundred pages, divided into seven chapters. It gives a fresh and thoughtful look at contemporary essays and how we might, with Catholic social teaching, respond to them. Rooted in Scripture, tradition, and living experiences of holiness, its timeliness informs and inspires the reader to service. It would be an excellent guide for college courses on Catholic social thought. Throughout, it is based on a meditation as to what is really important in our existence — the good earth and the people who inhabit it.

Thomas Massaro, S.J. points out nine themes in Catholic social teaching: 1) the dignity of every person and human rights; 2) solidarity, common good and participation; 3) family life; 4) subsidiarity and the proper role of government; 5) property ownership in modern society: rights and responsibilities; 6) the dignity of work, rights of workers, and support for labor unions; 7) colonialism and economic development; 8) peace and disarmament; and 9) option for the poor and vulnerable.[46] This is an excellent book for the initiate and the novice and it would be a perfect complement to Canon Aubert's historical explanation of Catholic social teaching.

The same author recently updated us with an article entitled *Judging the Juggernaut: Toward an Ethical Evaluation of Globalization*.[47] In this article, Massaro points out what globalization is. It is everything and its opposite. It raises a number of ethical questions and gives us an empirical challenge to measure the extent of the increased worldwide interchanges. The ethical challenge is to evaluate the quality and morality of these relationships. His main point is twofold. First, only by making globalization an instrument of inclusion and opportunity will we live up to the Gospel mandate to love our neighbor. And second, without a sober assessment of power and its use, any ethical advice offered by religious voices is relegated to mere high-minded moralizing. He gives two appendices: papal statements and miscellaneous statements from Catholic thinkers and organizations involved in social ethical issues.

For the benefit of our readers, let us now add two lists of the key doctrines of the social teaching. First, a general outline of twelve major lessons of Catholic social teaching. Any list of "major lessons" of Catholic social teaching is difficult to draw up (there is such a large body of Church teaching) and dangerous to publish (What about all the important items left out?). Offered with all due caution, therefore, is the following list of key emphases which characterize Catholic social teaching today. The documents suggested in parentheses illustrate the major lesson particularly well.

1. Link of religious and social dimensions of life. The "social" — the human construction of the world — is not "secular" in the sense of being outside of God's plan, but is intimately involved with the dynamic of the Reign of God. Therefore, faith and justice are necessarily linked together (The Church in the Modern World, #39).

2. Dignity of the human person. Made in the image of God, women and men have a preeminent place in the social order. Human dignity can be recognized and protected only in community with others. The fundamental question to ask about social development is: What is happening to people? (Peace on Earth, 8-26).

3. Political and economic rights. All human persons enjoy inalienable rights, which are political-legal (e.g., voting, free speech, migration) and social-economic (e.g., food, shelter, work, education). These are realized in community. Essential for the promotion of justice and solidarity, these rights are to be respected and protected by all the institutions of society (Peace on Earth).

4. Option for the poor. A preferential love should be shown to the poor, whose needs and rights are given special attention in God's eyes. "Poor" is understood to refer to the economically disadvantaged who, as a consequence of their status, suffer oppression and powerlessness (Call to Action, #23).

5. Link of love and justice. Love of neighbor is an absolute demand for justice, because charity must manifest itself in actions and structures which respect human dignity, protect human rights, and facilitate human development. To promote justice is to transform structures which block love (Justice in the World, 16 & 34).

6. Promotion of the common good. The common good is the sum total of all those conditions of social living — economic, political, cultural — which make it possible for women and men readily and fully to achieve the perfection of their humanity. Individual rights are always experienced within the context of promotion of the common good. There is also an international common good (Christianity and Social Progress, #65).

7. Subsidiarity. Responsibilities and decisions should be attended to as closely as possible to the level of individual initiative in local communities and institutions. Mediating structures of families, neighborhoods, community groups, small businesses, and local governments should be fostered and participated in. But larger government structures do have a role when greater social coordination and regulation are necessary for the common good (The Reconstruction of the Social Order).

8. Political participation. Democratic participation in decision making is the best way to respect the dignity and liberty of people. The government is the instrument by which people cooperate together in order to achieve the common good. The international common good requires participation in international organizations (Pius XII, "Christmas Message," 1944).

9. Economic justice. The economy is for the people and the resources of the earth are to be shared equitably by all. Human work is the key to contemporary social questions. Labor takes precedence over both capital and technology in the production process. Just wages and the right of workers to organize are to be respected (On Human Work).

10. Stewardship. All property has a "social mortgage." People are to respect and share the resources of the earth, since we are all part of the community of creation. By our work we are co-creators in the continuing development of the earth (On Human Work).

11. Global solidarity. We belong in one human family and as such have mutual obligations to promote the rights and development of all people across the world, irrespective of national boundaries. In particular, the rich nations have responsibilities toward the poor nations, and the structures of the international order must reflect justice (The Development of Peoples; The Social Concerns of the Church).

12. Promotion of peace. Peace is the fruit of justice and is dependent upon rights, order among humans and among nations. The arms race must cease and progressive disarmament take place if the future is to be secure. In order to promote peace and the conditions of peace, an effective international authority is necessary (Peace on Earth).
[Taken from *Our Best Kept Secret: The Rich Heritage of Catholic Social Teaching*, revised and enlarged edition, 1987]

We should add to this list ten points the American Catholic Bishops made on the economy in the United States:

1. The economy exists for the person, not the person for the economy.

2. All economic life should be shaped by moral principles. Economic choices and institutions must be judged by how they protect or undermine the life and dignity of the human person, support the family, and serve the common good.

3. A fundamental moral measure of any economy is how the poor and vulnerable are faring.

4. All people have a right to life and to secure the basic necessities of life (e.g., food, clothing, shelter, education, health care, safe environment, economic security).

5. All people have the right to economic initiative, to productive work, to just wages and benefits, to decent working conditions as well as to organize and join unions or other associations.

6. All people, to the extent they are able, have a corresponding duty to work, a responsibility to provide for the needs of their families and an obligation to contribute to the broader society.

7. In economic life, free markets have both clear advantages and limits; government has essential responsibilities and limitations; voluntary groups have irreplaceable roles, but cannot substitute for the proper working of the market and the just policies of the state.

8. Society has a moral obligation, including governmental action where necessary, to assure opportunity, meet basic human needs, and pursue justice in economic life.

9. Workers, owners, managers, stockholders, and consumers are moral agents in economic life. By our choices, initiative, creativity, and investment, we enhance or diminish economic opportunity, community life, and social justice.

10. The global economy has moral dimensions and human consequences. Decisions on investment, trade, aid, and development should protect human life and promote human rights especially for those most in need wherever they might live on this globe.[48]

A recent book by Jean-Yves Calvez, our teacher and precursor in all these matters, begins to show what now needs to be done to update and complement the existing Catholic social teaching.[49] He compliments John Paul II for initiating a period in which the social teaching of the Church becomes active again. During the 1960s, the Social Doctrine of the Church was reproached for its conservative nature. An old saying had been heard once again about the pope: we love the singer but hate the song. However, in recent times, documents coming out of Rome have been too long, for the most part poorly written, and, moreover, poorly translated.

Also, John Paul II has said that the "social doctrine" is "moral theology." He wants to make it stronger, but does making it "moral theology" not actually weaken it? To whom is the teaching addressed? Only to believers?

John Paul II also emphasizes "man" as the main focus of work. Has there not been radical redefinition in and of today's workplace and of the nature of work? The Church more than any other institution, under John Paul II, advocates a sharing of labor and a sharing of revenue. Who does all the work? This gives a whole new dimension to collective bargaining.

No papal authority before John Paul II has spoken so favorably of the free market. Yet, as the Pope points out, the goal of free enterprise is not exclusively the production of profit, but the very existence of the community of people which it comprises. The community counts as well as people.

On the subject of financial operations, we have virtually no directives in the various documents of the Church. Thus, capital has an overwhelming advantage in our world. We have a lack of thought here; a lack of fundamental questioning; a silence, in Calvez's words.

Capitalism is and is simply the fact that capital is in the hands of a few. Thus, only a few are empowered. And even if the means of production should become the property of the State, this does not mean, in and of itself, that property is "socialized." The enemy is not only class warfare or the denial of property. Justice is more than that and it needs to be spelled out.

Again, how do we avoid succumbing to an overly mechanized system of majority rule or, inversely, to the suppression of other people's ideas in the name of a *dogma*?

The Protestants have always reproached the Catholics for basing their social doctrine on natural law, which is then superimposed on the Gospel without the Gospel justifying that manner.

The present pope, John Paul II, is very concerned with basing his anthropology directly on theology. For John Paul II, the dignity of man comes from Christ. Man himself is derived, becomes himself from this central fact. However, Calvez indicates, if the social doctrine is theological, is it not marked by more clear cut limitations than has been previously thought? Does not using the word "theology" devalue the Church's social doctrine, then making it only discussable by theologians? How can we dialogue with others? How can we get the truth of others without being open to their truth? Do we not have to include them in the dialogue? Is not belief a monologue?

Calvez indicates four questions on which the Roman Catholic Church must break its silence: 1) the problem of employment; 2) the financial sector — the financialization of the economy; 3) the capital gains of financial enterprises; and 4) the rights of humans and democracy.

In this unipolar world we live in, the Church's social doctrine must have the audacity to question vigorously and in a most precise manner capitalism in all its manifestations. This questioning by the Catholic Church will be listened to all the more if it is based not on the imposition of norms coming from on high, but on a constant dialogue with people of good will.

In the world we live in, faith, politics, and social forces all jostle one another. Former points of departure, once thought solid as a rock, seem to come undone. We need to clarify our vision and reestablish, once more, our ancient loyalties, in order to be able to follow without denials and without contradiction all the twists and turns imposed on us today.

Thus, we need a series of vigorous interventions to offer new solutions, new precisions, without any artifice or hidden questions or agendas. In the Social Doctrine of the Church, not all has been said. It remains an intention, not an actuality. Why not begin then, begs Calvez, by simply discussing it?

Let us close this already too long essay by addressing ourselves to one of the major problems of the Catholic social teaching. Namely, why is it not heard, followed, obeyed, and used in our social and individual world?

Some old friends of mine wrote a book in 1985 called *Catholic Social Teaching: Our Best Kept Secret*.[50] This book and its insights haunt us all.

The late Father Richard A. McCormick, S.J., described the social responsibility of the Christian in these words, quoting Pope Paul VI, who said we should hear the Social Doctrine with a "lively awareness of personal responsibility and by effective action."[51]

McCormick proposed three components affecting our responses to the Social Doctrine of the Church. They are ignorance, inadequacy, and apathy.

Ignorance has two subtle roots:

First, there is the separatist or dualistic mentality. There is discontinuity between this life and the afterlife, between piety and practice. On one hand, there are prayer, preaching, church attendance, and domestic virtues. On the other, there are business, education, and politics.

The second intellectual root of a socially dormant conscience is individualism. Social responsibility is conceived exclusively in terms of one-on-one relationships: I donate to charities, I hire an underprivileged secretary, I treat some indigent patients free. These forms of social responsibility are essential but hardly exhaust the notion. They might not even be the best or most appropriate response to need.

Separatism and individualism in the face of contemporary social evils are the roots of this kind of ignorance and lead to the other components of a socially dormant conscience — inadequacy (programs for the poor which unwittingly maintain the institutions responsible for poverty) and apathy (a sense of hopelessness and powerlessness). To reverse the process, to create a socially sensitive conscience, we must cultivate the opposite qualities. Against apathy we must learn to feel right, against ignorance we must learn to think right, and against inadequacy we must learn to act right.

Feeling right is a delicate thing to explain and it is a very personal matter as well. Feeling right involves our sensitivity to the harm and hurt of other people. Judgments of moral "ought" derive not only from rational analysis. They have deep roots in our sensitivities, feelings, and emotions.

We need moral concern, we need passion; merely cerebral analysis won't do. But isn't it true that we get angry at injustice only when it hits us or our family personally? We celebrate the liturgy, we theologians play with fancy terms like *koinonia, kerygma, interpersonal encounter, eschatology* — and the world goes stale, secular, and cold. Passion is the source of any true moral responsibility, and therefore, it is the source of social responsibility.

Thinking right means correcting these twin errors of separatism and individualism. For correcting separatism the contemporary theology of liberation can help. I would summarize it as follows:

First, Christ came to liberate us from sin and death into the fullness of our humanity. This liberation will be completely realized at the final coming of the kingdom of God, but it must begin to arrive right now if it is to occur at all. Secondly, liberation theology points out that our enslavement is twofold: bondage to the selfishness of sin itself and to its effects in the social order. This means that the oppressive and alienating structures of society are embodiments of our sinful condition. The impoverishment of the exploited embodies the selfishness of the exploiter. Therefore, thirdly, Christ's liberation must be also twofold — from personal sins and from its institutional expressions. Fourthly, the Church, the Christian community, as a continuation of Christ's presence among men, must be a sign of the liberating presence of the Lord. The Church's main task is liberation from all enslavement, both personal and institutional.

Thinking right also means correcting individualism. The sources of social enslavement are structural and institutional. When blacks cry out against social inequities, when Chicanos point to exploitation in the agricultural system, when youth seek escape from frustration in drugs and crime, when the elderly are shunted from the world of the living — what are all these alienated people telling us? They are saying the system, the organization, the structure's wrong.

Acting right means influencing structures. Since structures, then, are a principal source of injustice and alienation, social responsibility today means influencing government, community, business, and Church decision making. One affects such structure by using power, using corporate persuasiveness, public opinion, political pressure. This sort of observation doesn't tell anyone exactly how to go about structural change. There is no neat formula for that, so beware of prophets bearing certainties. Christianity doesn't tell us what to do in the face of structural inequality or how to do it; experience tells us that.

But any such corporate effort demands at least the following qualities. First, we need a participatory attitude: not leaving it to the pastor, the boss, the government. Secondly, there must be willingness to enter into a process: an open, flexible, listening experimental attitude, willing to learn from mistakes and from experienced hands. Thirdly, patience is required. Changing structures means changing many minds and hearts, and that takes time. There is no surer way for enslaving structures to thrive than for good people to make only short-term efforts.

Sticking to this task requires what Archbishop Helder Camara calls Abrahamic people: those who hope against hope. We must pattern not only our personal life but also our social hopes on Christ. Just as resurrection comes out of death, the Christian knows that the kingdom is somehow now mysteriously aborning. It is Christ urging the coming of His kingdom, urging us to feel right, think right, act right — to be socially responsible.[52]

Before I bring this essay to a close, let me point out one interesting historical fact. Canon Aubert, from time to time, indicates that one of the advantages of the Social Doctrine of the Church is psychological, i.e., the pope is on the side of the undeserving poor.

In the article entitled *On the Origins of Catholic Social Doctrine*, pages 111-112, Canon Aubert makes an interesting historical point. Sometime between the 10th and the 15th of May, 1891, Pope Leo XIII, in his own hand, probably the only thing in his own hand, wrote these memorable words:

> It is gratifying to know that there are actually in existence not a few societies of this nature, consisting either of workmen alone, or of workmen and employers together; but it were greatly to be desired that they should multiply and become more effective. We have spoken of them more than once; but it will be well to explain here how much they are needed, to show that they exist by their own right and to enter into their organization and their work.[53]

The important words are "consisting either of workmen alone," as Canon Aubert is quick to point out, and that this is a recognition of syndication. These "societies" are unions. We owe this affirmation to Leo XIII himself. He is on the side of the worker, of the undeserving poor. In the halls of labor, his name is sacrosanct. For that reason alone, the recognition of labor unions, he stands as the keenest pope of our age.

What now has to be done is make the justice described in the social Teaching of the Church come true in our life. History points the way. Our own and collective consciousness, formed by it and the Social Doctrine of the Church, become our best friend and our champion. To the future we must then commit ourselves with much resignation to its demands.

Notes

[1] Höffner, Joseph Cardinal, *Christian Social Teaching, With an Introduction and Complementary Notes by Lothar Ross* (Ordo Sociales, Köln, 1968, pp. 258).

[2] Boswell, McHugh; Verstraeten, Eds., *Catholic Social Thought: Twilight or Renaissance* (Bibliotheca Ephemeridum Theologicarum Lovaniensium, Leuven University Press, 2000, CLVII, pp. 307). Hereafter BETL.

[3] Curran, Charles E., *Catholic Social Teaching, a Historical, Theological, and Ethical Analysis* (Georgetown University Press, 2002, pp. ix-261). Hereafter Curran.

[4] Massaro, Thomas, S.J., *Living Justice, Catholic Social Teaching in Action* (New York: Sheed & Ward, 2000, pp. 254).

[5] Boileau, David A., Ed., *Principles of Catholic Social Teaching* (Marquette University Press, 1998, pp. 204). pp. 9-10.

[6] Schuck, Michael J., *That They Be One: The Social Teaching of the Papal Encyclicals, 1740-1989* (Georgetown University Press, 1991). pp. 1-43.

[7] Camp, Richard L., *The Papal Ideology of Social Reform* (Leiden, E.J. Brill, 1969, pp. 180), p. 165.

[8] *Op. Cit.*, BETL, p. xiii.

[9] *Sharing Catholic Social Teaching: Challenges and Directives* (USCC-NCCB) June 1998. I use the summary printed by the Minnesota Catholic Conference.

[10] *Catholic Social Thought, the Documentary Heritage*. O'Brien, David J., and Shannon, Thomas A. (Maryknoll, N.Y.: Orbis Books, 1992), pp. viii-688, p. 3. Hereafter O-S.

[11] *Ibid.*, p. 4.

[12] *Ibid.*, pp. 6-7.

[13] See note #6.

[14] *Things Old and New, Catholic Social Teaching Revisited*. McHugh, Francis P., and Natale, Samuel M., eds. (New York: University Press of America, 1992), pp. 429.

[15] *Catholic Social Thought and the New World Order, Building on One Hundred Years*. Williams, Oliver F. and Hauch, John W., eds. (South Bend, IN: University of Notre Dame Press, 1993), pp. 383.

[16] *Ibid.*, p. xi.

[17] *Christian Social Teaching* (*Ordo Sociales*, Cologne, 1962), pp. 258). English Edition, 1964, with an Introduction and Complementary Notes by Lothar Ross.

[18] *Op. Cit.*, BETL, p. xiv.

[19] *Ibid.*, p. xiv.

[20] *Ibid.*, p. xv.

[21] Duprè, Louis. *Passage to Modernity, an Essay in the Hermeneuticss of Nature and Culture* (Yale University Press, 1993), pp. x-300, p. 253.

[22] *Op. Cit.*, BETL, p. xvi.

[23] *Ibid.*, p. 249.

[24] *Ibid.*, p. 251.

[25] *Ibid.*, p. 254.

[26] *Ibid.*, p. 254.

[27] *Ibid.*, p. 235.

[28] J. Milbank, *The Politics of Time* (*Telos*, 1998, no. 113), p. 61.

[29] Curran, Charles E. See note #3.

[30] *Ibid.*, pp. 114-19.

[31] *Ibid.*, pp. 1-2.

[32] *Ibid.*, pp. 129-30.

[33] Burggraeve, R., *From Self-Development to Solidarity.* (Peeters, Leuven, 1985, p. 135); p. 102 gives Levinas' explanation of human equality.

[34] *Op. Cit.*, O-S, p. 132.

[35] *Op. Cit.*, Curran, p. 133.

[36] Boileau, David A. *Cardinal Mercier, A Memoir* (Peeters, Leuven, 1996, pp. xxvii-417). p. 40.

[37] *Op. Cit.*, O-S, p. 421. *Sollicitudo Rei Sociales*, n. 38.

[38] *Op. Cit.*, Curran, p. 134.

[39] See note #33, Burggraeve's book, pp. 98-100, for Levinas' explanation of responsibility.

[40] *Op. Cit.*, Curran, p. 136.

[41] See note #21.

[42] *Op. Cit.*, BETL, p. 71.

[43] *Op. Cit.*, O-S, p. 266.

[44] *Op. Cit.*, Curran, p. 81.

[45] *Op. Cit.*, Curran, pp. 84-85. See also Levinas for an excellent description of conversion and the responsible I (note #33, Burggraeve).

[46] Massaro, Thomas. See note #4.

[47] *Blueprint for Social Justice* (Vol. LVI, No. 1, September, 2002, Twomey Center, Loyola University, New Orleans, LA).

[48] *Op. Cit.*, O-S, pp. 572-680.

[49] Calvez, Jean-Yves, *Les Silences De La Doctrine Sociale Catholique* (Les Éditions de l'Aletier Ouvrières, Paris, 1999, pp. 160).

[50] Henriot, Peter J., Edward P. DeBerri, and Michael J. Schultheiss. *Catholic Social Teaching: Our Best Kept Secret* (Maryknoll, N.Y.: Orbis Books, 1985).

[51] Paul VI, *Octogesima Adveniens* (May, 1971).

[52] McCormick, Richard A. *The Social Responsibility of the Christian*, reprinted in *The Blueprint* (Loyola University, New Orleans, LA., Vol. LII, No. 3, November, 1998).

[53] *Op. Cit.*, O-S, p. 33, paragraph 36, lines 1613-18.

Index

A

A. C. Jemolo, 93, 94
Abbé Daens, 146, 157
abbés démocrates, 57, 61
actio benefica in populum, 170
Action française, 59, 61, 69, 70
Adéodat Boissard, 151, 157
Aeterni Patris, 188
Alfons Ariëns, 145, 157
American Catholicism, 47
American Protestantism, 120, 121
anarchism, 197, 198
anarchists, 188
Ancien régime, 69, 70
André Siegfried, 31
anti-clerical bourgeois oligarchy,
   183, 187
anti-clerical politics, 124, 131
Aristotelian-Thomistic, 265, 266
Armand de Melun, 42, 46
asbestos strike, 34
Association catholique, 96
atomization of the workers, 189,
   190
authentic social democracy, 69, 70
authoritarian, 19, 22

B

Baron K. von Vogelsang, 140, 144
Baron von Hertling, 147, 157
Baron von Vogelsang, 83, 85
Belgian Democratic League, 164,
   170
Belgian School, 184, 187
Berliner Richtung, 166, 170
Bishops' Conferences, 14
bourgeois secular state, 212, 214
bourgeois society, 67, 68

C

Cardinal d'Astros, 76, 79
Cardinal de Bonald, 77, 79
Cardinal de Croij, 77, 79
Cardinal Manning, 192, 193
Cardinal Mazzella, 101, 103
Cardinal Mercier, 165, 170
Cardinal Pecci, 91, 94
Cardinal Zigliara, 100, 103, 194
Catholic Church in Canada, 29, 30
Catholic congresses in Liège, 51, 52
Catholic doctrine of property, 23,
   27
Catholic faith, 251
Catholic fundamentalists, 125, 131
Catholic Jurists Association, 90, 91
Catholic Romanticism, 82, 83
Catholic Social Movement, 161,
   163
Catholic social teaching, 13, 14
Catholic social thinking, 253, 254
Catholic theologians, 20, 22
Catholic thought, 259
Catholic University of Washington,
   47
Center Party, 27, 83
Centesimus annus, 182
*Centrale Jociste du Boulevard Poin-
   caré*, 33, 34
charity, 221, 223
Charles Curran, 13, 14, 242, 244
Charles de Coux, 43, 46
Charles Périn, 138, 144, 184, 187
Christian anthropology, 259
Christian conscience, 41
Christian corporation, 90, 91
Christian democracy, 19, 22
Christian duty, 32
Christian ethos, 261

Christian progressives, 226
Christian Social Order, 93, 94
Christian social order, 27
Christian trade-unions, 217, 219
Christian-Democratic, 56, 61
Christlich-soziale Volkspartei, 145, 157
Circle of German Jesuits in Königswinter, 171
civil order, 189
civil rights, 13, 14
class struggle, 134
clericalism, 56, 115, 121
communism, 49, 51
Communist Manifesto, 75
communist-style socialism, 162, 163
communitarian ethic, 243, 244
communitarianism, 267
Confederació national catolico-agraria, 158, 160
Confédération française des travailleurs chrétiens, 58, 61
confessional movement, 155, 157
Congress of Liège, 100, 103
Congress of Modena, 169, 170
Congress of Naples, 65
Congress of the Professional Association of Industry, 37, 38
Conseil des études, 89, 91
corporatist doctrinaires, 98, 99
corporatist formulas, 129, 131
corporatist theory, 141, 144
corporative patrimony, 90, 91
corporatively-based social organicism, 185, 187
Count Medalago-Albani, 95, 96
Count von Blome, 94
Count von Kuefstein, 93, 94
counter-revolution, 79, 137, 144
Culturkampf, 27

D

David Boileau, 18, 22
democracy, 15, 22
Democratic-Christian movement, 44, 46
Democrazia cristiana, 64, 65
deontological model, 270, 271
DesCartes, 265, 266
dignity of humans, 265
Dock Strike of 1889, 98, 99
Don Albertario, 152, 157
Don Luigi Cerutti, 152, 157
Don Sturzo, 58, 61
Donal Dorr, 259
Dorothy Day, 171
Dr. Howard Margot, 14
Dr. Sharon Harbin, 14
dualistic mentality, 278, 281

E

economic liberalism, 39, 90, 91, 209, 210
Ecumenical Council of Churches, 128, 131
egalitarian utopias, 210
Émile Poulat, 125, 131
Enlightenment, 243, 244
equality, 15, 22
Erweckungsbewegung, 118, 121
Étienne Borne, 60, 61
Eugène Duthoit, 172, 176
evangelical tendency, 117, 121

F

F. D. Maurice, 116, 121
Fabian Society, 158, 160
fascist regimes, 134
Fascist Revolution, 63, 65
Fédération française des syndicats d'employés, 152, 157

Federation of Catholic Entrepreneurs, 256
Flemish Movement, 71, 73
Flemish Question, 62
France, 19, 22
Francisque Gay, 59, 61
Franco-Canadians, 30
Frédéric Le Play, 158, 160
freedom, 15, 22
Freemasonry, 48, 49
Freie Kirchliche-soziale Konferenz, 118, 121
French Revolution, 92, 94
fundamental Catholicism, 217, 219
fundamental positions, 210
fundamentalist, 217, 219

G

Gaspard Descurtins, 191
Gaudium et Spes, 232
General Assembly of German Catholics, 24, 27
Georges Bidault, 59, 61
Georges Goyau, 57, 61
Georges Helleputte, 95, 96, 164, 170
German Empire of the Middle Ages, 185, 187
German Jesuits, 223
Germany, 19, 22
Gesamtband christlichen Gewerkschaften Deutschland, 147, 157
Gesamtverband der evangelischen Arbeitervereine De, 119, 121
Gesellenverein, 81, 83
Gilbert Clive Binyon, 116, 121
Giuseppe Toniolo, 92, 94
Graves de communi, 19, 132, 134
Great Depression, 173, 176

H

Heinrich Pesch, 171
Henri Bazire, 151, 157
Henri Lorin, 57, 61, 87, 91
Henri Rollet, 42
Holy Office of the Knights of Labor, 192, 193
Holy See, 29, 30
human dignity, 265
Humanum genus, 189, 190
hyper-spiritualism, 77, 79
hyper-capitalism, 162, 163

I

Immortale Dei, 192, 193, 236, 239
individualism, 13, 79, 82, 102, 140, 184, 245, 246, 262, 266, 267, 270, 279, 280
industrial proletariat, 75
industrial revolution, 42, 46
institutional Church, 261
integral Catholicism, 156, 157
intelligent paternalism, 72, 73
International Union of Social Studies of Malines, 171, 176
Internationale Arbeitsgemeinschaft evangelischer Arbeitnehmerverbänder, 119
Italian Catholic Movement, 136, 144
Italian Jansenism, 63, 65
Italian Social Catholics, 91, 94
Italian *transigenti*, 135, 144
Italy, 19, 22

J

J.-B. Duroselle, 42, 46
J.O.C. (Young Christian Workers), 33, 34
Jacobean State, 102, 103

286

Jacques Leclercq, 171
James Gibbons, 48, 49
Jean-Marie Mayeur, 182
Jeanne Caron, 125, 131
Jeunesse ouvrière chrétienne, 58, 61
Johann Christoph Blumhardt, 118, 121
John A. Ryan, 16, 22
John F. Cronin, 17, 22
John K. Ryan, 242, 244
John Milbank, 262, 263

K

Katholiekentag, 81, 83, 92, 94, 96
Knights of Labor, 47
Kölner Richtung, 166, 170

L

L.O.C. (League of Christian Workers, 33, 34
La question ouvrière et le christianisme, 82, 83
laity, 251
law of bronze, 183, 187
Lega democratica nazionale, 155, 157
Léon Harmel, 47
Leopold Kunschak, 164, 170
liberal conservatives, 71, 73
liberal indiviualism, 185, 187
liberal theology, 120, 121
Liberatore, 103
Libertas, 192, 193
Liège School, 99
Ligue démocratique belge, 62, 145, 157
London dock workers' strike of 1889, 122, 131
Louis XV, 29, 30
Lutheranism, 118, 121

M

Manifesto, 124, 131
Marc Sangnier, 57, 61, 73
Marcel Prélot, 58, 61
marginalization, 260, 261
Marius Gonin, 57, 61
Marxist, 41
Mater et Magistra, 106, 107, 229, 230
materialist socialism, 32, 34
materialistic pantheism, 92, 94
Maurice Defourny, 172, 176
Maurice Meignen, 45, 46
Maurice Vaussard, 55
metaphysics, 268, 269
methodological approaches, 264
Michael J. Schuck, 242, 244
Ministry of Labor, 62
Mirari vos, 65, 66
Mitbestimmung, 224
Modernity, 249
Mönchen-Gladbach, 81, 83
moral and religious education, 212, 214
moral obligations, 13, 14
moral reformism, 196, 198
Msgr. Affre, 77, 79
Msgr. Antonazzi, 100, 103, 123, 131
Msgr. Belmas, 77, 79
Msgr. Charbonneau
Msgr. de T'Serclaes, 51
Msgr. Delmotte, 36, 38
Msgr. Desranleau, 37, 38
Msgr. Domenico Jacobini, 94
Msgr. Doutreloux, 98, 99
Msgr. Frepel, 184, 187
Msgr. Giraud, 77, 79
Msgr. Ireland, 50, 51
Msgr. Isoard, 150, 157
Msgr. Keane, 50, 51

Msgr. Korum, 148, 157
Msgr. Lienart, 220, 223
Msgr. Mermillod, 94
Msgr. Roy, 37, 38
Msgr. Taschereau, 48, 49
Msgr. Turinaz, 150, 157
Msgr. Volpini, 101, 103
Mussolini, 64, 65
mutatis mutandis, 57, 61
Myron Taylor, 225

N

natural law, 13, 14, 255, 256
neo-corporatism, 164, 170
neo-Guelfe, 168, 170
neo-Thomism, 244
non-Roman Churches, 131
Nova et Vetera, 236

O

Octogesima adveniens, 182, 235
Octogesimo adveniens, 269
Œuvre des Cercles, 57, 61
Œuvre des congrès, 64, 65
Opere di Religione, 226
option for the poor, 259
Orleanist regime, 43, 46
Oswald von Nell-Breuning, 21, 22
Oxford Movement, 117, 121

P

P. Drouler, 21, 22
Pacem in terris, 230
Parti socialiste chrétiens, 60, 61
Pascendi, 156, 157, 217, 219
Pastoral Constitution on the
  Church in the Modern, 15, 22
paternalistic, 19, 22
Patrons du Nord, 87, 91

People's Christian Social Party, 164,

170, 217, 219
phenomenology, 268, 269
political modernism, 156, 157
Pope Benedict XIV, 13, 14
Pope Benedict XV, 66
Pope John XXIII, 15, 22
Pope Leo XIII, 13, 14
Pope Paul VI, 15, 22, 233, 234
Pope Pius IX, 125, 131
Pope Pius X, 58, 61
Pope Pius XI, 15, 22, 17, 22, 69,
  70
Pope Pius XII, 15, 22, 129, 131,
  224, 225
Popular Party, 64, 65
Populorum Progressio, 233, 234
positivism, 13, 14
Prefect of Propaganda, 48, 49
President Bill Clinton, 254
President George Bush, 254
Prince von Loewenstein, 95, 96
private property, 196, 198, 209,
  210
Programme of Milan, 153, 157
proletarianization, 73
Protestant Reformation, 92, 94
psychological point of view, 198

Q

Quadragesimo anno, 15, 22
Quanta cura, 79, 80
Quod apostilici, 189, 190
Quod apostolici muneris, 97, 99

R

R. Talmy, 91
reformist socialism, 213, 214
Religiös-sozialen, 119, 121
religious education, 45, 46
René de La Tour du Pin, 47, 87, 91
Rerum novarum, 13, 14

Rerum novarum excitata cupidine,
209, 210
Rhineland, 81, 83
Richard A. McCormick, 21, 22,
278
Richard L. Camp, 244
Roger Aubert, Canon, 13, 14, 181,
241, 244
Roger Cardinal Etchegaray, 181
Roman Committee of Social Stud-
ies, 94
Roman Question, 64, 65, 170
Romantic Socialism, 78, 79
Russian Revolution, 219

S

Sacerdotal Commission on social
issues, 35
Salvatore Talamo, 200, 203
Samuel Huntington, 19, 22
Sapientiae christianae, 192, 193
Sapiniere, 156, 157
scriptures, 252, 254
Secrétariats sociaux, 151, 157
secular state, 196, 198
Semaines sociales, 130, 131
Separatism, 279, 281
Simon Deploige, 165, 170
Social Catholicism, 41, 42
social insurance, 154, 157
social modernism, 156, 157
Social Protestantism, 120, 121
Social Reign of Jesus Christ, 127,
131
Socialism, 49, 51
Socialism-Communism, 221, 223
Socialist Party, 27
Sollicitudo Rei Socialis, 247
Sozialaristokratismus, 131
Sozialdemokratie, 197, 198, 213,
214
Soziale Gerechtigheit, 175, 176

St. Thomas, 174, 176
Stimmen aus Maria Laach, 175, 176
subsidiarity, 173, 176
Swiss Federal Council, 96
Syllabus, 79, 80
*Syndicat des employés du commerce et
de l'industrie,* 152, 157

T

Terrence Powderly, 48, 49
Theses of Haid, 84, 85
Third World development, 259
Third World liberation theology,
244
Thomas Massaro, S.J., 272, 273
Thomist distinction between *dominium* and *usus,* 210
Thomist doctrine, 24, 27
Thomist synthesis, 165, 170
totalitarian communism, 197, 198
totalitarian regimes, 173, 176
traditional social authority, 183,
187
transformation agent, 268, 269
transigenti, 92, 94
triumphalism, 18, 22
triumphalistic Church, 263

U

ultramontane, 131
ultramontane conservatives, 72, 73
*Union d'études des catholiques so-
ciaux,* 151, 157
Union of Fribourg, 96
Unione economico-sociale, 156, 157
Uniore cattolica per gli studi sociali,
153, 157
University of Louvain, 184, 187
Usufruct, 232, 234

V

Van Zeeland experiment of 1936, 63
Vaterland, 140, 144
Vatican Council of 1870, 80
Verband Katholischer Arbeitervereins Nord und Ostd, 148, 157
Volksbond, 52
Volksverein, 81, 83

W

Western Europe, 32, 34
Wilhelm II, 96
William-Emmanuel von Ketteler, 23
Wirkungsgeschichte, 263
workers' humanism, 162, 163
workers' rights, 69, 70
working classes, 122, 131
World War II, 31, 32

Z

Zentrumspartei, 207, 210

Canon Roger Aubert, Doctor and Master in Theology and Doctor in History, is Professor Emeritus at the University of Louvain. Author in 1945 of a monumental thesis on *The Problem of the Act of Faith*, in 1952 he published a book on the *Pontificate of Pius IX*. He is director of the prestigious *Revue d'histoire ecclésiastique*. He has, through his publications, achieved a prominent place among church historians. He is a priest of Malines-Brussels Archdiocese.

Father Charles E. Curran, Ph.D., is the Elizabeth Scurlock University Professor of Human Values at Southern Methodist University in Dallas. He has written and edited more than forty books in the area of Moral Theology. His most recent publications are *Catholic Social Teaching 1891-Present: A Historical, Theology, and Ethical Analysis* (Washington: Georgetown University Press, 2002), and *The Catholic Moral Tradition Today: A Synthesis* (Washington: Georgetown University Press, 1999). He is a priest of the Diocese of Rochester, New York.

Father David A. Boileau, Ph.D., Louvain 1961, is Chair of the Philosophy Department at Loyola University New Orleans, where he teaches Ethics. He is the former Dean of St. John's Seminary, Little Rock, Arkansas, and former Director of Human Services for the International Brotherhood of Teamsters. He has authored two books on Cardinal Mercier and has edited a number of books on the Social Doctrine of the Church. He is a priest of the Archdiocese of New Orleans.